Cultural Diversity, Educational Equity and the Transformation of Higher Education

Group Profiles as a Guide to Policy and Programming

Michael Benjamin

Westport, Connecticut
London

LC
1099.3
.B45
1996

Library of Congress Cataloging-in-Publication Data

Benjamin, Michael.
 Cultural diversity, educational equity and the transformation of
higher education : group profiles as a guide to policy and
programming / Michael Benjamin.
  p. cm.
 Includes bibliographical references and index.
 ISBN 0–275–95544–3 (alk. paper)
  1. Multicultural education—United States. 2. Minorities—
Education (Higher)—United States. 3. Universities and colleges—
United States—Administration. I. Title.
 LC1099.3.B45 1996
 370.19′6—dc20   95–26520

British Library Cataloguing in Publication Data is available.

Copyright © 1996 by Michael Benjamin

All rights reserved. No portion of this book may be
reproduced, by any process or technique, without the
express written consent of the publisher.

Library of Congress Catalog Card Number: 95–26520
ISBN: 0–275–95544–3

First published in 1996

Praeger Publishers, 88 Post Road West, Westport, CT 06881
An imprint of Greenwood Publishing Group, Inc.

Printed in the United States of America

The paper used in this book complies with the
Permanent Paper Standard issued by the National
Information Standards Organization (Z39.48–1984).

10 9 8 7 6 5 4 3 2 1

Contents

Illustrations

Acknowledgments

I would like to take this opportunity to express my appreciation to the handful of readers who, despite their chronically clogged schedules, still took the time to read, digest and comment upon several drafts of this volume. While their help has been invaluable, I, of course, take full responsibility for the text, including any errors that it might contain. At the University of Guelph (Guelph, Ontario, Canada): Brian Sullivan (V.-P., Student Services); Dr. Peggy Patterson (Assistant to the V.-P., Student Services); Indira Ganasellal (Human Rights Officer); Dr. Loraleigh Keashly (Psychology); Dr. Jean Turner (Family Studies). At Brock University (St. Catherines, Ontario, Canada): Dr. Sybil Wilson (Education).

PART I

Introduction

1

The Roots of the Cultural Diversity Movement

Advocates of cultural diversity want nothing less than to transform higher education. When they call for colleges and universities that are more inclusive, they envision institutions that are more accessible, more welcoming and supportive, and more relevant than at any time in the past.

The roots of this movement can be traced to an earlier one, the civil rights movement of the 1960's (Orlans, 1992). Initially dedicated to winning the vote for southern Blacks, student supporters soon shifted their attention to higher education. Greater access for ethnic minority students was only one of their many demands. And higher education authorities listened. Accordingly, throughout the 1970's and early 1980's, minority enrollment in higher education rose steadily (Nora, 1993).

But all was not well. Ethnic minority students enrolled in predominantly white colleges and universities were seldom happy. Incidents involving racism, discrimination and violence were not uncommon (Dalton, 1991). Compared to white students, ethnic minority students got lower grades, were much more likely to complain of alienation, isolation, loneliness and depression (Tierney, 1993), and were in consequence much more likely to drop out (Smedley et al., 1993). From about the mid-1980's to the present, ethnic minority enrolment rates have slowly but steadily declined (Fisher, 1992; Nora, 1993).

The significance of these negative trends derives, first, from the personal pain and wasted talent they denote and, as important, from their intersection with two structural changes in society. The first change is demographic and refers to the proportional increase of minority populations relative to their white counterparts. Representing 25% of the American population in 1990, minority populations are projected to increase to 35% by the year 2000 and to 50% by 2025 (see Table 1.1). More urgent in terms of higher education, however, is the fact that minority populations already represent 50% or more of the population in selected states, such

Table 1.1
Ethnic Minority Populations in the United States and Canada

	Census Data (in millions)			
	United States (1990)		Canada (1991)[a]	
Group	No.	%	No.	%
Blacks	30.0	12.1%	0.34	1.3%
Hispanics	22.4	9.0%	0.16[b]	0.6%
Asians	7.3	2.9%	1.62	6.0%
Natives	2.0	0.8%	0.47[d]	1.7%
Total Population	251.0[c]	100.0%	27.00	100.0%
Minority Population	61.7	24.8%	2.59	9.6%[e]
Projection to 2001[f]	78.6	35.0%	5.68	17.7%

Notes:

a. Includes single origins only representing 70% of the total; multiple origins are distributed across 14 categories which only distinguish between British, French, Canadian and "other."

b. Based on reported mother tongue, single responses only.

c. Total population, 1994 (in millions): United States, 261.1; Canada, 29.2.

d. Including multiple origins increases this total to just over one million or 4% of the total Canadian population in 1991 (Vanier Institute of the Family, 1994: 21).

e. Including multiple origins and those in a residual *other* category increases this proportion to 16% (Vanier Institute of the Family, 1994: 22).

f. Sources: United States: Dana (1993); Canada: Samual (1992, cited in Toronto Star, May 30, 1992: A1-A2).

as California and Florida (Bouvier, 1991; Dana, 1993). The second change is technological, such that the link between a college degree and occupational success is becoming ever more crucial (Volti, 1992). There was a time when jobs for unskilled workers were plentiful and paid well enough to support a family. By the 1990's, such jobs had all but vanished. Instead, minimal skill and education requirements have risen steadily. For a rapidly increasing proportion of well-paying jobs, a college or university degree is now a prerequisite (Skolnick, 1991).

In recognition of the explosive potential of rising ethnic minority populations blocked from advancement by an unresponsive higher education system, the cultural diversity movement was born. Amid warnings of impending crisis (Altbach & Lomotey, 1991) and renewed calls for educational reform (Miller, 1994), advocates called for major change, in the form of cultural diversity policies and programs (Barr & Strong, 1989; Woolbright, 1989). As in the early 1970's, such calls struck a responsive chord (Kramer & Weiner, 1994; Manning, 1994; Manning & Coleman-Boatwright, 1991; Stage & Hamrick, 1994). Cultural diversity programs rose in the hundreds across the United States (Mintz, 1993), with positive consequences (Astin, 1993), as the movement continued to gather momentum.

While the goals of the movement are laudatory, the means by which these goals are to be achieved are another matter altogether. As writers passionately trumpeted the importance of respect for differences, there was the very real danger that the baby might be thrown out with the bathwater. As Cheatham (1991: 28) explains,

Simplistic interventions result from describing racial and ethnic minority persons *not as they are but as they are different* from the modal individual. In that comparative context, the emphasis remains on validating the majority experience as opposed to studying the ethnic minority experience. Those embracing intervention models that ignore the unique and vital heritage of ethnic minority persons and treat them rather as deficient Whites reveal an ethnocentric or, more specifically, Eurocentric bias. (Emphasis in original.)

Here, Cheatham (1991) calls our attention to two critical weaknesses in current approaches to cultural diversity. The first weakness involves reliance on a deficit model of ethnic minority groups (Trickett et al., 1994), that is, the tendency to see characteristics of the dominant group (Whites) as the norm around which other groups vary, and against which the latter are invariably judged inferior. As will later be apparent, the most recent literature in the field has recognized and begun to address this thorny issue. The second and more fundamental weakness is to leave implicit any substantive description of the ethnic minority groups in question, save for their presumed difference. The results are extraordinary: a rapidly growing literature in which there are few and very limited descriptions of such groups, and a multiplicity of programs grounded on little more than good intentions, in the absence of substantive knowledge. Ironically, Cheatham (1991) himself is guilty of this sin of omission, for his otherwise excellent book of 205 pages contains only six pages (2.9%) of substantive content.

Only brief consideration suggests how variation across these groups might affect their experience of university life, with significant implications, in turn, for university administration and management. For example, consider only three areas: academic work, student services and student extracurricular activities. In each case, underlying assumptions may, to varying degrees, be at odds with fundamental attributes of the groups in question.

In the academic sphere, universities assume that students: can read, write, speak and understand standard English; are able and willing to be overtly critical of ideas; can think abstractly and synthesize information; can think and write analytically; can be verbally assertive, in terms, for example, of asking and answering questions in class or making contact with professors; can take notes in class and then study those notes in preparation for examinations; can get along with other students, both in large classes as well as in group projects; and, most recently, can understand and operate computers, in terms of preparing papers, doing assignments and using the library.

In the student services area, universities assume that students: can acknowledge personal problems and thus seek assistance for them; can accept advice from and divulge highly personal information to adults who are strangers to them; are prepared to enter into debt to finance their university education; are prepared to admit that they do not know how to use the library system; are willing to consume food prepared, for example, with the use of milk and/or pork products (such as lard); and are prepared to attend Christian religious services.

In the matter of extracurricular activities, universities assume that students: are willing to live (in residence) apart from their families of origin; are willing to accept a roommate from a different ethnic group; are untroubled by social activities in which men and women mingle freely, without adult supervision, and during which they may have unrestricted access to alcohol; are willing to live under coeducational conditions; are willing to live (off campus) independently of their parents, either alone or with peers as roommates; are willing to participate in cultural and group activities that reflect the interests of the White majority; and will be untroubled by interaction primarily with persons of a different ethnic group.

To the extent that these assumptions are true, students from ethnic minority groups will likely encounter few obstacles in their effort to adjust to the demands of university life. However, to the extent that some, many or all of these assumption prove false, students from these groups are likely to experience university life as profoundly challenging. Having large numbers of students who are "challenged" in this way is likely to pose a serious problem for university administration and management, ranging from increases in student attrition rates, or campus unrest, to rates of vandalism.

In this context, a detailed profile of the groups in question would go some way in clarifying what cultural diversity and educational equity policies should mean in practice. Such a profile would elicit the ways in which Asians, for example, might be similar to and different from Whites, *and* ways in which specific Asian subgroups, such as the Japanese, might be similar to and different from other subgroups, such as the Chinese, Korean or Vietnamese (Jones, 1994). In turn, having access to such information would be extremely valuable in helping university administration, management, staff and faculty develop the methods and prepare for the consequences of implementing such a policy. It would likely also serve to highlight our own unconscious biases, given "the power of culture to make us relatively oblivious to the limitations of our own perspectives, behaviors, and values." (Patton, 1985: 1).

Accordingly, the thrust of this volume is to construct a detailed profile of selected ethnic minority groups and then use those profiles as a basis for reconstructing cultural diversity policy and programming. I begin, in Chapter 2, by selecting the six core categories around which these profiles will be constructed, and by briefly exploring supplementary mediating factors that may affect the experience of ethnic minority groups. Next, in Chapters 3 to 6, I will develop profiles of four minority groups (African American Blacks, Caribbean Canadian Blacks, Hispanics, and Asians) as well as a fifth comparative group, the Jews (Schoem, 1991). The Jews are especially useful for my purposes, for despite the fact that they are typically White, they nevertheless share with other ethnic minority groups a history of oppression. In Chapter 7, I turn to a variety of important contextual matters, including a report on the current (1995) status of cultural diversity policy across North America, and an ecosystemic model of the university as a complex organization. Finally, in Chapters 8 and 9, using the model previously constructed, I propose and explore a version of cultural diversity policy in higher education informed by the group profiles.

Before proceeding, *five* important caveats are in order. First, the following profiles rely heavily on American sources. While descriptive Canadian data are available, they are hardly abundant. There appear to be two main reasons for this disparity: population size and scholarly interest. As seen in Table 1.1, above, ethnic minority groups make up a much larger proportion of the population in the United States compared to Canada (Allen & Turner, 1987), and, with local exceptions,[1] are likely to do so for the foreseeable future. In practice, this has meant that ethnicity has received both less and different attention in Canada. For example, both Peters (1990) and Tavuchis (1989) have noted the meager character of the Canadian ethnicity literature as regards both size and (narrow) range, with the emphasis on history and demography, as opposed to family life. Similarly, Canadian treatments of poverty tend either to ignore ethnicity (National Council of Welfare, 1981; Ross & Shillington, 1989) or to restrict attention to native groups (Ryerse, 1990) or immigrant women (National Council of Welfare, 1990, 1992). By contrast, in the United States, Buenker and Ratner (1992: 232) observe that "[t]he explosion of ethnic studies in every discipline over the past quarter century has produced a flood of literature, and the torrent is not likely to crest in the near future." In part, this "flood" reflects the much greater abundance of academic programs in the United States devoted to ethnic concerns, with more than 300 programs, for example, concerned exclusively with Jewish life, 27 of them at the doctoral level (Silberman, 1985). In light of these differences, despite every effort to balance out American and Canadian data, Canadian and other non-American readers are advised to examine the profiles to follow, with attention to their local applicability. They should also note differences in terminology, with "cultural diversity" an American term, while "educational equity" is its Canadian equivalent.

Second, the study of culture or ethnicity encompasses a range of disciplines, including: cultural anthropology (Westermeyer, 1976); family therapy (Brown & Root, 1990; Carter & McGoldrick, 1988; McGoldrick et al., 1982a, 1982b, 1989; Hansen & Falicov, 1983; Saba et al., 1990); cross-cultural psychology (Adler, 1989, 1991, 1993; Adler & Gielen, 1994; Kim et al., 1994; Lamb, 1987; Triandis, 1980); transcultural psychiatry (Cox, 1986); social work (Devore & Schlesinger, 1987);[2] family sociology (Alba, 1990; McAdoo, 1993; Ishwaran, 1979, 1983); and social demography (Breton et al., 1990; Driedger, 1987; Halli et al., 1990).[3] Regrettably, much of this work focuses on international comparisons rather than the study of ethnic minority groups within North America (McGoldrick, 1982), and so is not useful for my purposes. Accordingly, the following profiles lean heavily on the clinical literature (in family therapy, social work and psychiatry), and to a lesser extent on the anthropological, sociological and psychological literatures. Indeed, such an interdisciplinary focus is unavoidable. As Buenker and Ratner (1992: 231) explain, "[e]xploring these [ethnic] topics absolutely requires that all of us make a serious effort to break through the disciplinary boundaries that separate us."

Third, for *two* reasons, substantive limitations on my discussion were unavoidable. The first reason concerns the collective size of the literatures in question, which require that any comprehensive treatment necessarily be encyclopedic in size. Since the intent of the present volume was more modest, the following profiles provide coverage that is at best only selectively complete. I have been at some pains, for example, to ensure that all references frequently cited in the literature have been included for each ethnic group. Even so, substantive limitations were unavoidable so that a short monograph not balloon into a three volume work. The second reason concerns the criteria used to select the groups to be profiled, namely: (a) ethnic minority group status; (b) group size relative to the North American context; and (c) the availability of literature describing fundamental beliefs (attitudes and values), family practices and help-seeking behavior. Concern with ethnic minority status derives from the rationale for cultural diversity, noted above. Reliance on American sources explains the use of a North American rather than a solely Canadian context. And the reasons for my concern with specific substantive content will shortly be apparent in discussing the profile categories (see Chapter 2). In combination, these selection criteria dramatically limited the groups that could be included in the profiles. For example, the profile of Asians deliberately omitted consideration of several large and important subgroups, notably the South Asians of India, Pakistan and Bangladesh (Anderson, 1987; Buchignani et al., 1985; Chadney, 1984; Dana, 1993; Dasgupta, 1989; Herbert, 1989; Ishwaran, 1971, 1976; Joy, 1989; Luthar & Quinlan, 1993; Malik, 1989; Suglnasiui, 1985). Similarly glaring is the omission of North America's aboriginal groups: Native Indians, Metis, Inuit and Alaskan Natives (see Dana, 1993; Gareau, 1981; Flanagan & Foster, 1985; Ishwaran, 1971; Baker, 1990; Snipp, 1992).

Fourth, as will become clear shortly, each of the groups is heterogeneous, made up out of multiple subgroups that, in turn, vary in size, social class distribution, religious affiliation, and so on. Given this complex reality, any set of profiles are at risk of stereotyping the groups being described. Conversely, systematic attention to such heterogeneity would similarly be at risk of losing sight of any general trends by the sheer weight of detail. By carefully specifying the categories to be used in creating the profiles, I try to strike a balance between the general and the specific. That is, these profiles should be seen as general descriptions that will apply to varying degrees to any given member of the groups in question.

Finally, a word is in order about my choice of the phrase "ethnic minority group" as opposed to any of a variety of alternative words or phrases that might have been selected. The focus of this monograph is on the basic beliefs, practices and experiences of various groups as seen *from the inside*. "Ethnic minority group" captures this reality better than any other choice. For example, "designated group," a label in common use in Canada, is useful for political but no other purposes; it says nothing about the groups in question other than they have been selected for special attention. "Minority group" or "visible minority group" has more substantive content. They are sociological terms which locate a group in a status hierarchy,[4] and thus concentrate on how other people perceive these groups rather than how they see themselves. Finally, "race" or "racial group" are terms in wide popular use, but for that very reason obscure more than they clarify (Radcliffe, 1994). Anderson (1991), for example, shows that not only does "race" have little genetic or biological meaning, but its social use varies dramatically, with people seen as "Black" in the United States seen as "White" in Brazil. Thus, "race," while it may be a component of how *some* members of *some* groups see themselves, typically says more about how others see them and is consequently less useful than "ethnic minority group" for my purposes.[5]

NOTES

1. For example, Samual (1992, cited in the Toronto Star May 30, 1992: A1–A2) projects that by the year 2001, visible minorities will represent 45% of the population of Metropolitan Toronto.

2. The extent and quality of attention to ethnicity in the social work literature is a matter of some debate, some arguing attention has been scanty and ill-conceived (McMahon & Allen-Meares, 1992), others that it has been voluminous and systematic (Harrison et al., 1992; Irish et al., 1993).

3. Favazza and his collegues (Favazza & Faheem, 1982; Favazza & Oman, 1977) have compiled the most comprehensive bibliography in this area. Buenker and Ratner (1992) provide an excellent overview of the American ethnicity literature. Less adequate and rather dated overviews of the Canadian literature are available in Gregorvich (1972), Kralt (1977) and periodically in the journal "Canadian Ethnic Studies."

4. Shibutani and Kwan (1965) define "minority group" as "the underprivileged in a system of ethnic stratification."

5. Those advocating for an Africentric perspective, one seeking to highlight and enoble the African cultural roots of Africa American Blacks, have a rather different view of "race." For further discussion, see Nobles (1986).

2

The Choice of Categories

INTRODUCTION

Ethnicity may be defined as membership in a "human group that entertains a 'subjective belief' in its common descent because of similarities of physical type or customs or both, or because of memories of colonization and migration." (Alba, 1985: 17).[1] Such "imagined communities" (Anderson, 1983: 14) create and maintain boundaries between their own and other peoples (Barth, 1969), based on various prominent symbols, such as "race," religion and national or geographic origin (Yinger, 1985). The profound impact of these shared beliefs cannot be overemphasized, for they pervade all aspects of members' lives. In the words of McGoldrick (1988: 69), "[Ethnicity] plays a major role in determining what we eat, how we work, how we relate, how we celebrate holidays and rituals, and how we feel about life, death, and illness. We see the world through our own cultural filters and we often persist in our established views in spite of evidence to the contrary." In short, ethnicity helps establish the fundamental bases upon which we relate to ourselves and to others in the world, with these bases typically outside our conscious awareness (Schwartzman, 1982). Finally, ethnic identity is also shaped, at least in part, by how others see us. That is, ethnicity is partly subjective but also partly structural (Anderson, 1991; Gordon, 1964).

In this context, any given ethnic minority group may be described in terms of tens or even hundreds of relevant categories. However, not all categories are equally salient. Following Devore and Schlesinger (1987), Herberg (1989), McAdoo (1993) and McGoldrick (1982b), the profiles presented will be based on *six* categories selected for the extent to which they capture the core meanings and behavioral systems of the groups in question. Each of these categories is briefly described below. This will be followed by an equally brief note on six additional factors that are less central and, as a function of individual circumstances, may or may not operate to mediate or qualify the core categories.

CORE CATEGORIES

Modal Social Class

Social class, based on available resources and completed education, plays a central role in shaping life experience. Compared to the impoverished, the affluent eat better, live in families that are better organized, have access to better health care and even live longer (Aponte, 1976, 1986; Benjamin, 1994). Given that ethnic minority groups tend to be poor (Blalock, 1990; Cross, 1992; Dana, 1993; Katz, 1986), and that the last twenty years have seen the gap between rich and poor widen (Harrison & Bluestone, 1988; Michel, 1991; Mincy & Ricketts, 1990), it is unreasonable to speak about a given ethnic minority group without simultaneously specifying the social class of its members. As Sollars (1989: xvi) argues, "it is not any a priori cultural *difference* that make ethnicity. It is always the specificity of power relations at a given historical moment and in a particular place that trigger off a strategy of pseudo-historical explanation that camouflages the inventive act." (Emphasis in original.) In a similar vein, Gordon (1964) regarded the nexus of class and ethnicity as so crucial that he coined the term "ethclass" to refer to it, the underlying assumption being that both dimensions together are needed to gain some sense of the perspective of those being described.

That said, comprehensive data regarding the intersection between the five ethnic groups of interest here and at least three social classes (upper, middle and lower/working) simply do not exist. Rather, researchers have tended to concentrate on a modal class which accounts for a majority of those in a particular group. That practice will be followed here, with end notes used to cite material concerning group members in other social classes.

Definition of the Family

Across ethnic groups, great variation exists concerning the definition of who is inside and who is outside the family (Benjamin, 1983; McDaniel, 1988; Skolnick, 1991). At one extreme, family boundaries may be tightly defined, so that family refers to the immediate family and no others. At the other extreme, family boundaries may be loosely defined, so that family includes extended family members (both living and dead) as well as others treated "as if" they were blood relations. As such, these are not true extended families in anthropological terms, since they do not live under the same roof. Nevertheless, loose boundaries define a family arrangement which, with their nuclear counterpart, describe the variation which obtains across ethnic groups. Moreover, the ways in which families define their boundaries have practical consequences, for example, with regard to whom one might turn for support in times of need or what happens to children when their parents are experiencing difficulty caring for them.

Life Cycle

A closely related category concerns variation in life cycle phases. That is, ethnic groups vary widely as regards all aspects of life cycle processes, including the number of phases that are recognized; their respective duration and salience; and the markers used to signify transition between stages, for instance, from the status of adolescent to that of adult. As Fulmer (1988) makes clear, this is not solely a function of ethnic group membership per se, but is importantly shaped by social class. Affluent professional families typically display an "elongated" life cycle compared to their lower-income counterparts whose life cycle is typically "compressed." Children in affluent families may spend many years completing the educational requirements of a professional degree and thus a corresponding numbers of years in the "young adult" phase of their life cycle, in which they remain single and financially dependent on their parents. This phase is therefore "elongated" relatively to others in "average" middle-class families. By contrast, their lower-income counterparts may leave education early, marry, become a parent and take full-time employment (if they can find it), all before their twenty-first birthday. In their case, then, the "young adult" phase has been "compressed," again relative to others in "average" middle-class families.

Marital Relations

Another way in which ethnic groups vary is in terms of their perspective on appropriate relations between marital partners (whether heterosexual, homosexual or lesbian). This turns on two issues. The first issue concerns the relative salience of spousal relations in comparison to parent-child relations. Some groups regard spousal relations as primary or at least concurrent with parent-child relations, while other groups accord it secondary or even tertiary place, with parent-child relations taking precedence. The second issue concerns the extent to which groups vary in their perception of how marital partners should relate to each other. Some groups expect that one spouse should be more powerful than their partner, while other groups see the marital partners as equal in most, if not all, respects.

Parent-Child Relations

In addition to the salience of the parent-child relationship, groups vary in two additional respects: the character of parent-child relations and the responsibility for child care. With respect to child care, some groups take literally the Christian biblical adage that "children should be seen and not heard," whereas others adopt a more democratic stance (Yip, 1985). Further, in some groups child care is seen as the mother's responsibility, perhaps shared with other females in the extended family, while in others fathers are expected to participate to varying degrees.

Perspective on Help-Seeking

Finally, groups vary widely as regards help-seeking, by which I refer to the definition of distress (both physical and psychological) and its consequences for help-seeking. In this context, help is necessarily relative to what is regarded as "normal" or "normative." Since, as noted above, what is seen as normative is defined by ethnic membership, Vargas (1991, cited in Koss-Chioino & Vargas, 1992) argues, and I agree, that help giving is a "culturally defined enterprise." In turn, that same process makes help giving potentially problematic. As Pedersen (1984: 340; Pedersen & Ivey, 1994) explains, "[c]ultural differences introduce barriers to understanding in those very areas of interaction that are most crucial to the outcomes of therapy, through discrepancies between counselor and client experiences, beliefs, values, expectations and goals."

Such discrepancies are exemplified by the extent to which groups vary in their approach to help-seeking (Sue & Zane, 1987; Waxler-Morrison et al., 1991; White, 1984). Some groups find somatic illness the only acceptable basis for help-seeking, while others legitimize both physical and psychological complaints. Similarly, some groups are reluctant to seek help for any reason, seeing this as an admission of weakness, and so typically go for help only after the problem in question is serious and well-advanced. Others go for help readily, often when the problem in question is at an early stage in its typical course. Either strategy yields differential prognostic results and has divergent social consequences. Finally, groups differ in their preferred relationship with the caregiver, ranging from formal and authoritarian to familiar and informal. While such information is important in understanding student/client behavior, Devereaux (1967) and Stein (1985) are both correct in arguing that consideration should also be given to the values and attitudes that help givers (such as personal counselors or faculty members) bring with them into help giving, since these will act as filters through which they perceive and interact with student/clients. Hardy (1990) adds that while modern help givers may recognize differences between ethnic minority and majority students and/or families, they do not similarly recognize differences across ethnic minority subgroups. Consequently, help givers can be "seduced" into treating ethnic minority students and/or families stereotypically, minimizing subgroup differences or overgeneralizing similarities.

Taken together, data across these six categories will yield detailed, three-dimensional portraits of the groups in question, with the emphasis on how group members see themselves. Later, these same data, suitably reorganized, will support a systematic comparison of these groups across twenty-seven dimensions of family, work and educational experience. Not surprisingly, this will show that across some dimensions these groups are remarkably similar, while across other dimensions they are strikingly different. Unfortunately, these data are incomplete as regards ethnic minority subgroups, and would not support equally systematic description or comparison. However, available data do indicate that subgroups are similar in some respects while being quite different in other respects. More generally, on the basis of these profiles, I will argue that the inclusion of group profiles enormously enriches the potential of diversity policy, while simultaneously complicating its implementation, since no single inter- pretation, however generous or respectful of difference, can possibly encompass this range of similarities and differences.

MEDIATING FACTORS

While these six categories stand at the core of an ethnic minority group's identity, their impact can be significantly mitigated by a variety of additional factors. My reading of the literature suggests that *six* such factors warrant careful attention as part of any assessment of an individual student. However, precisely because of their variable status, they will *not* receive detailed exploration in the profiles which follow.

Immigration

Perhaps the single most important mediating factor concerns immigra- tion (Shuval, 1993) and its local variant, migration (Massey et al., 1994). This is applicable in *three* senses. First, all authorities agree that immigra- tion can be intensely disruptive of individual and family processes (Cole et al., 1992; Devore & Schlesinger, 1987; Landau-Stanton, 1985; McGoldrick, 1988; Pedraza, 1991). However, it is important to note that it is not immigration per se that increases the risk of distress and disorder. Rather, it is the contingencies associated with it, which are, in turn, associated with a significantly elevated risk of breakdown, either physical, psychological and/or interpersonal. Known risk factors (Aronowitz, 1984; Health & Welfare Canada, 1988; Munro-Blum et al., 1989; Vega & Rumbaut, 1991; Ying, 1988) include: decreased material resources; inability to speak the local language; separation from family and friends; a hostile reception by local people; isolation from others of the same ethnic group; traumatic experience (such as torture) and/or prolonged stress prior to immigration (such as internment); and age, either very young or very old. Further, such elevated risk typically applies in the period three to eighteen months following immigration together with a sleeper effect that may not be evident for years and is typically manifest in interpersonal problems. Thus, immigration not only increases the risk of distress, but may also act to disrupt or undermine ethnic identity. For some, this will mean primary identification with the dominant culture (known as acculturation or assimilation). For others, it may involve clinging tenaciously to their culture of origin while rejecting the dominant culture (known as separation or traditionalism). For still others, likely in the majority, the rigors of immigration notwithstanding, cultural values will persist for generations (Gelfand, 1982; McGoldrick, 1982b, 1988), and may evolve into true biculturalism in which members feel equally comfortable in both (or several) cultures (Birman, 1994).[2]

Second, immigration is important in another sense, namely, the impact of immigration policy (Cohen, 1991; Drachman, 1990, 1995; Jasso & Rosenzweig, 1990).[3] Government immigration policies act to selectively attract some immigrants while rejecting others. In Thompson's (1989: 156) words, "immigration laws have selected for those occupations characteristic of advanced industrial societies - managers and professionals, intermediate white collar clerical and sales workers, and blue collar manufacturing and construction workers." Thus, European immigrants were strongly favored by the United States and Canada until about the mid-1960's when both abandoned their respective "quota" systems. Since then the tide of immigrants has increasingly come from the Third World, most notably Asia, the Caribbean and Africa (Logan, 1991; Vanier Institute of the Family, 1994).[4] In similar fashion, government policies may cause the numbers of immigrants to rise and fall; may favor single persons or families; may concentrate on laborers or skilled workers; and may vary widely in their receptivity to refugees (the Cuban "Marielitos" and the Vietnamese "Boat People" are recent examples) and the statuses and services accorded or withheld from them (Drachman, 1995). In short, such policies profoundly affect the size, shape and composition of ethnic minority group populations in North America.[5]

Finally, immigration is important in a third sense regarding government policy at federal, state or provincial and even municipal levels. However, the impact of such policies has largely been ignored in the literature, which typically treats ethnic group identity as an entirely endogenous phenomenon (Anderson, 1991; Li, 1990a), that is, as arising solely from relations among group members. An alternate view characterizes group identity formation, maintenance and change as more complex (Anderson, 1991; Dawson, 1967; Light, 1974; Miller, 1969; Steinberg, 1981; Thompson, 1989; Ward, 1990). On the one hand, this view acknowledges the role of endogenous forces within ethnic communities. On the other hand, it gives much greater weight to the hegemony of elite groups to shape public policy in their own interests, including the manner in which ethnic groups are conceptualized, perceived and characterized. In response, the ethnic groups in question may either consciously use these "stereotypes" to further their own economic ends, or they may succumb to their potence by internalizing them into their own definition of self.

Degree of Identification
Ethnicity was defined above in terms of self-identification with the group. However, this too may vary. Landau-Stanton (1985), for example, suggests that families may respond to immigration in one of three ways: they may become isolated from other members of their ethnic group, and thus ambivalent in their group identification (acculturation); they may reject the dominant culture and identify totally with their ethnic group

(enmeshment); or they may reject traditional values and embrace the dominant culture (disengagement). Similarly, others note divergent responses of family members to the stresses of ethnic minority group status (Devore & Schlesinger, 1987; Driedger, 1987). Blacks and Hispanics, for example, may abandon speech patterns distinctive of their respective groups. Black women may straighten their hair or rely on wigs. Jews may anglicize their surnames, while Jews and Asians may have plastic surgery to remove or create distinctive facial and other features. Finally, Buenker and Ratner (1992) distinguish between cultural and structural assimilation. The former refers to loss of ethnically distinct values and behaviors. The latter refers to income and status mobility. For group members, cultural assimilation may be perceived as the necessary price of structural assimilation. As will shortly become evident, the expectation of a causal link from one to the other may be more illusion than reality, with discrimination and racism acting to block status mobility despite assimilation.

Thus, regardless of the specific dimension, ethnic groups distribute on a continuum (Lee, 1989), from the completely traditional, who reject the dominant culture, to the completely assimilated, who embrace the dominant culture. Broadly, assimilation or acculturation is directly related to the length of time spent here (Sodowsky & Plake, 1992).

Intermarriage

Variation in group identification may also be affected by the process of intermarriage (Ministry of Industry, Science & Technology, 1990). This appears to involve a dynamic relationship between social mobility, years since immigration, sex ratio, and ethnic identification. Typically, years since immigration, upward mobility and a low sex ratio (more men then women) are strongly associated with rising rates of intermarriage (Guttentag & Secord, 1983; Heer, 1974; Kitano & Yeung, 1982; McGoldrick & Preto, 1984; Murguia & Cazares, 1982; Schneider, 1984; Sue & Morishima, 1982). Such increases notwithstanding, rates of intermarriage tend, generally, to be low, for example, 8.4% in the United States in 1989 (Hegar & Grief, 1994). Finally, among those that make this marital choice, intermarriage tends to be associated with the loss of ethnic identity (Bruce & Rodman, 1973; Cretser, 1982; Goldstein & Segall, 1985; Larson & Munro, 1990; Ram, 1990).

Gender

Much will be said about gender, especially as regards spousal and parent-child relations. However, there are three senses in which gender operates as a mediating variable. The first concerns the speed and flexibility with which different family members become familiar with the dominant culture, particularly in situations involving immigration. In this respect, women appear to have an advantage over men (Duryea & Gundison, 1993; McGoldrick et al., 1989). As a function of their child care responsibilities, women are more likely to be exposed to the dominant culture and thus learn the local language. Further, they may have an easier time than men finding employment, in light of their superior language skills, but also because the jobs they seek (as cleaners or seamstresses, for example) are less likely to require advanced mastery of English. This greater flexibility means that women and children often act as cultural brokers, introducing the ethnic group to the dominant culture, but in the process putting at risk traditional patterns of spousal relating, especially in regard to dominance and power (Duryea, 1992).

The second sense in which gender mediates ethnicity concerns immigration. To date, the immigration literature has largely ignored women, under the rubric that "the men followed the money and the women followed the men" (Little, 1976: 17). In contrast, a recent and extensive literature review by Findley and Williams (1991) shows that this view is unjustified, and that the motives and experiences associated with immigration are often quite different for women as opposed to men. Among Hispanic women, for example, immigration may be motivated by a desire to escape spousal abuse (Takash & Zavella, 1993).

The final sense in which gender mediates ethnicity concerns the disparity between gender stereotypes or ideals and actual behavior (Davenport & Yurich, 1991). As will shortly be apparent, much of the available literature portrays men and women in traditional terms, that is, with men dominant, powerful and active, and with women submissive, weak and passive. Such a portrayal completely disregards either changing patterns of interpersonal conduct or the bases of variation in such conduct. Thus, in the words of Baca Zinn (1979: 65) speaking about Hispanic women, "[o]ne of the most apparent contradictions may be ·found in the disparity between the patriarchal ideal and women's [real] power in the family." This suggests the importance of being critical of the existing literature in the effort to construct a contemporary description of the groups in question, especially with regard to sources of within-group variation (Hardy, 1990).

Age/Generation

Gelfand (1982) finds that the salience of cultural norms and traditions increases with age. Thus, the clash between minority and dominant cultures often gets played out in cross-generational conflict. As a function of their age, children may have had limited exposure to the ethnic group in which they were born. Conversely, through contacts at play, through the media and in school, children are virtually immersed in the dominant culture whose values and norms may be sharply at variance with those daily espoused by their parents. In a single generation, this divergence increases the likelihood of parent-child conflict (McGoldrick et al., 1989), especially insofar as children's (more advanced) language skills often afford them power over their non-English-speaking parents (Duryea & Gundison, 1993). Over multiple generations, it increases the chances that ethnic group values and expectations will gradually converge with those of the dominant culture

(Connor, 1974a), including loss of ethnically distinct values, lifestyles and language skills.

Family Functioning

Finally, throughout this volume I will assume adequate family functioning, used here in a clinical sense (see McGoldrick, 1988). This is a convenient fiction. Regardless of group membership, the level of family functioning can be expected to distribute on a continuum, with a varying proportion of families functioning poorly (Logan et al., 1990). In turn, this is inversely related to social class (Kolody et al., 1986); as resources decline, the risk of family dysfunction (including divorce, substance abuse, child abuse and spousal violence) and the level of stress (Colon, 1980) increase.

NOTES

1. For other definitions, see Herberg (1989), Mindel et al. (1988), Sollars (1989), and Stern and Cicala (1991).

2. Biculturalism has recently become the focus of considerable study and debate. For an overview of this burgeoning area, see Birman (1994).

3. See also Gelfand and Bialik-Gilad (1989), Gelfand and Yee (1992), Glazer (1985), Hawkins (1988, 1991), Kasinitz (1992), Richard (1991), Sanjek and Colen (1990), Takaki (1993), and Walker (1980, 1984).

4. In the United States, this includes between 100,000 and 300,000 illegal immigrants annually (Chavez, 1990). While recent statutory changes, such as the Immigration Reform and Control Act (1986), has served to legalize some of these "illegals," Gelfand and Bialek-Gilad (1989) argue that such changes have also prevented many of them from achieving satisfactory living conditions.

5. Gelfand and Yee (1992) report that more than 35% of the population growth in the United States during the 1980's was due to immigration, both legal and illegal. The result is that, by the year 2000, in many states no single group (including Whites) will constitute a majority (Bouvier, 1991).

PART II

Ethnic Profiles

In this and the next three chapters, I profile five ethnic groups: African American Blacks, Caribbean Canadian Blacks, Hispanics, Asians and Jews. In each case, the profile is summarized in a Figure, followed by detailed elaboration in the text.

3

The Blacks

INTRODUCTION

The Blacks, like each of the groups to be profiled, represent a heterogeneous group, drawing members from Canada, the United States, the Caribbean, Africa and South America, with each subgroup distinctively different from the others (see Allahan, 1993; Anderson, 1985; Brice, 1982; Christiansen et al., 1982; Elliston, 1985; Gibson with Lewis, 1985; Kasinitz, 1992; Lau, 1986; Walker, 1984).

This profile will focus on *two* groups, both the largest of the Black groups in their respective nations: African American Blacks (hereafter referred to as *Blacks*) and Caribbean Canadian Blacks (hereafter referred to as *Caribbean Blacks*). Blacks are those originally brought here as slaves (Pinderhughes, 1982), with the majority still resident in the South (Hacker, 1992).[1] They have received the most attention of any group in the literature (Anderson, 1990; Billingsley, 1988; Boyd-Franklin, 1989, 1993; Dana, 1993; Dickson, 1993; Edelman, 1993; Fisher, 1992; Hacker, 1992; Hines, 1988, 1990; Hines & Boyd-Franklin, 1982; Jaynes & Williams, 1989; Marks, 1991; McAdoo, 1988, 1993; McGoldrick et al., 1989; Porter & Washington, 1979, 1989, 1993; Reddy, 1994; Stack, 1974; Staples, 1988, 1991; Staples & Johnson, 1993; White & Parham, 1990; Williams, 1987).[2] For quick reference, the profile of African American Blacks is summarized in Figure 3.1, below, with detailed description in the following text.

In contrast, there are at least *three* good reasons for thinking that this portrait of Blacks in the United States does *not* generalize well to their counterparts in Canada, that is, African Canadian Blacks and Caribbean Canadian Blacks. First, Canadian Blacks have a very different history (Walker, 1980: 160).[3] For example, Canada had a comparatively short history of slavery, no Civil War and no Reconstruction period.[4] Unlike their American counterparts, Canadian Blacks have had, at best, an in-

Figure 3.1
Summary Profile of Blacks in the United States

Modal Social Class:	lower/working
Definition of the Family:	multigeneration informal extended, including "kept" children and "fictive" kin
Life Cycle:	compressed, three phases, with emphasis on adulthood
Husband-Wife Relations:	role flexibility, matrifocal/matriarchal
Parent-Child Relations:	authoritarian; corporal punishment
Perspective on Treatment	community sources of help preferred, especially kin and church pastor

complete hierarchy of professions and institutions; their much smaller numbers and greater geographic dispersion mean they simply are not found in all possible occupations nor are they represented in all universities, law offices, government agencies, and so on. Further, unlike the United States, Canada has had no large scale inner city urban ghettoes. Indeed, a recent study of the inner-cities of twelve Census Metropolitan Areas (CMAs) during the period 1981-1985 (Statistics Canada, 1990) yields a rather different profile than that found in most large American cities (see below, Blacks, modal class). Three facts were especially noteworthy: the relative absence of children (only 9% of those sampled), the relatively high level of education (36% with at least some university), and an income split (39% reporting annual earnings at or below $20,000 compared to 15% reporting more than $60,000).

Second, the Black population in Canada involves a much higher proportion of Caribbean Blacks. Not more than 5% of Blacks in the United States are Caribbean immigrants, with the vast majority relatively recent (Kasinitz, 1992; Sowell, 1981). By contrast, 27% of Blacks in Canada (in 1991: 94,000) identified themselves as being from the Caribbean, the majority (64%) living in the Toronto CMA[5] (population: 3.4 million; Walker, 1984).[6] Further, approximately 20% of the Caribbean Blacks in Toronto are second generation Canadians (Toronto Star, June 21, 1992: A1, A6-A7). Indeed, this last fact suggests that 27% may be a conservative estimate. The Canadian census allows Blacks to identify themselves in two ways other than "Caribbean", namely, as "Black" (224,000 [65%]) or "African" (26,000 [7.5%]).[7] Given their duration in Canada, many Blacks may have chosen to identify themselves as "Black" rather than as "Caribbean," a choice especially likely among those born in Canada.[8]

Finally, Caribbean Blacks remain a distinct subgroup within the Canadian Black community. For example, Walker (1984: 23) observes that,

"[West Indians] can see very little in common between themselves and indigenous [Canadian] blacks beyond the coincidence of colour." This is so for several reasons. Not only are Caribbean Blacks more numerous than their African Canadian counterparts in all areas of Canada except the Maritime provinces (D'Oyley, 1977/1982), but having come from majority Black nations in the Caribbean,[9] Walker (1984) suggests that they are more sensitive to discrimination and more ready to challenge it. For their part, African Canadian Blacks may resent what they perceive among Caribbean Blacks as an air of superiority. Further, the two subgroups are divided on the basis of language, specifically "dialect" or "patois" (Gibson with Lewis, 1985),[10] a variety of languages unevenly distributed across the Caribbean (Christiansen et al., 1982) but absent among African Canadian Blacks.[11]

In light of these various differences, I will systematically distinguish between Blacks and Caribbean Blacks. This is not an ideal solution, but the paucity of material regarding African Canadian Blacks (Clairmont & Magill, 1987; Foggo, 1990) offers no alternative. Further, it suggests the need to develop a separate profile of Caribbean Blacks. For quick reference, that profile is summarized in Figure 3.2, below, with detailed description in the following text.

Figure 3.2
Summary Profile of Caribbean Blacks in Canada

Modal Social Class:	lower middle
Definition of the Family:	modified "Christian" or nuclear family, including child lending
Life Cycle:	no information
Husband-Wife Relations:	role segregation, matrifocal/matriarchal
Parent-Child Relations:	authoritarian; corporal punishment
Perspective on Treatment	community sources of help preferred, especially kin and church pastor

MODAL SOCIAL CLASS

Blacks

Despite major advances in equality and equity in recent years (Farley, 1984; Fisher, 1992), the United States remains a hostile environment for Blacks (Berry & Blassingame, 1982; Wilkinson & Spurlock, 1986). A brief glimpse at current demographic data reveal just how hostile:

- In the United States, on average, employed Black males earn only 58% of the income of their White counterparts (Allen, 1994; Dickson, 1993; Hacker, 1992), such that a well-educated Black man still earns less than a poorly educated White man (Staples, 1985, 1991). Consequently, while in 1991 the median income among White families was $38,000, it was only about half that ($22,000) among Black families (National Center for Educational Statistics, 1993).

- Chronic unemployment (Farley, 1987; Hines & Boyd-Franklin, 1982; Boyd-Franklin, 1989; Wilson, 1987); subemployment (Lichter, 1988); and underemployment (Giddings, 1985), especially among the young (Freeman & Holzer, 1986), remain commonplace, as do anti-minority stereotyping (Bobo & Kuegel, 1993; Kirschenman & Neckerman, 1991) and racial discrimination (Turner et al., 1991) as barriers to employment (Braddock & McPartland, 1987). The salience of this state of affairs for family life can hardly be overstated. In the words of Menaghan (1991: 439), "a variety of workplace conditions--restriction of opportunity to exercise self-direction, work overload, poor quality of interpersonal relations on the job, low opportunity for cooperative problem-solving, job insecurities, job loss, and loss of earnings--have emotional repercussions that have negative implications for family interaction."

- The majority (76%) of married Black women with children work (Piotrkowski & Hughes, 1993), earning (in 1992) about 68% of black men for work of equal value (Chapman, 1995). Most of these women work out of financial necessity and are relegated to jobs characterized by low pay, unskilled menial work, and close supervision (Tomaskovic-Devey, 1993). Even professional women must confront discriminatory stereotypes which limit their opportunities for advancement (Jacobs, 1989; McGoldrick et al., 1989).

- The result is that in 1990, 35% of two-parent Black families in the United States reported income below the poverty line, and a further 20% earned only slightly more (Dickson, 1993; Gilbert & Kahl, 1987). Among inner city Black families, the poverty rate exceeded 60% (Hacker, 1992).

- Single mothers represented 56% of all Black families in 1990 (Walsh, 1993). Of these, 70% reported income below the poverty line (Billingsley, 1988), that is, less than $10,530 per year for a family of three (Hacker, 1992). Consequently, 50% of Black children will spend all or part of their childhood growing up in poor families (Hines, 1989; Jaynes & Williams, 1989). Indeed, a recent study of twelve of the largest inner-city school districts in the United States found that more than 50% of the children surveyed came from poor families (Billingsley, 1988).

Other indicators are closely associated with poverty:

- McGoldrick (1993: 355) reports that there is an "epidemic number of Black teen parents."[12] [13] For example, Gibbs (1989a, 1989b) reports that in 1985, the birth rate among Black teenage girls was 163 per 1000 pregnancies, twice the comparable rate (of eighty-three) among Whites.[14] [15] This meant that of all teenagers less than fifteen years of age who gave birth in that year, 60% were Black (Ho, 1992b).[16] It also meant that by age eighteen, twice as many Black girls have been pregnant (41%) compared to their White counterparts (21%; Hacker, 1992).[17] Further, Walsh (1993) notes that while 25% of all births in the United States are to single mothers, the comparable figure among Black teenage mothers is more than 90%. Some have stressed the link between such pregnancies and the heigtened risk of long-term poverty, poor parenting, and health and psychosocial problems (Brooks-Gunn & Chase-Lansdale, 1993; Burton, 1990; Chase-Lansdale & Brooks-Gunn, 1991; cf. Webster & D'Allesandro, 1989). Others have argued that such pregancies arise out of poverty, and especially geographic residential segregation in crumbling inner-city ghettoes (Breunster, 1994; Franklin, 1988a; Massey, 1990; Wacquant & Wilson, 1989; Wilson, 1991).[18] Only cursory inspection suggests that cause and consequences are interwined, implying that many young Blacks are caught in a vicious circle that serves to perpetuate Black disadvantage.

■ Black geographic residential segregation is not limited to teenage mothers, but applies generally, affecting Blacks across all income levels (Sassen, 1990). Based on his comparative analysis of census data for 1950 and 1980, Allen (1994: 59) observes that "[to] eliminate the geographic isolation of blacks in the 16 largest metropolitan areas in 1980 77% of whites (or blacks) would have to be relocated. In the USA today, as was true 50 years ago, residential areas continue to be starkly delineated by race, and segregation by race in where people live and where their children attend school is therefore the rule rather than the exception."

■ Gang violence among inner-city Black youth is a serious problem (Garbarino, 1992; Horowitz, 1983; Sampson, 1987; Sanders, 1994; Sullivan, 1989).[19] In part, such violence, coupled with the ready availability of handguns,[20] has meant three things. First, Black males are ten times as likely as their White counterparts to be murdered (Hawkins, 1990, 1993, 1994; Staggers, 1989; Tienda, 1990).[21] Second, whereas the national murder rate is about 9.0 per 100,000, the comparable rate in large cities is much higher (U.S. Justice Department, 1991), for example, 58.5 in Detroit, 28.9 in Los Angeles, 30.4 in Chicago, 30.7 in New York City, 31.4 in Philadelphia and 35.5 in Houston. Finally, among Black males 18 to 24 years of age, murder is currently the leading cause of death (Hawkins, 1986; Staggers, 1989). Indeed, in a number of large cities young Black men are twenty times more likely to be murdered than their White counterparts (Nettler, 1982). This is one among a variety of facts (see below) that have caused some observers to characterize young Black men as an "endangered" species (Allen-Meares & Burman, 1995; Majors & Gordon, 1994).

■ In 1982, Staggers (1989) reported that the third leading cause of death among Black adolescents, especially males, was suicide, at a rate of 11.0 per 100,000.[22] In addition, Staggers (1989) argues that the second leading cause of death among Black adolescents, automobile accidents, may involve a classification error, since an unknown proportion of such fatalities may be disguised forms of suicide.

- In 1990, the infant mortality rate per 1000 births was 8.1 among Whites but 16.5 among Blacks (Hacker, 1992; Tienda, 1990).

- In large American cities, 63% of all children in foster care are Black (Jenkins & Diamond, 1985).

- In addition to higher rates of unemployment than their White counterparts, Newman (1988) reports that Blacks (especially Black females) tend to be unemployed for longer periods of time. This makes middle class Blacks more vulnerable to downward social mobility (Duncan, 1986). It also renders poor Blacks more vulnerable to homelessness (Hopper et al., 1985), recently abetted by state attacks on the welfare system (Block et al., 1987; Katz, 1989), with nearly half of all the homeless in the United States (44%) comprised of single Black males (Hopper et al., 1985; Rossi, 1989; Shlay & Rossi, 1992). In either case, Newman (1988) documents the terrible toll downward mobility takes in personal self-esteem, marital relations, parent-child relations, and relations with extended kin and friends.

- In 1990, the overall life expectancy among Whites was 76.0 years compared to 70.3 years among Blacks (Hacker, 1992).

In short, American society in the 1990's is characterized by "savage inequalities" (Kozol, 1991), with the majority of Blacks belonging to the lower/working class (Bonacich, 1990), and with a significant minority belonging to the "underclass" (Auletta, 1982; Glasgow, 1981; Katz, in press; Marks, 1991; Massey & Eggers, 1990; Wilson, 1987).[23] [24] Such experience is the basis for widespread alienation and cynicism among Blacks, especially Black youth (Powell, 1985), whose attitude is often that "there ain't no making it" (MacLeod, 1987; Harris & Wilkins, 1988).

Caribbean Blacks

On the basis of admittedly slim evidence, it appears that Caribbean Blacks come closer than African Canadian Blacks to income parity with Whites. In the United States, Kasinitz (1992) used 1980 census data for New York state to compare the poverty rates among Whites, Blacks, Koreans and Jamaicans. The results show Jamaicans with a rate (16%) nearly half that of their Black counterparts (27%; Allen & Farley, 1987).

In Canada, the findings are less clear. Moreau (1991), for example, using data from the 1986 census for the Toronto CMA, compared men and women in three ethnic groups ("Black," Chinese and Indo-Pakistani) across a range of dimensions. Among other things, this showed that Blacks were twice as likely to be poor (26%) as Whites (12%). The National Council of Welfare (1990: 119) notes that Caribbean women "receive significantly lower salaries than immigrants from other countries who have comparable qualifications," while several studies have reported discriminatory hiring practices aimed at Caribbean Blacks (Head, 1975; Henry & Ginzberg, 1986; Ramcharan, 1976). In the same vein, Sev'er et al. (1993), based on data from the late 1970's, found that, of seven ethnic groups studied, "West Indian" and Italian men had the lowest level of education and income, the lowest overall level of occupational status, and the highest level of anomie, that is, of perceived powerlessness. In contrast, Shadd (1987), using data from the 1971 census, showed that the average income of Black males in Ontario (typically Caribbean) was much closer to parity than their counterparts in Nova Scotia (typically African Canadian). Similar evidence (using data gathered in the early 1980's) of income close to parity, especially among Caribbean Black women, have been reported by Breton et al. (1990) and Halli et al. (1990). Most recently, using data from the 1986 census, DeSilva (1992) found that when years of education and Canadian work experience were controlled, there was no difference in the average incomes of Caribbean Blacks and Whites.

Combining the work of Breton et al. (1990) and Walker (1984) suggests a possible resolution of this apparent contradiction in terms of an occupational split based on education. Breton et al. argue that with the elimination of the tight restrictions on Caribbean immigration to Canada, two groups of immigrants began to arrive in large numbers: the highly educated who sought professional jobs (in law, medicine and management) and the poorly educated who sought unskilled and semi-skilled jobs (as taxi drivers and security guards). In turn, Walker argues that with immigration comes a period of downward dislocation caused by language problems, failure to recognize Caribbean qualifications, and the strain of reestablishing in a new society. Failure to distinguish between professional and unskilled workers in demographic analyses, then, may produce uneven results regarding income parity.

Finally, data regarding indicators associated with poverty support the inference that there are few marked differences between Caribbean Blacks and Whites, while there are sharp differences between the United States and Canada. Consider the following:

- In Canada, the homicide rate has historically hovered around 2.5 per 100,000 population;[25] as important, the comparable rates in Canada's major cities have hovered at about the same level. In Metropolitan Toronto, for example, the average homicide rate during the period 1990-1993 was 2.9.[26] While the Canadian Centre for Justice Statistics only began collecting crime data by ethnicity in 1991 (Centre of Criminology, 1991), local newspapers in Toronto periodically publish the pictures of murder victims: nearly all are White.

- The birth rate among Canadian teenage women was 26.6 per 1000 women in 1990, up marginally from 26.5 in 1989 and down substantially from 33.7 in 1971 (Nett, 1993: 215).[27] Regrettably, these data are not available by ethnicity. However, there is no reason to believe that such an analysis would show large differences between Caribbean Blacks and Whites.

- Finally, Breton et al. (1990) report on an analysis of residential segregation in Metropolitan Toronto, based on survey and census data collected during the period 1979-1981. This showed that Caribbean Blacks displayed an "intermediate" level of segregation, that is, higher than several European ethnic groups (Germans, Italians), on a par with Asian groups (Chinese, Japanese) but lower than the group showing the highest level of segregation, the Jews. Put differently, these data suggest that residential segregation among Caribbean Blacks, unlike their African American counterparts, is neither involuntary nor centered on the inner-city.

These various observations support two conclusions. While there does appear to be a disparity between Caribbean Blacks and Whites in terms of income, it is not nearly as great as that reported between Blacks and Whites in the United States. Further, despite the higher proportion of poor Caribbean Blacks compared to Whites, the modal class of Caribbean Blacks is likely within the middle-class range.

DEFINITION OF THE FAMILY

Blacks

Among Blacks, the basic family unit is the multigeneration, informal extended family (Edelman, 1993; Martin & Martin, 1978; Shimkin et al., 1978; Staples, 1991; White, 1990; Wilson, 1986). In addition to one or both parents and their biological children, it may also include: true kin (grandparents, in-laws, aunts and uncles, cousins); fictive kin (Ogbu, 1986), composed of long-time friends; informally adopted children (Hill, 1977), a process known as "child-keeping" (Stack, 1974); and visiting relatives, a process known as "doubling up" (Hill, 1977). Further, irrespective of the specific individuals included, relations among family members are built on expectations of loyalty and mutual support (Ball, 1983; Dressler, 1985; Hines & Boyd-Franklin, 1982; Lindblad-Goldberg & Dukes, 1985; McAdoo, 1979, 1981; McGoldrick,1988; Raymond et al., 1980; Stack, 1974; Taylor, 1986).[28]

This family form represents an adaptive response to the confluence of three longstanding structural processes: poverty, the scarcity of eligible males and the degraded status of males. Poverty places the very survival of the family at continuous risk (Boyd-Franklin, 1993; Fulmer, 1988). While sudden job loss, illness, death, marital separation, imprisonment and other untoward circumstances may each be unpredictable, having such "troubles" is generally expected. Material resources, meager to start with, can rise and fall without warning. The end result is a heroic effort to ensure family survival (Willie, 1974). Towards that end, the extended family is a more stable and enduring base than any one individual or family standing alone, ensuring that all members have access to some resources.

Next, there is a significant imbalance in the number of eligible adult men and women (Guttentag & Secord, 1983; Madhubuti, 1990; Staples, 1981), with the ratio of men to women in some regions of the United

States as high as one to seven.[29] This is largely a concomitant of poverty. At birth, this involves a much higher infant mortality rate among Blacks than Whites (Reddy, 1994), especially among male infants since they are biologically less robust than their female counterparts (Guttentag & Secord, 1983). Among children, it involves a higher rate of accidental deaths among Blacks than Whites, especially among males (Guttentag & Secord, 1983). And, among adults, Black men, especially young Black men (aged fifteen to twenty-four), have a much higher mortality rate than women due to elevated rates of illness, such as heart disease, hypertension, and sickle cell anaemia (Devore & Schlesinger, 1987); automobile and industrial accidents; alcoholism and drug overdoses (Guttentag & Secord, 1983); imprisonment (Hacker, 1992: Langan, 1985; Painter, 1977; Petersilia, 1983);[30] capital punishment (Gross & Mauro, 1989; see Flowers, 1988); suicide (Gibbs, 1989b; Howze, 1979; National Center for Educational Statistics, 1993) and murder (Hawkins, 1986). This shortage of men produces a dilemma, as women are unable to find eligible men of equal class and education, while men seek to marry up.[31] Indeed, this dilemma may be greatest for Black women who strive and succeed in gaining upward mobility. As Staples (1988: 189) observes, "the greater a [Black] woman's educational level and income, the less desirable she is to many Black males. While a [Black] man's success adds to his desirability as a mate, it detracts from a [Black] woman's." Consequently, compared to their White counterparts, Black women are more willing to enter into a common-law relationship and to bear children in that relationship (Staples & Johnson, 1993), but less willing to consider either abortion or formal adoption (McGoldrick, 1982a).

On the one hand, such norms help explain the high proportion of single mothers noted earlier. Indeed, even if such mothers can marry, they may be discouraged from doing so by their extended family, who may view marriage as threatening to both the safety of the woman and the stability of the family network (Kenkel, 1981). In some cases, this may mean that each of several children may have different fathers (Fulmer, 1988; Hunter & Ensinger, 1992). On the other hand, such norms account for a higher fertility rate among Black women compared to White women (Hacker, 1992).[32] For example, compared to Whites, Black women who do marry tend to do so younger, have more children, and wait less time between marrying and having their first child (Halli et al., 1990; Spanier & Thompson, 1984).

Third, the degraded status of males contributes significantly to a family form that is often female-centered or matrilocal in character (Comas-Diaz & Greene, in press; Madhubuti, 1990; Sanua, 1985). While men may be given respect as the head of their household, many experience grave difficulties in living up to these expectations. Compared to women, men are more vulnerable to job loss, a result of three related processes: unskilled or semi-skilled jobs characterized by low stability; racial discrimination on the job; and what Franklin (1992) has called the "invisibility factor," the tendency of Whites to perceive Black men as hostile and dangerous, and thus react in encounters with them as if they were invisible.[33] In addition, men are subject to group norms (see below) which accord them greater freedom to socialize away from home (McGoldrick et al., 1989).

Both employment experience and group norms mean that women frequently have the primary responsibility for supporting the family (Jones, 1985).[34] Consequently, Black women are more likely than their White counterparts to be employed (Beckett, 1976) and to see work as a family obligation (Leggon, 1983). In turn, Black women are more willing to delegate family responsibilities to others, in particular relying on a network of extended female kin to help with child rearing (Burton, 1985; Malson, 1983). Additional processes accentuate the focus on women. For example, the emphasis on informal solutions to marital problems may mean long periods of marital separation with no effort to obtain a formal divorce, typically leaving mothers to provide child care alone (Hines & Boyd-Franklin, 1982). Further, the involvement of non-resident fathers is discouraged by welfare regulations that may cut off support on evidence of male involvement (Danziger & Radin, 1990). The results are predictable: women are encouraged to claim that they are the head of the household while maintaining men as peripheral to the family, a further basis for their invisibility (Franklin, 1992).[35] The scarcity of men may mean that women who divorce are more likely than their White counterparts to remain single longer before remarrying (Staples, 1985). Taken together, these processes often deny Black men the positions of husbands and fathers (Devore & Schlesinger, 1987), placing a corresponding burden on the shoulders of the women in the network to be strong, independent and resourceful, if not for themselves, then for the sake of their children (Hines, 1990; McGoldrick et al., 1989). The result is that female centered families now represent the majority,[36] placing a special emphasis on mother-daughter relationships (Martin & Martin, 1978). Paradoxically, the enormous strength of Black women often means that while extended family support offers men some relief from stress, the same buffering effect does not extend to women (Dressler, 1985); their "labor of love [is often a] labor of sorrow" (Jones, 1985; Omolade, 1986; Pratt et al., 1984; Reid & Comas-Diaz, 1990; White & Parham, 1990).

Finally, these various processes have profoundly affected Black attitudes toward education and work. The attitude of Black parents toward education is marked by ambivalence. Black parents tend to have high aspirations for their children (McGoldrick et al., 1989; Nora, 1993).[37] However, they daily confront realities that limit the likelihood that those aspirations will be achieved. Many parents are themselves high school dropouts (National Center for Educational Statistics, 1993). This increases the likelihood that they will adopt a passive attitude toward their children's education, feeling powerless to intervene (Calabrese, 1990; Lareau, 1987). They will also have had first-hand experience of schools that are dangerous and disorganized, of teachers that have low expectations and of an employment market in which Blacks have limited opportunities, irrespective of their education (Edelman, 1993; Gibson & Ogbu, 1991; Hale-Benson, 1982; Hines, 1988).[38] For example, Kunjufu (1985) speaks of "fourth grade failure syndrome" in which White teachers, intimidated by the violent reputation of Black males, are likely to perceive the behavior of Black boys as indicative of aggression and hyperactivity and thus predictive of academic failure. Similarly, a recent analysis found that of public schools in thirty-two states containing 98% of all Blacks, more than half were segregated, that is, between 50% and 83% of the students were Black, although Blacks represented a much smaller proportion of the populations in those states (Hacker, 1992). Findings such as these have led some observers to conclude that the United States is sliding back into a form of "American apartheid" (Massey, 1990).

Further, Black children may be unprepared for the expectations of the White school system, never having had the experience of being systematically questioned by adults and thus having no conception of what "testing" is (McDowell, 1992; Ogbu, 1981). Entwisle and Alexander (1993: 405) capture these difficulties when they observe that "for children brought up outside the middle class mainstream, differences between home and school are dramatic. The conventions of the school, with its achievement orientation, its expectations that children will stay on task and work independently without close monitoring, its tight schedule of moving from lesson to lesson, its use of "standard" English, its insistence on punctuality, and its evaluation of children in terms of what they can do instead of who they are, all can be daunting."

One consequence of such cultural divergence may be active resistence by students who perceive the educational system as hostile to their needs. The following observation by Wolcott (1994: 307), while concerned with American native children, seems equally applicable to the Black experience:

Formal teaching is predicated on the notion of learner incompetence. Education across cultures exacerbates the magnitude of that incompetence by identifying worthy knowledge as something located entirely outside the cultural system of the student. We continue to perceive multicultural education as a problem of the student, a problem to which teachers and schools are the answer. We are correct with this approach often enough. Education apparently "takes," and we witness wave upon wave of refugees and immigrant and minority groups successfully incorporated into new communities and nations.

But sometimes the lines are drawn differently, especially in cases where indigenous minorities see themselves as overrun, dislocated, or threatened with involuntary assimilation. In such settings, resistance to "the system," or to the teacher as its spokesperson, may become an entrenched student strategy.

Another consequence of such divergence is that Black children perform less well in school than their White counterparts across all levels, from public school (Alexander & Entwisle, 1988; Alexander et al., 1993; Entwisle and Alexander, 1993; Neisser, 1986) to high school (Coleman, 1990) to university (Beaudry, 1992; Nettles et al., 1984; Nettles, 1988; Stikes, 1984; Thomas, 1981). While Black girls are more likely than boys to complete high school, the combined junior and senior high school dropout rate is about 60% (Nora, 1993). Even so, while high school completion rates have historically risen, they are now in decline (Postsecondary Education Opportunity, 1993b).[39] Moreover, as a function of parental education and income (Persell et al., 1992; Postsecondary Education Opportunity, 1993c), and weak student academic preparation (Hacker, 1992),[40] both girls and boys are increasingly likely to decline the opportunity to advance to postsecondary education (Fulmer, 1988). While Black enrollment rates rose in the 1970's and early 1980's, they have since been slowly falling (Fisher, 1992; Mow & Nettles, 1990; Nora, 1993).[41] In the words of Smedley et al. (1993: 434),

African-American students attending predominantly white colleges are less likely to graduate within five years, have lower grade point averages, experience higher attrition rates, and matriculate into graduate programs at lower rates than white students and their counterparts at predominantly Black or minority institutions. (See Astin, 1982, 1993; Pallas et al., 1989.)

In addition, such experience is often associated with discrimination, alienation, isolation and depression (Feagin, 1992; Lang, 1992; Loo & Rolison, 1986; Mow & Nettles, 1990; Nora, 1993; Stewart et al., 1990; Suen, 1993). In turn, such alienation helps explain Stewart and Vaux's (1986) finding that nearly all Blacks (98%) enrolled in a predominantly White university interacted only with other Blacks. Finally, the most recent data indicate that Blacks are 45% as likely as Whites to earn a university degree by age twenty-five to twenty-nine (Postsecondary Education Opportunity, 1993a, 1993b; Commission on Minority Participation in Education and American Life, 1988).[42]

In light of these sad realities, Black parents have come to value education in a different way than their White counterparts. Black parents are less likely than Whites either to perceive the benefits of educational achievement (Davis, 1992) or to withdraw their love should their children fail to meet their educational expectations (Hines, 1990; McGoldrick et al., 1989).[43]

As regards work, Black attitudes are similarly mixed. Most Black adults have a positive attitude toward work. McGoldrick et al. (1989) indicate that Black parents strive to instill in their children the importance of morality, honesty, hard work and keeping a good name, while Devore and Schlesinger (1987: 63) note that Blacks maintain a "puritan ethic" toward work and success (Hill, 1972; Lewis & Looney, 1983). Even so, Black experience in the labor force has often been negative, exacerbated by the

fact that many Blacks, especially men, come to work both with negative
expectations and weak academic skills. Their overall commitment to work,
then, especially among the young, may be ambivalent (Hines, 1988; Staples
& Johnson, 1993).

Caribbean Blacks

The generalizability of this portrait to Caribbean Blacks is limited by
culture and immigration. At the risk of oversimplification, life in the
Caribbean Islands may be characterized as poor, authoritarian and
matriarchal. The basic family unit falls somewhere between the White
nuclear family and the Black extended family (Brice, 1982; Christiansen et
al., 1982; Gibson with Lewis, 1985; Ho, 1993). That is, while the two-
parent family is central, it is linked to a rich support network of relatives
and friends. Friends can drop in any time, whenever they please, make
themselves at home and share in anything being offered. Inpromptu parties,
held in the street, are commonplace. Family life is thus further characterized by relatively diffuse boundaries, including a longstanding tradition
of "child lending" in which, during hard times, children may temporarily
live with relatives or family friends. The poor economy means that
husbands are often absent for extended periods in search of work and that
hard work and "thrift" are central cultural values. The practical consequence is that women, many of whom work, are expected to be self-
sufficient, strong and resourceful. Moreover, given a history of British
colonization, authority is hierarchical, based on age. This is especially
evident in Island schools in the respectful and dependent way in which
students interact with teachers. Such behavior also highlights education as
another central cultural value. However, the utility of education as a basis
for mobility intersects with a class system based on skin color. Historically,
"light" skin has been associated with high status, although this has changed
somewhat in recent years (Walker, 1984); with national independence has
come increased pride in native culture and language.

This approach to family life, work and education is complicated by
immigration. Christiansen et al. (1982) and Ho (1993), for example,
distinguish between five patterns of immigration to Canada: (1) one spouse
(typically female) arrives first, obtains employment and the others follow;
(2) both spouses arrive first and the children follow; (3) the entire family
arrives together; (4) one spouse (typically male) arrives first, completes
university or professional training, gets a job and then the others follow;
and (5) a single parent (typically female) arrives first, obtains work and
then the children arrive later (sometimes much later).

These various patterns of immigration clarify two of several ways in
which Caribbean Blacks are different from their Black counterparts,
namely, extended family support and gender parity. As seen above, Blacks
are typically embedded in an extended family support network. In contrast,
in moving away from the Islands, Caribbean Black families typically leave

behind their support system. While many live with or near relatives (Moreau, 1991), and prefer to live in neighborhoods with high concentrations of Caribbean Blacks (Breton et al., 1990), the web of reciprocal relations that typify Island life takes generations to reconstruct. It will thus be unavailable to most Caribbean Black families that have immigrated recently.[44] This loss extends considerably the time it takes Caribbean Black families to adjust to life in Canada.

As for gender parity, as noted above, this is highly problematic for Black women. In contrast, there is no shortage of men among their Caribbean Black counterparts. For example, Moreau's (1991) study of Metropolitan Toronto found that men made up 48% and 45% of the White and Black populations, respectively. Further, such figures must be placed in the context of assimilation, one aspect of which concerns intermarriage. Thus, Ram (1990), using census data for 1981, found that between 22% (among Trinidadians) and 34% (among Jamaicans) of Caribbean Blacks married someone not of the same national origin.

Finally, while Black and Caribbean Black children both encounter problems in education, this is so for very different reasons (Anderson & Grant, 1987; Christiansen et al., 1982; Gibson with Lewis, 1985). In contrast to Black children, Caribbean Black children have been socialized in a very different school system (La Belle, 1986). This is characterized by schools which are small; populated mostly by Caribbean Blacks; use language which includes dialect or patois; and instruction in which teachers issue detailed instructions and maintain strict discipline. For these children, problems with education in Canada have less to do with a hostile and dangerous environment than with "culture shock." For the first time, they will constitute a minority of the students and may be subject to various forms of racism and discrimination. Their school will be comparatively large, leading to feelings of disorientation and isolation. They will be offered instruction in standard English which some will understand rather imperfectly and which others may misunderstand, since many English words have different meanings in dialect (see below). Perhaps most important, much of the teaching process will involve relations with teachers designed to foster child independence, which will be foreign to Caribbean Black children. Indeed, the combination of passivity (seen as appropriate in Island schools); confusion (in response to the lack of explicit instruction); and lack of participation (given the absence of "correct" answers that they would expect to know in Island schools) may lead some teachers to erroneously conclude that such children are "slow" or academically incompetent.

In any event, the school adjustment of many Caribbean Black children is slow and painful, with negative consequences for conduct and academic performance. The former may involve anger leading to acting out and, for some, the formation of cliques of like-minded adolescents (Christiansen et al., 1982). As to their academic performance, recent reports concerning elementary and high school students in the Toronto CMA (Cheng et al., 1989; Peel Board of Education, 1989; Wright, 1985) show that "Black" students, comprising 7%-8% of the student body, do less well than their White counterparts, both in grades and credits earned. This was especially true of those that came from poor families and/or were recent immigrants. While we know of no Canadian study tracking the movement of Caribbean Black high school graduates on to university, data from the 1986 census concerning the educational attainment of "Black" and Caribbean Black adults show that both groups have the lowest proportion reporting either some university education (10.6%, 10.1%, respectively) or university graduation (8.6%, 9.4%, respectively). As to Caribbean Blacks who do enter university, available data are quite sparse, but suggest that their experience may be much less negative than their American counterparts. Grayson (1994c), for example, has recently surveyed approximately 1,100 Caribbean Black, Chinese, East Indian and White students at York University in Toronto. He concluded that

In contrast to much of the research carried out in the United States, the experiences of minorities in the first year [at York University] are not all negative and the experiences of non-minorities are not all positive. Considerable variation exists from experience to experience and from one racial group to the other. In addition, while university experiences have implications for certain first year outcomes, race per se has only a marginal impact on a couple of outcomes. As a result, at least with regard to the first year experience, there is a considerable degree of racial equality in outcomes. (p. 36)

LIFE CYCLE

Blacks

The life cycle of lower/working class Black families tend to be compressed (see above) and accelerated compared to their middle-class counterparts (Fulmer, 1988; Hines, 1988; Hogan, 1981; McAdoo, 1988), women feeling the effects of such compression earlier than men (Hogan, 1985; Nicholson, 1990).

Whereas the life cycle of middle-class Black families is elongated (see above) in light of the need for extended education, that of poor Black families is shaped in response to the demands of survival in a dangerous and hostile environment with meager resources. The result is a three-phase process in which adolescence early fades into adulthood, often ambiguously marked by parenthood, especially among girls (Furstenberg, 1986; Gibbs, 1984). Further, child care and other demands associated with mutual support mean that there may be no clear demarcation between adulthood and old age. Having been overburdened as young women, they later support the view that struggle, sacrifice and the denial of personal satisfaction are inevitable (Hines, 1990).[45] Confirmed in light of later experience, such attitudes are simply carried over into old age. Thus, despite support from their adult children (Mutran, 1985; Taylor, 1986), the elderly often continue to work, either in the home or in paid employment (Burton, 1985), despite ill health, with the result that males in particular risk premature death, either before or shortly after retirement (Hines, 1988). Given the harshness of their lives, release through death is seen as an extremely important transitional event whose celebration can often be costly and elaborate (McGoldrick, 1988).

Caribbean Blacks

Regrettably, no comparable data are available with regard to Caribbean Blacks. It is consequently unclear how to characterize their life cycle processes.

HUSBAND-WIFE RELATIONS

Blacks

As implied above, there are an array of structural forces operating against the maintenance of stable marital relations among lower/working class Blacks (Fine et al., 1987). In addition to those already noted, another concerns the manner in which marriage is often initiated, that is, through pregnancy (Devore & Schlesinger, 1987).

Daughters often receive an ambiguous message from parents and from the community at large. On the one hand, they are pushed to grow up fast, with the experience of motherhood widely seen as essential to becoming a woman (Aschenbrenner, 1975; Hines, 1990). Indeed, motherhood may be regarded as more valued among Blacks than the marital role (McGoldrick et al., 1989). As for boys, they may be encouraged to father babies (Stack, 1974) as a test of manhood (Anderson, 1990; Wilson, 1987), but without social fatherhood (Aschenbrenner, 1975). Wilson (1987) argues that lacking any sense of a secure future fosters in young Black men an approach to life that is present-centered and pleasure-oriented. This is not inconsistent with community norms which approve an open and frank approach to sexual matters, with no rules prohibiting adolescent men and women from socializing together. In this context, the fact that a recent study found that 23% of single Black men intend never to marry (South, 1993) should hardly be surprising.

On the other hand, both parents and the church frown on premarital sex. Mothers may perceive that they have little control over whether or not their daughters become pregnant. The result can be an ambiguous response, encouraging adult behaviors while withholding sexual information and restricting freedom. Similarly, with boys, parents may feel powerless to counteract the pull of the peer group and the street, with its very real danger (McGoldrick, 1982b). Thus, the combination of weak interpersonal skills and sexual experimentation easily translates into pregnancy and parenthood (Gibbs, 1984, 1989a; Notman & Zilbach, 1975). However, with their partners unwilling to become involved in child care, many teenage mothers soon discover that they are unprepared for the emotional and practical demands of a baby; their own mothers or even their grandmothers (Burton, 1985) frequently assume responsibility for care of these children (McGoldrick, 1993; McGoldrick et al., 1989). In turn, this may initiate a series of relatively transient romantic relationships, thus creating a household comprising several generations of women and their respective offspring (Burton, 1985; Fulmer, 1988; Hunter & Ensinger, 1992).

While commonplace, this is only one of several variants on the extended family theme. For example, Boyd-Franklin (1989) calls attention to three additional family forms: (1) the subfamily, involving either two partners without children or with children living elsewhere; (2) the family with secondary members, that is, either an extended or a nuclear family form that includes other relatives (either children or the elderly) as well as family friends; and (3) the augmented family, that is, either an extended or a nuclear family form that includes non-related others, such as informally "adopted" children as well as boarders or lodgers.

Perhaps in defiance of the general tendency to pathologize Black families in the literature (Coner-Edwards & Spurlock, 1988), a number of authors (Billingsley, 1992; Hill, 1972; Lewis & Looney, 1983; Royse & Turner, 1980) have asserted and Lindblad-Goldberg et al. (1988) have confirmed that all of these variants can represent well-functioning families.

There is also a good deal of related evidence in the same vein. For example, in the face of frequent life changes, marital relations in poor Black families are often characterized by more balanced and flexible gender roles (Allen, 1978) and more egalitarian decision-making (Donohue, 1985) than would be expected among their White counterparts.[46] Black fathers, for example, are more likely to help out with household and child care tasks (Gary, 1981; Willie & Greenblatt, 1978). Women openly acknowledge enjoying sex; therefore, it is less often a source of marital tension (Scanzoni, 1971). While spouses are often not physically affectionate in public (McGoldrick et al., 1989), they are more affectively expressive than would be typical among White couples (Donohue, 1985). Blacks, for example, tend to interpret loud language (Kochman, 1974, 1981) and the avoidance of eye contact while listening (Mayo & LaFrance, 1978) as indicative of sincerity and interest.[47] They display sophisticated listening skills, especially as regards nonverbal communication (Erickson, 1979). In Hillard's (1986) terms, they are not word dependent and show a more fluid use of space than Whites, beginning a conversation some distance apart and coming closer together as the conversation intensifies (Connolly, 1975). They are more likely than Whites to make creative use of language, especially slang, laughter, gestures and idiomatic phrases (Cheek, 1976).[48] Finally, Blacks think and perceive in ways different than their White counterparts (Hilliard, 1986). For example, Blacks are more likely to respond to gestalts rather than parts, to prefer inferential to deductive reasoning, to approximate space, numbers and time rather than be exact, and to focus on people and interpersonal relationships rather than on things or events.

In addition, as suggested above, Blacks display community norms of conduct different from Whites. For example, husbands are much freer than their wives to socialize outside the family, including involvement in extramarital affairs (Rutledge, 1980). In addition, couples know they can turn to the larger community for support. For example, poverty encourages reliance on the "underground" or informal economy (Portes et al., 1989), in which barter and mutual aid stand in place of cash, thus indirectly promoting community solidarity. Similarly, the near-universal spirituality (Boyd-Franklin, 1989, 1993) rather than religiosity (Knox, 1985) of Blacks means that the church is a central source of solace, practical support and self-help as well as a focus of community organization and activity (Daniel, 1985; Goldsmith, 1989).

These sources of flexibility notwithstanding, the pressures on Black families are such that they are at considerable risk of dysfunction. For one thing, Black couples are at greater risk of separation and/or divorce than their White counterparts (Dickson, 1993; Teachman, 1982). In part, this may be related to a conflict style which emphasizes control (Ting-Toomey, 1986), and in which compromise is likened to defeat (Donohue, 1985). Given these norms and the enormous stress of poverty, conflict can lead to violence (Hampton, 1991; Lane, 1985).[49] For another, mothers in particular are at constant risk of becoming overburdened (Boyd-Franklin, 1989). Informal adoptions may become either a family secret or a source of conflict resembling a custody battle following divorce.[50] Intergenerational conflict may erupt when teenage mothers, growing older, indicate their desire to parent their own children. In response, their mothers or grandmothers, who had previously cared for these children, may now refuse to relinquish control (Franklin, 1988a).[51] More generally, child rearing efforts may be impaired by family underorganization (Aponte, 1976, 1986, 1994) such that children may be expected to take on adult roles prematurely or may fail to develop the discipline necessary for adult functioning (Boyd-Franklin, 1989). For example, parental disciplinary consistency may be impossible when daily confronted with life circumstances that are themselves unpredictable (Aponte, 1976; White & Parham, 1990); on a nightly basis, children may not know which room or even which bed they are to sleep in (Hunter & Ensinger, 1992).

Under these conditions, several adaptive responses are possible. Parents, overwhelmed by demand, may inadvertently encourage the emergence of one or more parental children, typically female (Hines, 1988). Alternately, such difficulties may encourage the active involvement of other adults, especially women, from among extended kin (Hines & Boyd-Franklin, 1982). Here, child-keeping may be seen as an adaptive response to family distress (Stack, 1974),[52] although it means that some children may spend at least part of their childhood in the care of adults who are unrelated to them (Davis, 1992). Finally, the efforts of well-meaning but intrusive service (welfare, counseling) and control (police, parole) agencies can make matters worse rather than better.

Caribbean Blacks

Turning to Caribbean Blacks, Brice (1982) and Christiansen et al. (1982) note one source of similarity between Caribbean Black and Black women. Both groups of women place equal importance on motherhood as the key to both femininity and adulthood.

These authors also note two areas of difference. The first concerns family variants, with six types distinguished:

- "Christian marriage," in the form of the nuclear family.

- "Faithful concubinage," in which partners cohabit over a period of years and bear offspring; they may or may not marry eventually. In this and the next variant, children are given their father's last name. Consequently, it is not uncommon in the Caribbean Black community to have mothers each of whose several children have different surnames.[53]

- "Serial polygyny," essentially a series of concubinage relationships each of which produces offspring. Since children are encouraged to remember their natural fathers (even if they never see them), their current stepfathers are not expected to play a parental role in their rearing.

- "Maternal family," a single parent mother and her children. This corresponds to the mobility pattern in which the parent in question immigrates, leaving the children in the care of a relative, often a grandmother, until she becomes well-established. This separation may last up to a decade or more. Both mother and father(s) contribute as much as they are able to the children's financial support.

- "Keeper family," a common-law arrangement in which partners live apart, the children living with their mother while the father provides financial support. Here, two subtypes may be distinguished. In one, the arrangement is temporary, leading first to concubinage and later (perhaps) to marriage. In the second subtype, the father is already married, his common-law partner being his "kept" mistress, an arrangement about which the father's legal wife may or may not be aware. Should the arrangement break down or the partner die, the father's legal wife would be expected to raise the children of this union.

- "Housekeeper family," a temporary common-law arrangement based on mutual convenience and consent, in which, by convention, the woman is referred to as the man's "housekeeper."

Irrespective of the family form, relations between spouses are typified by role segregation, with household chores and child rearing largely a female responsibility. Separation between the sexes is similarly played out in the importance accorded privacy in the Caribbean Black community, with extensive family secrets, even between spouses, commonplace.

Christiansen et al. (1982) describe the second source of difference, namely, the marrying of religion, spirituality and magic, especially among poor Caribbean Blacks. Many Caribbean Blacks are deeply religious, with a strong and abiding faith in God and a belief in the literal truth of the Bible. To this is added a belief in the reality of human spirits who are thought to live on after death. In turn, these spirits are thought to play an important role in human affairs, particularly in the form of dreams, visions, prophesies and spirit possession (evidenced by *speaking in tongues*). Accordingly, like Blacks but for very different reasons, it is essential that on death an individual be given a proper funeral so that his or her spirit is *sent off properly*. If not, his or her spirit (Jamaica: *duppy*; Trinidad: *old hag* or *jumbie*) may be *kindled*, bringing illness and/or bad luck (*a duppy deh pan 'im*, he is possessed by an evil spirit). While few will openly admit to it, some still continue to seek the aid of *obeahman* (witch doctors) or other healers who alone can remove the possession. More generally, such beliefs contribute to a sense of fatalism, thus commending the acceptance of suffering while discouraging active change efforts, since these will only fly *in God's face*.

PARENT-CHILD RELATIONS

Blacks

As suggested above, children are seen by Black parents as very important. Typical child care practices vary by child age and gender (Boyd-Franklin, 1989). Parents tend to be relatively indulgent with infants while using strict, even authoritarian discipline, with older children (McAdoo & McAdoo, 1985; Scanzoni, 1971), including corporal punishment (Phinney & Rotheram, 1987). For example, children are expected to obey parental commands immediately and are not permitted to talk back, question parental authority or have angry tantrums. McGoldrick (1993) argues that this approach to discipline is seen by Black parents as necessary to the survival of their children who must quickly learn to face the harsh realities of life. Nevertheless, feelings, both positive and negative, tend to be expressed openly, although nurturance is more likely to take the form of verbal praise rather than physical affection (McAdoo, 1981). Consequently, children are raised to be assertive, independent and positively self-accepting (McGoldrick et al., 1989).[54] In turn, they typically share feelings of loyalty and attachment to their parents. Indeed, Watson and Protinsky (1988) found that intense family closeness, also known as enmeshment, characterized as dysfunctional in White families (Minuchin, 1974), was a positive force in Black families. It helped family members, especially children, feel secure and develop a sense of ego integrity in the face of external oppression (Daly et al., 1995; Greenfield & Cocking, 1994). There is also a good deal of evidence that such support is crucial for children's later academic success (McAdoo, 1988; McAdoo & McAdoo, 1985), since, as indicated above, such support may be unavailable elsewhere.[55]

Child rearing also varies by child gender. While daughters usually share household tasks, sons are seen as harder to control and may be lost to the streets relatively early (McAdoo & McAdoo, 1985). Indeed, recent evidence indicates that sons make independent decisions much earlier (at thirteen years) than daughters (at seventeen years; Dornbusch et al., 1985).

Finally, given the focus on parental as opposed to marital roles (see above), Black families are more inclined to see child behavior rather than adult conduct as a particular source of difficulty (Hines & Boyd-Franklin, 1982; Minuchin et al., 1967). In turn, this perspective highlights the special role of the elderly, particularly elderly women, in Black culture (Gelfand & Barresi, 1987). By virtue of their very survival to old age, the elderly are viewed with respect, as sources of good advice, wisdom and stability (McGoldrick et al., 1989). The complexities of Black family life mean that elderly women seldom experience an empty nest, as their help is needed and valued in child care. Indeed, they may head a three or four generation family (Hines, 1988), a fact that helps explain the relatively small number of elderly Blacks in nursing homes (Devore & Schlesinger, 1987). Even so, many elderly Blacks, especially men, are often poor, live alone and cannot depend on emotional support from their children (Devore & Schlesinger, 1987).

Caribbean Blacks

As for Caribbean Blacks, their attitudes toward child rearing have much in common with their Black counterparts (Christiansen et al., 1982), although they are sustained in a different cultural context. For Caribbean Blacks, children are seen as a *gift from God and a blessing*, with women unable to conceive disparaged as *mules*. Consequently, contraception, abortion and formal adoption are all discouraged.

Despite such regard, children are typically seen as extensions of their parents rather than as individuals in their own right, and thus are not seen to have individual rights, perceptions or feelings. Accordingly, child socialization stresses obedience and passivity, with strong prohibitions against behavior labeled *rude* (impertinent), *fas'* (inquisitive) or *indecent* (disrespectful). This is thought especially important in public, since children's conduct is likely to affect the family's reputation in the community. Thus, disobedience or impropriety may be severely punished, either by scolding, threats or by *flogging* (spanking) severe enough to produce welts. On the one hand, it will be apparent that the independence and expressiveness that schools seek to foster (see above) may directly conflict with parental norms, and indeed, may become a key source of intergenerational conflict. On the other hand, Caribbean standards of discipline directly conflict with community standards in Canada, with charges of child abuse sometimes resulting from this discrepancy.

This general accent on propriety[56] is especially apparent in relations between mothers and daughters. For example, daughters are taught much about housekeeping and child rearing but little, if anything, about sex, though repeatedly enjoined to avoid *keeping bad company* or *playing with boys*. While their schooling in house- and family-keeping prepares them well for the helping professions (such as nursing or teaching), their lack of sex education may leave them unprepared for menstruation or sexual relations within marriage. More generally, this is an approach to child rearing which stresses emotional control, with the result that women often have fewer emotional outlets than men for dealing with frustration, conflict and trauma.

More generally, as regards child socialization, it is important to stress the sharp contrast between child rearing in the Caribbean and in Canada (Gibson with Lewis, 1985). In the Caribbean, children are left pretty much on their own. Life is lived on the street, with children and adults standing and talking or playing at street corners a normal sight. Social activities are routinely organized among the children themselves, while more formal outings are arranged informally among the families. Underpinning this loose and informal approach to child rearing is a large extended family. If the parents themselves are not present to supervise activities, they can rest assured that other adults will be. In coming to Metropolitan Toronto, this parenting superstructure is lost. Children are likely to feel trapped in the home, and offered little by way of recreation or stimulation. Further, naturally reticient, parents may feel deeply ashamed of being poor, and may feel powerless to control their children's improper behavior, as the children struggle to cope with the very different demands of life in this new country.

PERSPECTIVE ON HELP-SEEKING

Blacks

Finally, faced with psychological or interpersonal troubles, the first response of Blacks is to seek advice either from members of their extended family or from the church (Daniel, 1985; McGoldrick, 1988).[57] When they do, reluctantly, seek assistance from a formal institution, it is typically because no other alternative presents itself or because they have been referred for help by an agency upon which they depend for resources (Boyd-Franklin, 1989).

Thus, despite recent evidence of change (Baker, 1988; Gary, 1987), Blacks have traditionally underutilized mental health services (Cleary & Demone, 1988), and with good reason. Bitter experience with White, middle-class institutions (Logan et al., 1990; McGoldrick, 1982; see Adebimpe, 1981; Bass et al., 1982) have fostered what Grier and Cobbs (1968) call a "healthy cultural paranoia" (Newhill, 1990). Access to service may be limited because of inadequate resources as well as the lack of health insurance (Amaro et al., 1987; Stern, 1991). Mental health service providers are overwhelmingly White (Lassiter, 1990)[58] and, in the absence of culturally sensitive training (Lassiter, 1990), they may be inclined to deny that presenting problems are linked to ethnicity, something Thomas and Sillen (1974: 58) call "the illusion of color blindness." Partly in consequence, Blacks presenting to mental health institutions are consistently misdiagnosed with schizophrenia (Fabrega et al., 1988; Fulani, 1988; Pavkov et al., 1990). Finally, in the absence of direct experience, most Blacks will have little or no idea of why they have been referred for help, what they can expect, how the process is likely to be helpful to them or the nature of the relationship between their therapist and the other agencies with whom they are simultaneously involved (Hines, 1988).

Accordingly, intimidated and unaccustomed to being heard (or if heard, misunderstood),[59] Blacks will typically approach treatment in one of two ways, by being inarticulate or belligerent (Daniel, 1985), and may take some time to size up and check out the service provider (Gibbs, 1980). In family therapy, for example, they may interpret the therapists' attempt to take a family history as "prying" (Chapman, 1995: 25). They may also take much longer than Whites to engage or join with the therapist and risk being labeled as "resistant" or "difficult" as a result (Boyd-Franklin, 1989; Robinson, 1989). However, once trust has been established (by informal means), Blacks will often prove to be realistic, emotionally aware and comfortable with their feelings (Boyd-Franklin, 1989; McGoldrick, 1982). In turn, they respond best to an approach that is short-term, highly structured and problem-focused (Boyd-Franklin, 1989; Colon, 1980; Hines, 1988; Minuchin et al., 1967; Minuchin & Montalvo, 1967). Even so, Blacks have a high dropout rate and, given an approach to time which accords it less salience than Whites, they may often be late for scheduled appointments or fail to show up at all (Wilkinson & Spurlock, 1986).[60]

Caribbean Blacks

Like Blacks, Caribbean Blacks faced with troubles are likely to turn first to family, friends and the church. They too have historically been most reluctant to seek assistance from formal institutions (Christiansen et al., 1982), although for different reasons having to do with culture and language. The self-sufficiency and privacy so highly valued in Caribbean Black culture supports a prohibition against help seeking, with mental health service providers in particular likely to be seen as just plain nosey (*jus' wan' fas' in a mi business*). Similarly, referral for "counseling" is likely to be misinterpreted, since in dialect *counseling* variously refers to scolding, instructing or preaching, as in something a parent or teacher might do to a child, misconceptions that are easily sustained in the absence of any direct experience. However, once induced to attend, Christiansen et al. (1982) stress the need to respect family hierarchy by seeing only the parents at first and by delaying direct parent-child confrontation. They also commend the effort to combine religious parables and stories with psychological notions.

SUMMARY

This portrait of Blacks and Caribbean Blacks highlights three sets of similarities and differences. First, Blacks and Whites display both differences and similarities. The latter are both structural and social. Both groups have suffered the ravages of an American economy which has seen a widening gap between the rich and the poor, and thus an overall decline in the qualty of life of large segments of society, both White and Black. Shared economic struggle translates into broad social similarities, as Whites and Blacks alike value family, marriage and child rearing. Beyond that, however, cultural differences between Whites and Blacks appear pervasive. Given their history and ongoing experience of racism and discrimination, Blacks are much more likely than Whites to experience life as harsh, unforgiving and unpredictable. The results are sharp differences: in the way Blacks behave; in their beliefs and values; how they organize family life, spousal relations and child rearing; how they think and perceive; and how they conceptualize and respond to life problems.

Second, in related fashion, Blacks and Caribbean Blacks are also both similar and different. Especially striking are similarities regarding the central place of women in both cultures, and, in turn, the central importance of the maternal role. But conduct similarities can be deceiving. While both groups may look and often act alike, repeatedly we have seen that they do so for very different reasons, based on fundamental differences in culture. Further, given their very different histories as peoples and their different geographic and national contexts, the two groups are manifestly different in various areas, including language use, some family values, marital and child rearing practices, religious practice, and their approach to education and work.

Finally, while the above portrait applies generally to all poor Blacks, there is some evidence of intragroup differences, based primarily on geography and context. Thus, the above portrait will be most representative of Blacks living in large, urban settings, and especially those crammed into central ghettoes on the East or West coasts. It may be less true of Blacks living in smaller settings, in rural counties and in states where Blacks are less concentrated.

NOTES

1. The five states with the highest proportion of Black residents in 1990 were Mississippi (35%), Louisiana (31%), South Carolina (30%), Georgia (27%), and Washington, D.C (27%). Exceptions include several large Northern cities, such as Detroit (76%) and Washington, D.C. (66%), according to Hacker (1992).

2. For bibliographies, see Breyfogle & Dworaczek (1977), Davis (1986) and Walker (1980). For a discussion of "racially mixed" groups in the United States, see

Root (1992).

3. For a history of Canadian Blacks, see: Bramble (1987), Carter and Carter (1989), Henry (1973), Hornby (1991), Pachai (1987), Thomson (1979), Tulloch (1975), Walker (1980) and Winks (1971).

4. The first Blacks arrived in Jamestown, Virginia in 1619 (Ho, 1992b).

5. The population of Metropolitan Toronto per se was 2.3 million in 1991.

6. In contrast, French-speaking Haitians are more likely to go to Montreal (Goossen, 1976; Laguerre, 1978, 1984; Locher, 1977; Walker, 1984). For a discussion of Haitians in the United States, see Woldemikael (1989).

7. Such reasoning is consistent with the findings of Grayson (1994b). In a study of Caribbean Black undergraduate students at York University (Toronto), participants were most likely to identify themselves as "Black" than as either "Caribbean" or "Canadian."

8. Even "Caribbean" is not a unitary designation. As Walker (1984: 13) notes, "West Indians do not constitute a uniform group, nor do they accurately reflect the class and ethnic make-up of their home territories." (See also Allahan, 1993.)

9. Ganasellal (personal communication, 1994) notes three exceptions: Trinidad, Surinam and Guyana.

10. As Christiansen et al. (1982) explain, dialect combines elements that are distinctly African (nyam=to eat, oonoo=you) with African pronunciation of English words (ooman=woman, mi=me); modified versions of English words (ee=he, hask=ask); words involving letter transpositions (flim=film); and words of uncertain origin (bwoy=boy, cyap=cap). In contrast, patois involves a mixture of English and Creole, the latter originally derived from French (Gibson with Lewis, 1985).

11. Hall's (1976) discussion of Standard and Black English makes the identical point in relation to Blacks and Whites in the United States. (See Dillard, 1973.)

12. The period 1950 to 1988 saw a general rise in the proportion of births to never married women, although more so among Blacks-from 16.8% to 63.7%-than Whites-from 1.7% to 14.9% (Hacker, 1992).

13. Such statements have not gone unchallenged. Ruggles (1994), for example, notes that throughout the period 1880 to 1990, Blacks consistently exhibited a rate of single parenthood two to three times that of their White counterparts. He argues that while economic deprivation was likely the primary cause, different cultural norms, rooted in African culture, was also an important factor. (See also Vinovskis, 1988.)

14. The comparable rates among fifteen to nineteen-year-olds were 86.4 among Blacks versus 18.5 among Whites (Gibbs, 1989b). More recent figures show little change. In 1991, the pregnancy rate among White teenagers was ninety-three compared to 196 among their Black counterparts (Hacker, 1992).

15. In 1991, the total number of births per 1000 never married women of all ages was 127 among Whites and 1,020 among Blacks (Hacker, 1992).

16. Overall, nearly 10% of all Blacks girls between the ages of ten and nineteen gave birth to a child compared to 2% among their White counterparts (Gibbs, 1989b). However, Hacker (1992) notes that in 1990 the proportion of births to unmarried women varied by state. Among Whites, the lowest proportion (10.8%) was in Utah, while the highest proportion (27%) was in New Mexico. Among Blacks, the lowest proportion (15.3%) was in Hawaii, while the highest proportion (76.5%) was in Wisconsin.

17. De Ridder (1993) notes that the United States, with over one million pregnancies per year to teenage women, has the highest teenage pregnancy rate (10%) of all industrialized nations, despite comparable levels of teenage sexual activity

(Jones et al., 1986).

18. For further discussion, see Allen and Pittman (1986), Furstenburg et al. (1989), Lancaster and Hamburg (1986), Ooms (1981), and Pittman and Adams (1988).

19. Hawkins (1994) notes that the relatively high crime rate among Blacks is not new, going back at least to the 1930's. He adds that the crime rate is higher among native born Blacks than among Blacks born elsewhere, including the Caribbean and Africa (Farley, 1990).

20. In a study of 758 male high school students in ten inner-city school districts, Wright and Sheley (1993, cited in the Toronto Star, November 21, 1993: A18) found that 22% admitted owning a handgun, while 12% reported carrying them routinely.

21. In the United States in 1990, 20,045 people were murdered, a murder rate per 100,000 population of 9.0 (U.S. Justice Department, 1991). Half of those murdered were Black and most Black victims (85%) were male. Further, in 93% of all murders involving Blacks, both offender and victim were Black. Further, such ethnic minority differences do not only apply to murder, but rather to death from all causes. For example, in 1990, the death rate per 100,000 population among fifteen to twenty-four-year-olds was ninety among Whites compared to 160 among Blacks (National Center for Educational Statistics, 1993). Among men in this age range, this difference was even more striking: 131 among Whites compared to 252 among Blacks.

22. In the same year, the comparable suicide rate among Black female adolescents was 2.2 per 100,000 (Staggers, 1989).

23. The notion of the underclass has generated much debate. For the American perspective, see Jencks and Peterson (1991), Jencks (1992), Kasarda (1989), Massey and Denton (1993), and Wilson (1991). For the British perspective, see Gans (1990), Morris (1994), and Smith (1992).

24. Blacks who achieve middle-class status often do so at the expense of becoming cut off emotionally from their families of origin (Pinderhughes, 1982; cf. McAdoo, 1978; Wenger, 1980). This leaves them feeling insecure and isolated from the mainstream (Collins, 1989) and subject to intense stress (Coner-Edwards & Spurlock, 1988; Landry, 1987). Moreover, in contrast to their White counterparts, Black executives are often confronted by low job security and stability (Davis & Watson, 1983), and by positions that are "racialized" (Collins, 1993) insofar as their positions are linked to the needs of Black consumers. In contrast, in the sciences and engineering, Tang (1993) found little evidence of discrimination against Blacks (cf. Hacker, 1992). Thus, Blacks may exhibit one of three mobility patterns (McAdoo, 1981): upward in one or several generations, downward and long-term stability.

25. In 1989, there were a total of 649 murders in Canada, down slightly from 575 in 1988 and 642 in 1987 (Statistics Canada, 1988, 1989, 1990).

26. The numbers and rates for the years in question were: 1990 (55/2.4); 1991 (89/3.9); 1992 (65/2.8); and 1993 (58/2.5). If Toronto had a murder rate equivalent to Detroit's, there would have been 1,420 murders in 1993 instead of fifty-eight.

27. In Canada in 1990, the overall rate of out-of-wedlock births, regardless of age, was 23.1% (Statistics Canada, 1991: Table 4). This represented 25% of all births in 1990, with only 20% accruing to women less than twenty years of age (Vanier Institute of the Family, 1994: 58).

28. For the way in which this plays out among middle-class Black families, see Coner-Edwards and Spurlock (1988) and Willie (1974).

29. Sex ratio is defined as the number of men per 100 women in the population (Guttentag & Secord, 1983). In the United States in 1985, the average was 100 Black

females for every seventy-eight Black males (Dickson, 1993). In 1990, there were only sixty-seven Black men for every 100 college educated Black women (Hacker, 1992). Thus, Blacks in the United States may be characterizied as a low sex ratio culture (Guttentag & Second, 1983).

30. Hacker (1992) reports that in 1990, there were more than one million Blacks, mostly men, either in prison, out on parole or probation, or awaiting trial; up to a million Blacks have a criminal record. He notes too that in the same year, Blacks comprised 47% of those awaiting trial for a criminal offense, 41% of those sentenced to death, and 45% of those imprisoned in state or federal facilties.

31. Ironically, this may include marrying White women. The rate of intermarriage among Blacks in 1977 was 1%, 76% of the 125,000 couples in question involving Black men marrying White women (Bruce & Rodman, 1973; Guttentag & Secord, 1983; Heer, 1974). More recent data show little change. In 1992, there were just under 250,000 Black/White interracial marriages (Reddy, 1994), 157,000 (63%) involving Black men marrying White women, and representing 4% of all Black married men (Aldridge, 1989; Chapman, 1995; Giddings, 1984).

32. Demographers measure fertility as the number of live births per 1000 women between the ages of fifteen and forty-four. By that standard, in 1990, the fertility rate among Blacks was 83.2, while that among Whites was 68.3, a difference of 22% (National Center for Educational Statistics, 1993). However, for both groups, current figures represent a substantial decline from 1940 when the comparable rates were 102.4 and 77.1, respectively (Hacker, 1992).

33. Hooks (1992: 340) provides a rather different explanation, arguing that "in a white supremacist society, white people can 'safely' imagine that they are invisible to black people since the power they have historically asserted, and even now collectively assert over black people accorded them the right to control the black gaze."

34. It is noteworthy that Black women are more likely to marry men who either have a job or at least a prospect of obtaining one compared to their unemployed counterparts (Wilson, 1987).

35. However, absence does not necesarily mean that such men are uninvolved with their families (Danziger & Radin, 1990). Rather, as Boyd-Franklin (1989) explains, there are at least two alternatives. One is the creation of a "family secret," that is, one in which Black women present as single parents when in fact they have had a live-in "boyfriend" for some years. The other, following Stack (1974), is that paternal involvement may be indirect, through his extended family. In this way, children may maintain strong ties to a father who they never see.

36. In the United States during the period 1950 to 1992, the proportion of two-parent Black families with children declined from 64% to 39%, while the proportion of single parent mother-led families rose from 17% to 57% (Dickson, 1993; Hacker, 1992). In turn, this means that 58% of Black children under 18 years of age live in single paret mother-led homes (National Center for Educational Statistics, 1993).

37. In the 1986-87 school year, Blacks represented the majority of public and high school students in Chicago, Detroit, Los Angeles and New York City (Quality Education for Minorities Project, 1990).

38. Differences in educational opportunity between Blacks and Whites in the United States are hardly new. For a historical analysis of this phenomenon, see Perlmann (1988).

39. During the period 1967 to 1985, high school graduation rates rose from 60% to 86%. By 1993, they had dipped below 80% (Postsecondary Education Opportunity, 1993b).

40. A widely used indicator of academic preparation is a high school student's score on the Scholastic Aptitude Test (SAT). Hacker (1992) found that such scores are directly related to family income. For example, in 1990, among students from families reporting earnings of less than $20,000 annually, average SAT scores by ethnic group varied as follows: White (881); Asian (832); Hispanic (738); and Black (692). Similarly, across the full income sprectrum, SAT score ranges varied systematically by ethnic group: White (879-998); Asian (855-1066); Hispanic (756-932), and Black (704-854).

41. During the period 1960-1988, college attendance rates among Black high school graduates rose from 31% to 50%. By 1993, they had declined to 47% (Postsecondary Education Opportunity, 1993b).

42. In the 1986-87 school year, 995,000 Black undergraduates represented 9.2% of the total enrolled in higher education (Quality Education for Minorities, 1990). In the same year, nearly 57,000 Blacks graduated with a B.A., 5.7% of all students who did so. Historically, this represents a declining graduation rate. During the period 1965 to 1991, the proportion of Black undergraduates who completed college or university by age twenty-five to twenty-nine dropped from 46% to 34% (Postsecondary Education Opportunity, 1993b).

43. In contrast to their lower/working class counterparts, middle-class Black families place greater emphasis on education and on the control of sexual and aggressive impulses (McGoldrick et al., 1989).

44. Unable to interact with extended family members on a face-to-face basis, Caribbean Blacks, especially women, maintain kinship ties "back home" through other means, for example, by mail, telephone, visiting and through child lending (Ho, 1993).

45. Bagarozzi (1980) argues that middle class Blacks also diverge from White norms.

46. Cazenave (1979), however, argues that this varies by class, with middle-class fathers more directly involved in child care than their lower-class counterparts.

47. Whites in contrast tend to interpret loud language as indicating impending violence, while the avoidance of eye contact is seen as sullenness or fear. Conversely, Blacks see staring by Whites as hostile, solicitous behavior as suspicious, and silence as devious (Donohue, 1985; Jones, 1972).

48. Blacks similarly prefer novelty and personal distinctiveness in matters such as clothing and music (Hilliard, 1986).

49. In dealing with non-blacks, Black adolescents may engage in a related form of communication known as "sounding" (also known as basing, chopping, cutting, hoorawing, joning, ranking, screaming, signifying, snapping or woofing), a ritual form of verbal dueling which, depending on the other's response, may be good fun or deadly serious (Kochman, 1986).

50. Among intermarried couples, such battles extend to parental abduction (Hegar & Grief, 1994).

51. Several of these examples are consistent with Lipsky's observation (1978, quoted in Christiansen et al., 1982: 2) that "some of the patterned behaviors that we frequently recognize within Black cultures were originally developed to keep us alive. Today many of these responses to mistreatment have become embedded in our culture, but no longer serve a useful function. Instead, these so-called "elements of Black culture" operate to lock us into our roles as victims of oppression."

52. Hill (1977) notes several additional reasons for child-keeping. These include doing a kindness for a woman who wants to care for a child but is unable to have children of her own or whose children have left home, or to allow a child to live

closer to school or gain access to a particular school by living in the school district.

53. Brice (1982) explains that the terms given this arrangement vary across the Caribbean: "concubinage" in Jamaica, "menage" in Martinique and "living" in Trinidad.

54. While true, this statement is complicated by class and skin color. Helms (1990), for example, found that positive racial identity is more likely in middle-class than in lower-class children, while Spurlock (1986) reports similar findings in light rather than dark-skinned Black children.

55. For further discussion of the interaction between Black family dynamics and education, see Dilworth-Anderson and McAdoo (1988) and Dilworth-Anderson et al. (1993).

56. Christiansen et al. (1982) characterizes this approach as involving "rigid Victorian attitudes."

57. A minority of Blacks, especially those living in rural parts of the United States, continue to rely on folk medicine (Terrel, 1989; Watson, 1984; Wilkinson & Spurlock, 1986).

58. For example, Lassiter (1990) estimates that only 3% of the members of American Psychological Association are Black. (See Bernal, 1994; Stricker et al., 1990.)

59. Hall (1976: 74) attributes such misunderstandings (at least in part) to repeated miscues, given "great differences in the kinesic and proxemic, linguistic and other behavior patterns between working-class blacks and a wide range of whites (working to upper middle class)."

60. In this context, Hall (1976) distinguishes between monochronic (M-time) and polychronic (P-time) temporal perspectives. A monochronic approach typifies Whites (including Jews) and involves thinking about time in discrete units, working at one task at a time and giving task completion a higher priority than social relations. In contrast, a polychronic approach typifies Blacks, Hispanics and Asians and involves thinking about time as nonlinear and diffuse; working at a variety of tasks at the same time and with a variety of others; and according social relations a much higher priority than task completion.

4

The Hispanics

INTRODUCTION

Hispanics are a heterogeneous group comprised of Spanish-speaking peoples from Mexico, Puerto Rico,[1] Cuba, the Caribbean, Spain, and Central and South America. In the United States, the largest subgroup, comprising 62% of the total, are of Mexican origin (*Latinos* or *Chicanos*), with the majority (74%) concentrated in four states: California, Texas, Florida and New York (Dana, 1993; Martinez, 1986; Moore & Pachon, 1985; Nelson & Tienda, 1985; Portes & Truelove, 1987; Valdivieso & Davis, 1988).[2][3] Puerto Ricans (*Puertoriquenos*) and Cubans (*Cubanos*) are the next largest subgroups, making up 13% and 5%, respectively, with the former concentrated in New York City, and nearly all of the latter (97%) living in and around Miami. The balance derives from Central and South America (12%) or elsewhere (8%), including Spain.

In Canada, the demographic situation of Hispanics is less clear given that Statistics Canada does not recognize "Hispanic" as a category, although it includes Spanish as a mother tongue. What scanty data are available show (Berdichewsky, 1984, 1988; Duryea & Gundison, 1993; Hartzman, 1991; Logan, 1991; Mata, 1985) that most Canadian Hispanics originate from Central and South America, and are scattered in small pockets across the country. In 1991, the single largest concentration (48%) lived in the Toronto Census Metropolitan Area.

However, irrespective of location in both countries, Hispanic subgroups are characterized by different histories, traditions and beliefs (Alers-Montalvo, 1985; Devore & Schlesinger, 1987; Falicov, 1982; Garcia-Preto, 1982; Kumabe et al., 1985; Maldonado, 1991; Nelson & Tienda, 1985; Reimer, 1985).[4] In the words of Szalay and Diaz-Guerrero (1985: 121), "the average Hispanic American based on representative national averages is a statistical abstraction with little practical value."[5] Accordingly, the following discussion will focus on the Latinos and the Puertoriquenos, both newly arrived and long-resident, since they have received the most attention in the literature (Acosta-Belen & Sjostrum, 1988; Bean, 1987; Bean & Tienda, 1987; Blea, 1985; Falicov, 1982; Falicov & Karrer, 1980; Keefe & Padilla, 1987; Martinez, 1977; Martinez & Mendoza, 1984; McGoldrick et al., 1989; Moore & Pachon, 1985; Ramirez, 1983; Rodriguez, 1992).[6] For quick reference, the profile of the Hispanics is summarized in Figure 4.1, below, with detailed description in the following text. Given evidence of similarity (see below), no effort will be made to distinguish systematically between American and Canadian populations, save to note generic national differences examined above with respect to the Blacks.[7]

MODAL SOCIAL CLASS

The history of Hispanics in North America is typically one of migration, sometimes legal, sometimes not (Bean et al., 1983; Chavez, 1990), of a mostly rural, agricultural people seeking a better life for themselves and their children in urban, industrialized North America (Arizpe, 1981; Bean, 1987; Dinerman, 1978; Falicov, 1982; Massey & Schnabel, 1983; McGoldrick et al., 1989; Reichert & Massey, 1980). Data regarding a range of demographic indicators (Dana, 1993; Hacker, 1992; Martinez, 1986; Moore & Pachon, 1985; Nelson & Tienda, 1985; Portes & Truelove, 1987; Valdivieso & Davis, 1988; Tienda, 1983) tell a story of pervasive disadvantage.

Figure 4.1
Summary Profile of the Hispanics

Modal Social Class:	lower/working
Definition of the Family:	informal extended, including godparents (*compadres*) and "lent" children
Life Cycle:	compressed, six phases, with elongation of adolescence and middle adulthood
Husband-Wife Relations:	patriarchal, with clear role segregation
Parent-Child Relations:	authoritarian; double standard
Perspective on Treatment	community sources of help preferred, including spiritual healers (*curanderos*)

- Among Latinos, 26% of two-parent families and 47% of single parent families report income below the poverty line, with another 20% in both groups classed among the working poor. In California, while the median income among Whites in 1990 was $43,000, the comparable figure among Latinos was $27,000, with an overall poverty rate among Latinos of 22% (Hayes-Bautista, 1992). The related income figures among the Puertoriquenos are lower still (Porter & Washington, 1993). For Hispanics as a group, national figures are comparable. While median family income in 1991 (in constant 1991 dollars) was $36,000, among Hispanic families it was $24,000 (National Center for Educational Statistics, 1993), or 35% below average.[8] This means that in the same year, 40% of Hispanic children living in two-parent families were poor, while the same was true of 70% of such children living in single-parent families (National Center for Educational Statistics, 1993).

- The majority of Latinos (54%) and Puertoriquenos (67%) have a high school education or less. However, this is more likely among recent immigrants who originate in rural settings as opposed to those who originate in urban settings or who have lived in the United States or Canada for some time (Duryea & Gundison, 1993).

- While 90% of native-born Hispanics speak English, the comparable proportions among recent immigrants varies between 35% and 65%, with 80% of these reporting some language difficulty. Further, Portes and Truelove (1987), based on a longitudinal study, found that their acquisition of English was very slow (McManus et al., 1983).[9]

- The immigration status of many Hispanics is uncertain, with a substantial minority thought to be "undocumented aliens" (Bean et al., 1983; Chavez, 1990; Dana, 1993).[10]

- Out of financial necessity, the labor force participation rate among Hispanics is high, both among men and women (Mora & Del Castillo, 1980; Pedraza, 1991; Romero, 1986; cf. Fernandez-Kelly & Garcia, in press; Romero, 1988; Valdez, 1984). In light of the above, the majority of Latinos and Puertoriquenos are forced to accept unskilled or semi-skilled clerical, service or seasonal jobs characterized by low prestige, low pay and high rates of turnover and underemployment (Rodriguez & Melendez, 1992; Safa, 1984), often for longer periods of time than their White counterparts (Newman, 1988). Their immigration status and their ethnicity also subject many Hispanics to discrimination in hiring, working conditions and firing (Chavez, 1990; Cross et al., 1990; Turner et al., 1991).

That said, Duryea and Gundison (1993) suggest three important qualifications. First, immigrant women may have a much easier time gaining employment than men, *not* because women speak better English, but because the menial jobs they can take (for example, as cleaners or supermarket shelf stockers) require less sophisticated language skills. Such new found economic independence can have important repercussions for the marital relationship (see below). Second, urban Hispanics may arrive in the United States or Canada with professional skills in law, medicine, psychology and the like, only to discover that their qualifications are not recognized here. The resulting extreme status loss may be devastating for these individuals and their families who were accustomed to a middle-class lifestyle but are now reduced to poverty. It also deprives the Hispanic community of essential services not otherwise available in Spanish (Castex, 1994). Third, whereas "back home" they looked to an elaborate support network for help (see below), once in the United States or Canada, refugees (typically from Central and South America) are usually forced to leave all of that behind, thus arriving here feeling adrift and completely alone (Jacobs, 1994).

Other indicators are closely associated with poverty.

- The rate of births to single mothers in 1990 varied across Hispanic subgroups, from 53% among Puertoriquenos, and 31% among Latinos, to 16% among Cubanos (Hacker, 1992). Similar variation was apparent in the proportion of mother-led single parent families, from 44% among Puertoriquenos and 19% among Latinos, to 16% among the Cubanos (Hacker, 1992). This means that in 1992, of all Hispanic children under eighteen years of age, 29% lived with only one parent (National Center for Educational Statistics, 1993).

- Finally, gang violence and youth crime is a significant problem among Latino and Puertoriqueno communities (Hawkins, 1994; Horowitz, 1983; Olzak, 1992; Sanders, 1994; Sullivan, 1989), especially in poor, urban neighborhoods (*barios*).[11] In the United States, murder is the number one cause of death among Hispanic males aged eighteen to twenty-four, as it is for their Black counterparts (see above) (Morales, 1992; Garcia, 1992; Harris, 1986).[12] Such violence is significantly associated with drug trafficking and drug abuse among Hispanic youth (Mayers et al., 1993; Moore & Glick, 1991) and, not surprisingly, has resulted in an increasing rate of imprisonment (Farley, 1990).

Thus, for many Hispanics in the United States in the 1990's, life is only slightly less harsh, unforgiving and unpredictable than for Blacks, with the majority of Hispanics having income and education which places them in the lower/working class.[13] [14]

DEFINITION OF THE FAMILY

Among Hispanics, the basic family unit is the multigenerational, informal extended family (Devore & Schlesinger, 1987; Falicov, 1982; Griffith & Villavicencio, 1985; Sabogal et al., 1987; Sena-Rivera, 1979; Sewell, 1989). This explains their distinction between the immediate or nuclear family (*la casa*) and the extended kinship network (*la familia*). Such networks expand both vertically and laterally to include grandparents, uncles and aunts, cousins (to the third and fourth generation), godparents (*compadres, comadres*) and close family friends (*amistad* or *cuatismo*). Even relations with non-family members are family-like in intensity (Murillo, 1976), the children calling family friends "aunt" or "uncle." And, in times of crisis, family boundaries are sufficiently flexible and the norms of mutual support (*confianza en confianza*) sufficiently strong to sanction child lending (Garcia-Preto, 1982) as well as taking in relatives for varying lengths of time.

Relations within Hispanic kinship systems may be variously characterized by personalism, familism, hierarchical organization, honor, and cohesion (Dana, 1993; Taylor & Sanchez, 1991; Zinn, 1982/83).[15] Personalism refers to a meaning system in which members are encouraged to see the world in terms of personal relationships with others (Mindel, 1980; Sewell, 1989) rather than abstract concerns related to time or to task. Time is seen as flexible or elastic. Appointment times are treated casually, flowing out of mutual relationships rather than the tasks at hand. Similarly, tasks have no inherent significance apart from the relationships out of which they emerge. In short, the importance of relating to others stands as a cornerstone of the Hispanic meaning system.[16]

In turn, social relations among Hispanics may be typified as friendly, spontaneous, emotional and unorganized (Duryea & Gundison, 1993). This includes a variety of patterns of relating supportive of this approach. For example, relatives often live in close residential proximity (cf. Massey, 1981). Contact is frequent, and interaction typically involves hugging (*abraza*), public kissing and frequent touching (Axtell, 1985; Harris & Moran, 1991). In conversation, participants stand much closer together than would be comfortable for Whites, often with noses almost touching, and, among status equals, with eye contact unflinching and prolonged (Axtell, 1985).[17] Emotions are close to the surface, and are easily expressed in tears, rage, laughter or sentimentality (Axtell, 1985). Social interaction, varying from a comfortable chat, *platicando* (Triandis et al., 1984), to a lively argument (Duryea & Gundison, 1993), is based on assumptions of informal friendliness and hospitality. Indeed, much effort is directed toward creating a warm and accepting atmosphere (*ambiente*) in which nearly everything is highly personalized (Harris & Moran, 1991). Hispanics feel comfortable, for example, talking about a person's inner qualities of soul or spirit. Similarly, their notion of *simpatia* has no exact English equivalent but is intended as a descriptor of individuals who are perceived by others as likeable, attractive, sensitive to others, fun to be with, and easygoing (Martin & Triandis, 1985). In behavioral terms, these preferences distinguish Hispanics from their White (*Anglo*) counterparts. As Keefe (1984: 68) observes,

For Mexican Americans, it is important to see relatives regularly face-to-face, to embrace, to touch, and to simply be with one another, sharing the minor joys and sorrows of daily life. For Anglos, these things are integral to nuclear family life but less important with regard to extended family ties.

In a similar vein, familism describes a belief in the importance of interdependence and obligatory mutual aid (*compadrazgo*) among kin and quasi kin (Martin & Triandis, 1985; Mindel, 1980; Taylor & Sanchez, 1991; cf. Keefe, 1984). This not only discourages autonomy and independent achievement on the part of all members, but devalues all behavior that would interfere with cordial interdependence. In particular, direct confrontation and conflict are strongly prohibited, with indirect means (*indirectas*) of dealing with problematic issues preferred. Accordingly, Hispanics have evolved elaborate methods to insure control (*controlarse*) of sexual and aggressive impulses (Cohen, 1985). This relates to the social character of the "self" in Hispanic culture (Sewell, 1989).[18] As Hall (1959, 1976) explains, Hispanics are caught in a dilemma. On the one hand, Hispanics, men especially, are exquisitely sensitive to insult or criticism, particularly any comment or action which might offend their pride or honor (see below); only a weak person is thought to have neither pride, *orgullo*, nor shame, *verguenza* (Albert, 1986). On the other hand, there are prohibitions against direct confrontation which act as a source of contrary pressure. Thus, Hispanics tend to hold back until they can stand it no longer, after which, without warning, there is likely to be a violent response, so far overstepping the norms of propriety that there is no turning back. Confrontations can thus be bitter and, rejecting third-party intermediaries, prolonged. In handling conflict, then, Hispanics are characterized by a short, rapid escalation of steps; reliance on social rather than personal inhibitions; and a focus on control over social situations or processes rather than individuals.[19]

One of the key mechanisms for achieving such control is a strong emphasis on respect or honor (*respecto*) for authority (Falicov, 1982; Hofstede, 1984). Hispanic kinship systems are hierarchical, based on age and gender, with older males dominant. Such patriarchal attitudes mean that family members are expected to be sensitive to social contexts; willing to conform to group norms; and ready to be influenced by others, especially those above them in the kinship hierarchy (Martin & Triandis, 1985).

This approach to social relations is futher exemplified by the related notions of *machismo* and *honor*. Machismo applies only to men and may be loosely translated as manliness, courage, daring, competitiveness and virility (Davenport & Yurich, 1991; Gonzalez, 1982; Harris & Moran, 1991); in business, it is embodied in the *enchufado*, the man who makes things happen because of his good connections (Axtell, 1985).[20] While consistent with the stereotype of continuous sexual readiness among Hispanic men (Sluzki, 1982),[21] it is better understood as an expression of the relationship between authority and responsibility. According to group norms, men are obliged to protect and provide for their kith and kin. Indeed, this notion is taught early, with boys expected to protect their sisters, even if the latter are chronologically older (Murillo, 1976).

However, this obligation can only be understood in cultural context, on the one hand, in beliefs concerning personalism and familism, while on the other hand, in acceptance of one's fate (*resignarse*) and the need to be strong in the face of the inevitability of hard times (*aguantarse*). In business, for example, such fatalism may take the form of a boom and bust attitude (rich today, gone tomorrow) that accepts such notions as chance, luck, destiny, the determinant role of outside forces, and the inevitability of death (Axtell, 1985; Harris & Moran, 1991).[22] [23]

On similar grounds, many Hispanics take a lighthearted approach to work, one that emphasizes living for today (*chotao*). While married men are expected to be dignified and hardworking (Abad et al., 1974), they nevertheless do not see work as having an intrinsic value in and of itself (Murillo, 1970). Rather, its worth arises from the social relations which surround it. In turn, this has repercussions for Hispanic work experience. Harris and Moran (1991), for example, note that in the work context, deference to authority can mean saying what workers think managers want to hear, even though it may not be factual. Hall (1976) adds that Hispanic workers, aversive to confrontation, may prefer to quit without notice rather than complain about a problem. Notions of loyalty and mutual aid mean that when more than one member of a family or a friendship group works for the same employer, the firing of one member will likely mean that all will quit. And, notions of friendliness mean that business meetings are likely to be as much about social relations as economic affairs, and more likely to be conducted over coffee rather than across a desk.

Returning to the notion of honor (*respecto*), it applies both at the individual and the family levels. Thus, in one sense it refers to the dignity and esteem shown family members based on their inner, personal attributes (*fuerza de espiritu*), while in another sense it suggests behavior consistent with group norms, that is, an unwritten code of honor (Devore & Schlesinger, 1987). For men, this means providing for his family and acting honorably with his compradres, for example, exhibiting behavior in keeping with agreements based on a handshake. For women, it means behaving with modesty and decorum toward other men, while showing respect for their husbands, especially in public. For children, as status inferiors, it means showing respect for adults, especially their parents, for example, by avoiding direct eye contact (Duryea & Gundison, 1993) or in other gender-appropriate ways (see below).

In this context, it becomes clear why behavior of family or kin, which is seen as dishonorable or which shows disrespect, is taken very seriously, for it assaults the very core of machismo (Garcia-Preto, 1982). Indeed, given the employment status of many Hispanic men (see above), it is not hard to understand why some men would rather desert their families than face the daily shame of unemployment and/or welfare (Bean, 1987).[24]

Finally, by comparison with Whites, Hispanic kinship systems are extraordinarily close and cohesive (Dana, 1993; Delgado, 1985; Mizio, 1974;

Papajohn & Spiegel, 1975). As already noted, in addition to residential proximity, feelings of mutual emotional involvement are typically intense and frequent visiting is occasionaed by a variety of life cycle transitions (such as baptism and first communion) and religious ceremonies and festivals (see above). Strong ties among siblings and cousins are encouraged, whereas contact with non-family members is discouraged (Falicov, 1982). Indeed, until adolescence, it is still not uncommon for Hispanic children to have virtually no close friends outside their extended family (Murillo, 1976). Accordingly, not only are rates of intermarriage low (Fitzpatrick & Gurak, 1979; Salgado de Snyder & Padilla, 1985), but even in such cases, Hispanic ethnic identity tends to be retained (Salgado de Snyder & Padilla, 1985).

Such cohesion means that support for life is guaranteed so long as members remain within the system (Papajohn & Spiegel, 1975). It also means that members can become extremely distressed should such support be absent or the system begin to malfunction (Keefe et al., 1979).

LIFE CYCLE

By comparison with Whites, Falicov and Karrer (1980) describe the Hispanic family life cycle as consisting of six stages: an extended childhood, a shortened adolescence, a prolonged courtship, a brief couple stage, an elongated middle age and a shortened old age.

Hispanic's emphasis on the group means that children are encouraged to be dependent; they are not seen as individuals with minds of their own (Garcia-Preto, 1982). Accordingly, young children are indulged, with discipline becoming more and more strict with advancing age and focused on obedience (*malcriados*) and respect for authority (McGoldrick, 1988). As children enter adolescence, a double standard becomes increasingly evident. Whereas machismo reflects community expectations of boys, *marianismo* (Stevens, 1973) is the equivalent for girls, emphasizing modesty, submissiveness and virginity. Thus, the onset of menstruation marks an important change among Hispanic girls, for the family's honor is now linked to her virtue (Falicov, 1982). She will now be watched more closely, as she is expected to be a virgin at marriage (Devore & Schlesinger, 1987). In contrast, restrictions on boys begin to ease, with special privilege associated with the position of eldest son. Boys are expected to come to marriage with some sexual experience, experience that is both a rite of passage and one basis for their reputation among their social group or *palomillas*; Murillo, 1976).[25]

The shift from adolescence to adulthood comes with early marriage (Falicov & Karrer, 1980); women who wait to marry until their late twenties may be labeled spinsters. Since it is not uncommon for one female in the family to remain single as caretaker for older relatives, despite the risk this entails to the family's honor (McGoldrick et al., 1989), this label may well be self-fulfilling. Among the vast majority that do marry, child bearing is expected soon after (Devore & Schlesinger, 1987). Indeed, given that most Hispanics (80%-90%) are Roman Catholic (Dana, 1993), there is a strong tendency (at all class levels) to prefer large families (Alvirez & Bean, 1976; Bean, 1973, 1987; Bradshaw & Bean, 1972; cf. Bean et al., 1985).[26] [27] This fact highlights several facets of Hispanic family life, including: (1) their emphasis on parental as opposed to marital functions (see below); (2) the prolongation of the child rearing phase of the life cycle; (3) the frequent absence of an "empty nest" phase (Falicov, 1982); and (4) the disaster that infertility can bring, denying women a key component of their social identities (Devore & Schlesinger, 1987). Moreover, it makes clear that the level of closeness regarded as normal and desirable in Hispanic (especially Puertoriquena) families would be regarded as dysfunctional were it observed in White families (Canino & Canino, 1982; Zayas & Bryant, 1984).

In turn, these facts help bring into focus Hispanic attitudes toward education. Like Blacks, Hispanics' experience of education has often been far from positive. Obstacles to success include attendance at under-financed and sometimes dangerous inner-city schools and limited English language proficiency, which impedes both class participation and access to and use of school support resources (Stanton-Salazar & Dornbusch, 1995). Especially important, however, are group norms that (a) associate work with adult pursuits and school with childhood concerns (Falicov, 1982); (b) emphasize cooperative behavior at the expense of individual striving (Koss-Chioino & Vargas, 1992; Velez-Ibanez & Greenberg, 1992); and (c) favor respect for and obedience of authority over critical thinking skills (Delgado-Gaitan, 1994). In addition, for males in particular, there are very limited employment opportunities available.

Consequently, Hispanic involvement with education has been problematic at all levels. In elementary school, Hispanic children are often classified as underachievers (Bender & Ruiz, 1974; Burial, 1975; Ramirez & Castenada, 1974). At the high school level, they have traditionally displayed low achievement, a high (60%) dropout rate (Falicov, 1982; Nora, 1993; O'Brien, 1993) and limited motivation to pursue higher education (Olivas, 1986). As Marsiglia (1991) explains, based on a naturalistic study of Puertoriqueno students, Hispanic high school students are caught in a dilemma. Strict adherence to their culture, based on pride in their language (*el idioma*),[28] risks rejection by the majority group. Conversely, complete assimilation means loss of their ethnic community, their only refuge against a hostile and uncaring society. The result is that students distribute across a variety of groups, depending upon how they resolve this dilemma. "Warriors" maintain a strong ethnic identity and protect their peers but at the cost of low academic achievement. "Lawyers," in opting for a bilingual solution, are high achievers but with weak links to their ethnic identity. "Poets" adhere to *el idioma* in its purest form, seemingly untouched by inner-city cultures or dialects, while "traders" are truly bicultural, feeling completely at ease in both cultures.[29]

As for higher education, this has traditionally been tied directly to parental (especially father's) education and social class: as education and class decline, so do child aspiration and rates of enrollment (Postsecondary Education Opportunity, 1993c). Given the modal status of Hispanic families, reviewed above, Hispanic enrollment rates in higher education have traditionally been weak, and have slowly declined during the 1980's (Mow & Nettles, 1990; O'Brien, 1993). Moreover, those that do attend perform less well than their White counterparts (Duran, 1983; Quevedo-Garcia, 1987) and are more likely to drop out before completing their degree (Keller et al., 1991; National Center for Education Statistics, 1993; Pallas et al., 1989).[30] [31] The latter is likely to reflect not only their academic standing but also their non-assertive style and their reluctance to use existing campus resources (Duran, 1983; Nelson, 1994; Quevedo-Garcia, 1987).[32] Interestingly, Steward et at. (1992) found that among successful Hispanic university students, those that felt closest to Whites also felt the most alienated.

Finally, the focus on children and parenting has clear implications for their view of the elderly who are traditionally respected as a source of knowledge and child care (Maldonado, 1975). Moreover, life-long obligations of mutual support and their relatively intense sociability means that Hispanics are likely to view nursing homes as repulsive (Devore & Schlesinger, 1987). Rather, the aged are cared for in the home of a relative, with males providing financial support and females providing caregiving (McGoldrick et al., 1989). Old age apart from family respon-sibilities is often short, with elaborate rituals associated with death (Skansie, 1985). However, this traditional life course may be put at risk by immigration. In leaving their home country, the elderly, like their adult children (see above), may be exposed to status loss on arrival here (Duryea & Gundison, 1993). Family leaders at home, they may be reduced to babysitters, as their adult children search for work.

HUSBAND-WIFE RELATIONS

If community expectations of adolescent girls fall under the notion of *marianismo*, then for married women they are encompassed by *hembrismo*, that is, strength, flexibility, self-sacrifice and perseverance in the face of troubles (Comas-Diaz, 1989). These beliefs derive from the socialization practices already examined above; their thrust is that men are indispensable but undependable and that holding onto such a relationship is thus worth making major sacrifices (Espin, 1985). This implies a traditional power imbalance favoring husbands over wives (Meierding, 1992). With spousal relations organized around a gender-based division of authority and labour (Briody, 1985; McGoldrick et al., 1989), men may refuse to help around the house, since this would lower their dignity (Harris & Moran, 1991).

However, following Cromwell and Ruiz (1979), Ramirez (1983, 1985), Davenport and Yurich (1991), Diaz-Guerrero (1984), and most recently Takash and Zavella (1993), it is more useful to distinguish between the ways in which Hispanic couples present themselves to the world and the way they actually operate on a daily basis, that is, between social fiction and social reality.[33]

The fiction is that husbands exercise complete authority over their wives. Accordingly, the latter are expected to be humble, submissive, compliant and respectful (McGoldrick et al., 1989). Similarly, their respective roles in the family are segregated; husbands are responsible for supporting the family and thus focused on matters in the outside world, while wives are responsible for caring for their husbands and children and thus focused on matters in the home. Further, with the emphasis on parenting, relations between spouses can be somewhat formal (Falicov, 1982). Neither deep intimacy nor overt conflict are expected (Garcia-Preto, 1982). Given prohibitions against overt conflict, marital problems, should they arise, are typically handled indirectly (Duryea & Gundison, 1993). That is, no effort may be made to clarify issues. Rather, dealing with them may be indefinitely postponed in the common hope that time will heal any differences. If discussion of these issues occurs at all, it will be confined to family members and extended kin, never with children or strangers. Alternately, marital problems may be displaced as concerns over the children. Indeed, any lingering parental concerns about child rebelliousness or failure to show respect may suddenly take on special significance (McGoldrick, 1988). Further, the double standard, seen initially in adolescence, extends to the marital relationship. While men are free to engage in extramarital affairs, wives are expected to remain faithful, with dire consequences if they do not.

The reality is more varied, as Vazquez-Nuttall et al. (1987) demonstrate in a recent review (Harris & Moran, 1991). While wives may remain respectful of their husbands' authority in public, covertly they may be quite powerful behind the scenes, based especially on their alliance with the children (Comas-Diaz, 1989; McGoldrick et al., 1989). Spousal relations likely fall along a continuum, from husband dominant to husband submissive to egalitarian (Hawkes & Taylor, 1975). This appears related to three factors (Vazquez-Nuttall et al., 1987): time in the United States or Canada, education level and employment status. The longer their duration in North America, the greater their acculturation, achieved education and employment status, and, in turn, the greater the likelihood of a shift from "traditional" to "liberal" attitudes. For example, the fact that many Hispanic women work outside the home means that they have a source of income. This may significantly shift the balance of power in the marital relationship (Duryea & Gundison, 1993), challenging traditional male authority, especially if their husbands are unemployed (Mizio, 1974).[34] In some cases, this can lead to divorce.[35]

In this context, while wives are expected to be strong, in practice they may have fewer outlets than husbands for expressing dissatisfaction. However, the double standard now works in reverse, since "[w]omen are conceived of as frail creatures who could not possibly stand up to any man." (Hall, 1959: 89). Thus, women (but not men) have normative permission to express their feelings directly, through crying and hysterical seizures, or *ataques* (McGoldrick et al., 1989; Osterweis et al., 1978), ironically confirming the Hispanic male stereotype that women are weak and out of control.

PARENT-CHILD RELATIONS
Relations between parents and children are clearly hierarchical, with parents in charge (Diaz-Guerrero, 1975; Preto, 1990; Hines et al., 1992). While relations may be friendly, with each enjoying the company of the other, it is clear that parents are not friends. In this context, the supportive and nurturing role of mothers is central; fathers, the occasional role of enforcer aside, are not expected to help with child rearing (McGoldrick et al., 1989), especially when the children are young (Falicov, 1982). Relations between mothers and children are typically very close, although some distinctions can be made on the basis of child gender. While relations between mothers and sons can be close and dependent, sons, as noted above, are still expected to protect the females in the family, including their mothers. Similar closeness between mothers and daughters is evident but more reciprocal, since the former is expected to teach the latter all they need to know to become wives and mothers themselves. This includes not only extreme modesty and an obligation to maternal self-sacrifice, as seen above, but also a passive approach to sexuality (but in the absence of any sexual instruction). However, mothers will likely not be alone in advancing this message; the extended character of the kinship system ensures child rearing help from other women. Moreover, in instances of desertion, separation, divorce or widowhood, it is commonplace for the family to move in with relatives; these single mothers work to support their children, while their married kin care for both sets of children (McGoldrick et al., 1989).

As suggested above, the thrust of child socialization combines gender-specific skills and attitudes with a generic respect for authority. While discipline may involve spanking, it more typically relies on shame, threats and belittling (Falicov, 1982). Since Hispanics value private space more than Whites (Duryea & Grundison, 1993), they would be unlikely to send an errant child to his or her room, insisting instead that the child remain in the more crowded public space. Further, with the accent on interdependence, parents typically take a very relaxed approach to child achievement, either of developmental milestones when young, or skills indicative of self-reliance when older. While adolescents are encouraged to help out around the house, including taking care of their younger siblings, they are not encouraged to work outside the home. Moreover, as children enter adolescence, the control function of fathers becomes more obvious. As a result, an intense intergenerational struggle may erupt should the children, especially the girls, seek to pursue a more independent life outside the family (McGoldrick, 1988; Murillo-Rhodes, 1976). This is complicated in new immigrant families by the issue of language (Duryea & Grundison, 1993). Unable to speak English, parents may become dependent on their children to translate. In turn, this accords them much greater power than they would have "back home," and may encourage them to defy traditional parental authority. The resulting parent-child conflict can be explosive, in extreme cases leading to complete rupture, the children spurning their parents for the street and thus a life of delinquency and drug abuse.[36] Among those that remain at home, this intergenerational struggle may be played out in a different way, as children, empowered by their command of English, lose their ability to speak Spanish (Delgado-Gaitan, 1994).

PERSPECTIVE ON HELP-SEEKING

Hispanic perspectives on help-seeking are shaped by *four* interrelated beliefs: machismo, social selves, privacy and spirits (Miralles, 1989). First, machismo enjoins men in particular to resolve problems on their own, by the imposition of their will (*sobreponerse*). On the one hand, this makes it very difficult to admit failure and rationalizes delaying help-seeking until virtually no alternatives are available. On the other hand, this approach legitimizes somatic complaints while stigmatizing psychological problems seen as indicative of weakness. Thus, help-seeking, if it occurs at all, will more likely involve medical rather than psychiatric or psychological complaints (McGoldrick, 1982a; Sanua, 1985), such as "nerves," called *ataque de nervious* (Delacancera et al., 1986; Guamaccia, 1989). It also helps explain why mental health services tend to be underused by the Hispanic community (Griffin, 1984; Lopez, 1981; Martinez, 1986; Solomon, 1988).

Second, given their intense sociality, Hispanics tend to explain behavior in terms of circumstances rather than personalities (Hall, 1976). Accordingly, the idea that a person is mentally ill (*enfermidad mental*) is foreign to them. Thus, a person may be seen to behave strangely under certain circumstances. The solution to this situational problem is to keep the person away from circumstances in which this behavior is likely to arise while rejecting the notion that the problem may be "inside" the person. This explains why Hispanics tend to delegate responsibility for their presenting problems to others (Evans et al., 1986).

Third, I have already alluded to norms concerning privacy that prohibit discussion of intimate family matters before children or strangers. Indeed, given the respective expectations of spouses, wives are likely to feel highly ambivalent about voicing complaints about their spouses (Vazquez-Nuttall et al., 1987). Similarly, spouses are much more likely to seek help from relatives, compadres, friends and/or the church rather than therapists (Griffith & Villavicencio, 1985; Raymond et al., 1980).

Fourth, given their predominantly rural background, many Hispanics continue to believe that illness is the result of extrahuman forces (Dana, 1993; Miralles, 1989; Samora, 1978). This is either because troubles may cause the person's spirit or soul to leave their body (*susto*), or bad spirits may, as a result of jealousy or vengeance, be wilfully used to attack a person by means of hexes (*mal puesto*), the evil eye (*mal ojo*) and the like (Delgado, 1985). Thus, in explaining illness, Hispanics who hold such beliefs make no distinction between natural, supernatural and superstitious causes, and are likely to seek relief by consulting folk healers (Delgado, 1988). Among the Puertoriquenos, this involves the use of mediums or spirit guides (*espiritista*) who help ward off bad spirits and bad luck. Among the Latinos, this involves the use of herbalists (*curandera*) who operate out of local folk pharmacies, called *botanica* (Devore & Schlesinger, 1987), that double as social clubs and community centers (Delgado, 1985). Indeed, the success of folk healers among Hispanics has persuaded Ruiz and Langrod (1976) to argue that psychiatrists and folk healers should be seen as partners in community mental health.

Finally, Garcia-Preto (1982) warns that Hispanics who do seek formal therapy are likely to take a rather informal approach to appointments, prefer home visits, seek service only in crisis and drop out as soon as the crisis appears to have passed. Falicov (1982; in press) adds that of various forms of mental health service, family therapy is likely to be the most acceptable, especially if it is brief, highly structured, is conducted in Spanish and employs indirect techniques, such as allusion and storytelling. If successful, through time, family behavior toward the service provider is likely to gradually shift from the formality expected when interacting with strangers to the informal friendliness expected when dealing with kin.

SUMMARY

This portrait of Hispanics in North America is organized around two sets of similarities and differences. The first set concerns the comparison between Hispanics and Whites. Here, the similarities are broad and generic: both groups have lost ground in the face of recessionary economics; both value hard work, family life, and children; and, among the poor, both groups experience life as harsh and beset by multiple problems. Beyond that, however, the differences are pervasive, and center on a cluster of attributes which define Hispanic culture as allocentric in character, including intense sociality, family cohesion, conformity to group norms, and submission to authority. In addition, less central, but more striking, is Hispanic vulnerability to oppression, especially racism and discrimination.

The second set concerns comparisons between and among Hispanic subgroups. Here, Hispanic allocentrism is pervasive across all subgroups and, indeed, in the eyes of Whites, is a typification that has become the basis of stereotyping shading into racism. However, as with all stereotypes, on closer inspection they break down, revealing significant subgroup differences. One series of differences is sociodemographic, including such matters as population size, geographic distribution, average income, criminal involvement, and so forth. Another series of differences sees their allocentrism not as a set of fixed attributes, but rather as a set of continuua, with Puertoriquenos typically at one pole, Cubanos at the other pole, and Latinos and other Central and South Americans somewhere in between.

These differences are rendered still more complex, as they intersect with two additional dimensions, namely, generation and immigration. With rare exceptions, new immigrants, irrespective of their subgroup membership, are disadvantaged compared to their second and later generation counterparts. Similarly, the forces of acculturation are such that members of the younger generation are more likely than their elders to eschew traditional Hispanic beliefs, values, customs, and language, or to opt for a bicultural solution to the dilemma of cultural choice. Such differences mean in practice that any generic statement about "Hispanics" is likely to be both wrong and offensive.

NOTES

1. Puerto Rico is a commonwealth of the United States. Island residents, known as *puertoriquenos*, are thus American citizens and may pass freely to and from mainland United States without the need of a passport.

2. However, their concentration in those states varies widely, from 24% of the population (in California and Texas) to 12% (in Florida and New York).

3. As a group, in 1990, Hispanics were most concentrated in New Mexico (38%), California (26%), Texas (26%), and Arizona (19%; Hacker, 1992).

4. For a general history of Hispanics in the United States, see Acuna (1988) and Gann (1986). Histories of specific subgroups are also available: for Latinos, see Barrera (1980), Del Castillo (1984), Mirande (1985), and Murguia (1989); for Puertoriquenos, see Bonilla and Campos (1982) and Sanchez-Korrol (1983); for Cubanos, see Boswell and Curtis (1984), Llanes (1982) and Pedraza-Bailey, 1985); and, for other subgroups, see Henricks (1974). As far as I know, histories of Canadian Hispanics have yet to be written.

5. Szalay and Diaz-Guerrero (1985) had Latinos, Puertoriquenos, Cubanos, Columbians and Whites respond to stimuli from ten domains. While the scores of the Latinos and the Columbians were quite similar, both were quite different from the Puertoriquenos and Cubanos, and very different from the Whites.

6. Bibliographies concerning Hispanics in North America have been compiled by Foster (1982) and the U.S. Department of Housing and Urban Development (1975). For an interdisciplinary anthology, see de la Garza et al. (1985).

7. Even where systematically different treatments warranted, the absence of substantial data concerning Canadian Hispanics would render such an effort futile.

8. Such earning differentials persist despite higher education. For example, among adults with a B.A. degree in 1990, average earnings among Whites was $30,600 compared to $22,700 among Hispanics (O'Brien, 1993), a difference of 26%. In the same year, among workers who had graduated high school, average earnings among

Whites was $16,800 compared to $13,100 (O'Brien, 1993), a difference of 22%.

9. Harrison (1993) reports that in Canada in 1991, of those reporting Spanish as their mother tongue, only 6% of those aged five or over could speak neither English nor French.

10. Harris and Moran (1991: 356) estimate that in 1990, there were 8 million illegal Hispanic immigrants in the United States, mostly Latinos.

11. Hawkins (1994: 115, note 4) notes that crime rates vary across Hispanic subgroups, with Puertoriquenos higher than Latinos who are higher than Cubanos, with native-born Hispanics of all groups higher than their immigrant counterparts (Flowers, 1988).

12. Morales (1992) argues that gang members are much more likely than other delinquents to come from poor, dysfunctional families, with the gang serving as surrogate family.

13. The Cubans are an important exception, having achieved income parity with Whites (Aldrich & Waldinger, 1990; Light & Bonacich, 1988; Perez, 1986; Portes, 1987; Portes & Bach, 1985).

14. For a rare discussion of the Hispanic middle class, see Fischer (1986). Further, evidence suggests that among Hispanics upward mobility is associated with positive ethnic identity (Portes & Bach, 1985; Safa, 1988).

15. Taken together, this range of attributes classifies Hispanic culture as allocentric, that is, centered on the in-group, as opposed to Whites whose emphasis on individuality and individualism classifies them as an idiocentric culture (Diaz-Guerrero, 1984; Kim et al., 1994).

16. In Hall's (1976) terms, Hispanics are a good example of a high-context, polychronic culture.

17. Those who back away or avert their gaze may be seen as snobbish (Axtell, 1985).

18. As part of a critique of Western notions of a "transhistorical self," Cushman (1990) and Sampson (1988) argue that non-Western cultures (including Hispanics) operate with an "ensembled" or social conception of the individual.

19. In Hall's (1959: 50) words, centered on sexual relations but having much wider application, "In Latin America, both sexes expect their will power to be provided by other people rather than by personal inhibitions."

20. The word for this quality varies by location (Axtell, 1985). In Mexico, he is know as the *coyote*, while in Portuguese-speaking Brazil, he is the *despechante*. Related terms for men of status include *caudillo*, for men who own and/or manage companies, and *patron*, for men of wealth and great power (Harris & Moran, 1991).

21. Sluzki (1982) argues that in face-to-face encounters, the Hispanic definition of an intermediate or neutral distance apart is much shorter than that used among non-Hispanics. Consequently, what would be defined as merely "friendly" in the interaction between two Hispanics comes to be seen as "seductive" between a Hispanic man and a non-Hispanic woman, setting in motion a train of misunderstandings that has led to the non-Hispanic stereotype of the "Latin lover." Hall (1959) adds that differences in appropriate distance can be one source of generic misunderstanding. As Hispanics move forward to a comfortable interaction distance, Whites move back for the same reason. Consequently, Whites see Hispanics as pushy and forward, while Hispanics see Whites as cold and unfriendly.

22. Among Hispanics, bad luck is associated with the number thirteen and with the colors black and purple, reminders of the somber Lenten season (Axtell, 1985).

23. Death figures prominently in Hispanic religious celebrations and feastdays

(Harris & Moran, 1992), including *Quinceneras* (a major event for fifteen-year-old girls (Delgado-Gaitan, 1994), *Las Posadas, Nuech Buena* (Christmas Eve) and *La Virgen de Guadalupe* (Salgado de Snyder & Padilla, 1985).

24. While the rate of divorce among Hispanics is low compared to their White counterparts, the frequency of desertion and common-law relationships has risen among the urban poor (Alvirez & Bean, 1976). However, given the salience accorded marriage, and the closeness expected between marital partners, divorce can be even more devastating among Hispanics (Wager, 1987a, 1987b) than it is among Whites (Irving & Benjamin, 1995). This is so not only for the public shame associated with divorce, but even more importantly, for the extent to which divorce disrupts the kinship system (Wagner, 1987a, 1987b).

25. The necessary consequence of this double standard is a group of Hispanic girls who have been disgraced, having engaged in premarital sex, and who may now be seen as little better than prostitutes (*putas*).

26. In 1985, average household size among Hispanics exceeded four (Harris & Moran, 1991).

27. The United States Census Bureau (cited in the Toronto Star, Oct. 12, 1993: A23) estimates that by 2013, Hispanics will number forty-two million and will constitute the largest minority group in the United States (see Harris & Moran, 1991).

28. This is in contrast to the emphasis among Latinos on *La Raza*, the race or the people (Harris & Moran, 1991). See especially Ramirez's (1983) discussion of the "mestizo" perspective.

29. Triandis (1985) describes another cultural accomodation he calls the "pingpong effect," that is, the tendency to swing between poles, now traditional in support of Hispanic culture, now assimilated in support of the dominant culture.

30. In 1986-87, there were 569,000 Hispanic undergraduates representing 5.2% of the total enrollment in the United States (Quality Education for Minorities, 1990). In the same school year, nearly 26,990 Hispanics graduated with a B.A., 2.7% of all students who did so.

31. For an ethnographic study of Hispanic university students, see Reich (1989).

32. It also relates to their interpersonal sensitivity. Kaczarek et al. (1990), for example, found that compared to White university students, their Hispanic counterparts who were involved in a romantic relationship that ended were more likely to experience grief and depression.

33. A reminder of the formally patriarchal character of Hispanic culture is embodied in naming customs. Among many subgroups, surnames combine the surnames of both spouses. However, only the father's surname is used in conversation. Thus, Carlos Mendoza-Miller is called "Mr. Mendoza." In Portuguese-speaking Brazil, it is the other way around (Axtell, 1985).

34. Mizio (1974) notes that expectations of male protection and support are mutual, held by both spouses. One consequence of male unemployment is that wives may come to view them with contempt.

35. Duryea and Gundison (1993), on the basis of reports from Canadian respondents, indicate that there is a "high" divorce rate among Hispanic immigrants to Canada. This appears to be the result of a combination of factors: female financial and psychological independence; male status losss; change in parent-child relations; and the loss of the family's support system, including traditional norms prohibiting divorce.

36. Martinez (1986), for example, notes that the use of toxic inhalants is fourteen

times more common among Hispanic children and adolescents compared to their White counterparts (Trimble et al., 1993).

5

The Asians

INTRODUCTION

Asians in North America comprise thirty-two distinct groups (Dana, 1993; Sue & Sue, 1988). Of the total in the United States in 1990 (see Chapter 1, Table 1.1), 23% were Chinese, 19% Filipino, 16% South Asian (Indian),[1] 12% Japanese, 11% Korean, 8% Indo-Chinese,[2] and 16% other subgroups (Porter & Washington, 1993), including the Polynesians, Indonesians and Malays. While these subgroups are distributed throughout the United States, they tend to be concentrated on either coast (Dana, 1993).[3] Differential population growth across subgroups is also noteworthy, with the Filipinos likely to be the most populous by the turn of the century (Leung & Sakata, 1988).

As for Canada, the Asian population is distributed quite differently. Of the total in 1991 (see Chapter 1, Table 1.1), 42% were Chinese, 30% South Asian (Indian), 11% Filipino, 8.5% Indochinese, 3.5% Japanese, 3.1% Korean, and 1.9% other. While subgroups are located across Canada, over half (56%) are concentrated in Ontario (Chen, 1990), with specific subgroups well represented in British Columbia (including 31% of the Chinese and 43% of the Japanese). While comparable data regarding growth patterns are not available, sharp differences in subgroup size and relatively low fertility rates (Breton et al., 1990) predict that the Chinese and the South Asians will likely remain the most populous subgroups, at least over the next decade. Samual (1992, cited in Toronto Star, May 30, 1992: A1-A2) reaches the same conclusion with regard to the Toronto Census Metropolitan Area.

Like the Hispanics but even more so, Asian subgroups are marked by distinctly different histories, traditions and beliefs (De Mente, 1989; Devore & Schlesinger, 1987; Li, 1988a; Kitano & Daniels, 1990). Consider that if native speakers from each group were placed in a room together, they would not only be unable to communicate, having different written and spoken languages,[4] they would not even be able to share a meal, since the H'mong prefer sticky rice, the Japanese, short-grained rice and the Chinese, long-grained rice (Chao, 1992).[5] [6] [7] The following discussion will concentrate on the Chinese and Japanese, both newly arrived and long-resident, since they have received the most attention in the literature (Araneta, 1982; Baker, 1979; Connor, 1977; Dana, 1993; Devore & Schlesinger, 1987; Fugita & O'Brien, 1991; Gaw, 1982; Kendis, 1989; Levine & Rhodes, 1981; McGoldrick et al., 1989; Portes & Rumbaut, 1990; Shon & Ja, 1982; Sue & Morishima, 1982; Tan & Roy, 1985; Thompson, 1989; Ward, 1982; Yamamoto, 1976, 1982, 1986),[8] although occasional reference will be made to other subgroups. For quick reference, the profile of the Asians is summarized in Figure 5.1, below, with detailed description in the following text. Given substantial evidence of similarity (see below), no systematic effort will be made to distinguish between American and Canadian populations, save to note generic national differences examined above with respect to the Blacks.

MODAL SOCIAL CLASS

In North America, the social status of Asians has been shaped by the complex interaction among *six* dimensions: history, immigration, education, language, employment and cultural values.

Historically, Asians have been subject to unremitting oppression, discrimination and racism (Adachi, 1991; Chan & Helly, 1987; Con et al., 1982; Hirata, 1979; Kikumura, 1981; Li, 1988b; Makabe, 1981; McClain, 1994; Takaki, 1989), some of which continues to this day (Yee, 1992). In search of gold, the Chinese, for example, arrived in North America, which they called *Gold Mountain* (Chan, 1983), in the late 1840's, landing first in San Francisco and later (in 1858) migrating to Vancouver (Thompson, 1989).[9] In the late nineteenth and early twentieth centuries, Chinese men were recruited as cheap, disposable manual laborers in the construction of

---

Figure 5.1
Summary Profile of the Asians

Modal Social Class:	middle
Definition of the Family:	formal extended, including deceased ancestors
Life Cycle:	elongated, six phases, especially adolescence and early adulthood
Husband-Wife Relations:	patriarchal, with clear role segregation
Parent-Child Relations:	hierarchical interdependence
Perspective on Treatment	informal and community-based sources of help preferred

---

roads, bridges, railways, fisheries and the like (Boswell, 1986). The result were "bachelor" communities (Thompson, 1989) where men worked and died under appalling conditions (Ong, 1981). Those that survived, and who did not return to China, began drifting east, arriving in New York and Toronto by the late 1870's. Further immigration was blocked by exclusionary laws, including the infamous "Head Tax," first applied in 1885.

Those that remained made a life for themselves by establishing Chinese enterprises that did not compete with Whites, especially Chinese restaurants, hand laundries and small grocery stores. In the process, they established "Chinatowns" across North America (Godfrey, 1988; Kwong, 1987; Lai, 1988), the largest (in order of population size) in San Francisco (Salter, 1978), New York (Kuo, 1977; Kwong, 1979; Wong, 1977, 1985, 1987, 1988; Yuan, 1966), Vancouver (Anderson, 1991; Yee, 1988) and Toronto (Lai, 1973; Thompson, 1989).[10] [11] In each case, community evolution followed the same pattern: small size and slow growth;[12] a "segmentary" society (Crissman, 1967) organized around voluntary community associations based on district of origin in China (Cantonese: *hui guan*) and/or surname (Cantonese: *kung so* or *tong*); and, consisting almost entirely of men.

Later, through the period 1945-1967, while women were technically allowed entry, their numbers remained small. In addition, while more likely than men to be accepted into mainstream society (Kitano & Yeung, 1982), Chinese women were confronted by sexist stereotypes and other forms of discrimination (McGoldrick et al., 1989). Until recently (Yamamoto, 1976), such experience accounted for a relatively high suicide rate among Asians, especially women (Sung, 1967).[13]

In part, this was reflected in the relatively small numbers of Asian immigrants present in North America. As noted above, that has significantly changed. The repeal of exclusionary immigration policies in the mid-1960's has meant that what was once a trickle has since become a flood; Asians now represent the largest of the various national groups streaming into North America in record numbers (Dana, 1993; Logan, 1991).

That said, it is important to note that Asian subgroups vary widely in where they originate, how they arrive in North America, and the resources they bring with them. Among the Chinese, for example, early immigrants came from the rural Toisan district of southern China and spoke the local dialect (Thompson, 1989). Since the 1960's, political events in mainland China and Hong Kong have meant that the majority of recent immigrants originate in metropolitan Hong Kong where Cantonese and English are spoken. As to their status on arrival, many of the Vietnamese, for example, arrived as refugees, bringing with them only the clothes on their back and a few meager possessions (Bach et al., 1984; Cole et al., 1992; Muir, 1985); since then, differential acculturation across Vietnamese subgroups has been the rule (Matsuoka, 1990). The "Gucci Chinese" are at the other extreme

(Lam, 1993);[14] wealthy industrialists and entrepreneurs from Hong Kong seeking safe haven in light of the uncertainty following the transfer of Hong Kong from the British to the Chinese in 1997.[15] [16] Between these extremes, many Korean immigrants have managerial, professional or technical skills prior to immigration to North America (Almirol, 1985; Min, 1988).

However, more important than either national origin or material resources has been the sheer weight of their numbers. This has changed the shape of subgroup communities and rendered the Asians a dynamic force in North American (Aldrich & Waldinger, 1990). Among the Chinese, for example, the immigrant influx is responsible for a dramatic shift from communities of rootless "bachelors" to communities of families committed to a future in North America (Thompson, 1989).

An additional dimension shaping the status of Asians has been their outstanding educational attainment, second only to the Jews in North America (Breton et al., 1990; Fugita & O'Brien, 1991; Hirschman & Wong, 1986; Ho, 1994; Hsia, 1988; Schneider et al., 1994). In the United States, for example, Asians have been more successful in higher education than either Blacks or Hispanics and at least on a par with Whites (Levine & Rhodes, 1981; Nagasawa & Espinoza, 1992).[17] However, subgroup differences are noteworthy. Groups vary in the extent to which they see education as the best route to advancement. Thus, success in higher education has been more true of the Chinese, Japanese and Korean than the Filipinos or the Indo-Chinese (Endo, 1990). Comparable Canada data paint a similar picture, with the Chinese, Japanese and Koreans more likely to have achieved educational parity with Whites than the Filipinos or the Indo-Chinese (Li, 1988b; Moreau, 1991; Shamai, 1992; White, 1990; Winn, 1988).[18]

Following Sanday et al. (1977) and Wilson (1982), one basis for this success may be Asian acceptance[19] of a value system based on the work of the Chinese scholar, Confucius (551 b.c.-478 b.c.).[20] Among other things (see below), this places extraordinary emphasis on education as a primary route to upward mobility.[21] [22] Another is their level of English language proficiency (McDowell, 1992). This is clearly related to how long they have lived in North America, with recent immigrants at a distinct disadvantage. In the United States, Tsang (1989), for example, estimates that 65% of Asians speak a language other than English at home, and even five or more years after immigration only 20% have acquired only limited English proficiency. By contrast, Fugita and O'Brien (1991) observe that among the *Yonsei* (fourth generation) Japanese, virtually all are fluent in English and, indeed, more than half do not speak Japanese, a fact that can occasion considerable intergenerational conflict (Fugita & O'Brien, 1991; Ganesan et al., 1989; Ho, 1987, 1992a; Kendis, 1989; Nguyen & Williams, 1989).[23] In Canada, much the same applies (Maykovich, 1980). Harrison (1993) examined the question using data from the 1991 census. He found that 28% of those whose mother tongue was Chinese reported speaking neither English nor French. This was especially true of elderly women living in Toronto or Vancouver. By contrast, Breton et al. (1990) found the Japanese at the other end of the spectrum, with most having a good command of English and many having lost the ability to speak Japanese. Thus, across North America, language proficiency has contributed directly to Asian status mobility. It has also contributed indirectly to three additional factors linked to Asian financial success: (a) a high rate of intermarriage, now at or above 50% among the Japanese (Fugita & O'Brien, 1991; Goldstein & Segall, 1985; Kendis, 1989; Kitano et al., 1984; McCready, 1983; Montero, 1981; Ram, 1990: Tinker, 1982); (b) a low rate of residential segregation (Breton et al., 1990; Fugita & O'Brien, 1991; Halli et al., 1990; Kiefer, 1974), with many Chinese, for example, living in predominantly non-Chinese neighborhoods (Huang & Uba, 1992); and (c) a low rate of fertility (Halli, 1987a, 1987b), with small families of one or two children the norm.

Still another dimension of the status picture concerns employment, and especially self-employment. Among recent immigrants (especially women) and specific subgroups (especially the Indo-Chinese), language barriers, restricted skills, limited education, and discrimination have meant that many have been confined to low-level employment characterized by long hours and low wages (Boyd, 1975, 1990; Cabesas & Kawaguchi, 1988; Driedger, 1987; Li, 1978, 1987, 1988b; Moreau, 1991; Shon & Ja, 1982; Verma et al., 1980; White, 1990; Yamamoto, 1986).[24] In Thompson's (1989: 333) words, based on Canadian data but applicable across North America, "[t]here is one aspect of the Chinese working class about which there is no debate. The proletarians in Hong Kong remain proletarians in Canada."

In contrast, among Asians resident in North America for generations or those newly arrived but with professional skills, the majority have been concentrated in high-status, white collar employment (Breton et al., 1990; Levine & Rhodes, 1981; Levine & Montero, 1973; Li, 1992; Moreau, 1991). Among Hong Kong immigrants to Canada, for example, 50% arrive with managerial, professional or technical skills (Lam, 1993). Similar findings emerged from a recent study by Statistics Canada (reported in the Toronto Star, 1995: June 14: A1, A11), but with much variation across subgroups. More than 60% of Chinese and Japanese adults surveyed had professional or managerial jobs compared to 27% of Filipinos.[25] Tang (1993a, 1993b) reports comparable data for the United States, including income parity with Whites in science and engineering. Fugita and O'Brien (1991) found that 56% of the Sansei (third generation) Japanese in their California sample had professional or technical jobs.[26] [27]

As for self-employment, Asians, especially the Chinese, Japanese and Koreans have concentrated on some combination of two economic forms, both rooted in exclusion from mainstream economic activity: the ethnic economic enclave and the ethnic middleman (Aldrich & Waldinger, 1990; Bonacich & Modell, 1980; Chin & Cheung, 1985; Hurh & Kim, 1984; Kim, 1981, 1987; Light, 1972; Light & Bonacich, 1988). In the former, local ethnic markets reflect and cater to the concentration of Asians in a given neighborhood, forming what Modell (1977) has called a "vertically integrated ethnic economy." In turn, Wilson and Portes (1980) have argued that the success of such enclaves is based on the ready availability of an ethnic clientele, thus according such businesses a monopolistic advantage over their non-ethnic competition. However, the effects of this economic form have been doubled-edged (Thompson, 1989). On the one hand, it has enormously benefited Asian communities, made for dynamic economies, ensured international competitiveness, provided necessary work and, of course, returned handsome profits to their ethnic owners. On the other hand, it has created a vested interest in hiring immigrant workers who speak little or no English and are ignorant of North American labor codes; they work long hours for very low wages, and demand neither benefits nor job security in return. In short, it has created a context in which new immigrant workers are confined to the ethnic economy and thus open to exploitation.

As for the ethnic middleman, ethnic small businesses serve as a conduit, linking Asian producers and manufacturers with a largely nonethnic clientele (Aldrich & Waldinger, 1990; Bonacich, 1973; Bonacich & Modell, 1980; Kim, 1981; Light, 1972; Light & Bonacich, 1988; O'Brien & Fugita, 1982; Turner & Bonacich, 1980), as in the garment industry. In combination, these economic forms have been very successful, accounting for self-employment rates of 21% and 20% among the Koreans (Light & Bonacich, 1988) and the Sansei (third generation) Japanese (Fugita & O'Brien, 1991),[28] respectively, and virtual hegemony among the Japanese in specific segments of the California economy (Jiobu, 1988).

Finally, that success is based on yet another dimension: culture. This involves three interlocking elements (Fugita & O'Brien, 1991): economic adaptations in response to exclusion from mainstream economic activity (see above); socialization into middle-class family life (Goldscheider & Kobrin, 1980; cf. Ehrenreich, 1989); and, perhaps most important, a supportive cultural milieu. Middle-class socialization includes values emphasizing hard work; deferred gratification and a future orientation, with the roots of these values in a particular kinship system (see below); and a legacy of labor-intensive agriculture (Thompson, 1989).

As for the cultural milieu, this involves a complex, multifaceted belief system. At the heart of this system is support for what has variously been described as "ascriptive ties" (Light, 1972) or "structural intimacy" (Kiefer, 1971). That is, the belief that Asians are ethically bound to behave honorably in financial dealings with other Asians. In related fashion, they show a propensity to buy and sell to and from each other, in part because of a shared, nonassertive interactional style (Johnson et al., 1974; Kendis, 1989; O'Brien & Fugita, 1983).[29] Historically, this has been assisted by their development of small-scale, community-based financial institutions (such as the *tanomosho* among the Japanese or the *hui* among the Chinese) designed to assist small businesses (Fugita & O'Brien, 1991). Further, Asians are characterized by a high level of participation in voluntary community organizations dedicated to promoting harmonious interpersonal relations (Fugita & O'Brien, 1991). This reflects a collective or allocentric orientation (see below) emphasizing group preservation, even at the expense of individual interests (Hall, 1976; Ho, 1994; Wong, 1995; Zander, 1983). Accordingly, Asians tend to see and treat other Asians as quasi kin (Hall, 1976). Finally, and paradoxically, Asians have found a way to balance high levels of acculturation with equally high levels of group identification, based on a strong and abiding sense of "peoplehood" (Haglund, 1984; Reischauer, 1981). Indeed, various authors have argued that Asian business success has been a critical factor in promoting community solidarity (Connor, 1974a, 1974b, 1977; Makabe, 1976, 1978, 1979; Portes & Rumbaut, 1990; Wong, 1978, 1982). Thus, business success promotes community, just as community supports business success, a perfect loop, the circle being an important symbol among several Asian subgroups.

None of the above is intended to suggest that Asian communities are problem-free. For example, Asian crime rates, while historically low compared to their Black or Hispanic counterparts, have nevertheless always been present, especially among immigrants as opposed to native-born groups (Hawkins, 1994). Asian youth gangs are a fact of life (Sanders, 1994), as are rates of single parenthood which fall between 5% and 12% (Hacker, 1992). Even so, over the past twenty-five years interaction among the six dimensions discussed above has meant striking upward mobility for the Asian community. At present, the majority of Asians in most subgroups are solidly middle class (Hirschman & Wong, 1981; Kitano, 1976; Knoll, 1982; Li, 1988b, 1990b, 1992; Makabe, 1979; Nee & Wong, 1985; Verma et al., 1980).

DEFINITION OF THE FAMILY

Ethnic groups vary widely in terms of how they see the world. As noted above, the Asian approach is one of "consociation" (Plath, 1980) or "ensembled individualism" (Sampson, 1988). This emphasizes the family or group, and the individual's identification with and dependence on the larger whole (Chin et al., 1993; Cushman, 1990; DeVos, 1980; Doi, 1985; Harrison et al., 1984).[30] Thus, the individual is coextensive with and superseded by the family (Aylesworth et al., 1980; Dion & Dion, 1993; Kim, 1978; Marsella et al., 1985; Morales, 1974; Petersen, 1978; Tamura & Lau, 1992; Tseng & Char, 1974). Among the Japanese, for example, Roland (1988) refers to a "family-self," while among the Chinese, Chin et al. (1993) note that the written character for "human," *ren*, means "two men", and

Kim and Choi (1994) stress the Korean use of the inclusive "we" (*uri*).

In addition, the family is seen as extended in both place and time (Li, 1988). Following Sidel (1982) and Yung (1986), it is extended in place in the sense that it goes beyond the nuclear unit to include all blood relations (Cantonese: *gangi*), no matter how distant (Thompson, 1989), while giving less prominence to all others. This is reflected in the language, with Mandarin Chinese, for example, providing dozens of words for familial designations, such as *jie jie* for older sister and *mei mei* for younger sister (Chao, 1992). It is extended in time in the sense that it includes respect for and obligations to deceased ancestors (Chao, 1992; McGoldrick, 1988). This too is reflected in the language. As Chao (1992) notes, Asian women keep their family surnames when they marry, and it is through that name that each person is linked first to their family, then to their clan and ultimately to their ancestors.[31] It is also represented physically, in the altar to their ancestors some Asian families (especially the Indo-Chinese) still maintain (Chao, 1992).

Within this context, Asian families are organized hierarchically, based on age, gender and rank (Chen, 1983; Johnson, 1979; Lau, 1986). Asians are thus quite comfortable in relationships between individuals unequal in status (Hofstede, 1984), and are likely to resist external efforts at power balancing (Triandis et al., 1988). However, it will be useful here to distinguish between traditional and acculturated expressions of this arrangement. Among the Japanese, for example, the historical prototype for such an arrangement was the *iemoto*, literally, the "origin of the household or the household root" (Fugita & O'Brien, 1991; Hsu, 1975; McGill, 1987). This encouraged the development of superior-subordinate quasi kin relations among all members of the nation, from the emperor to the lowliest peasant farmer. Among the Chinese, Koreans and Indo-Chinese, the counterpart is filial piety (Chao, 1992; Duryea & Gundison, 1993; Shon & Ja, 1982) whereby every family member was obliged to honor, obey and show reverence for those above themselves in the hierarchy.

Further, kinship ties were traditionally highly structured in accord with patriarchal principles, with older males assigned the most authority. Inheritance was patrilineal, both property and rank passing from father to eldest son, and with sons generally preferred over daughters (Duryea & Gundison, 1993; McGoldrick et al., 1989). Authority and obligation were reciprocal (Korean: *shu*); just as fathers had authority over sons, so sons were obliged to obey fathers (Shon & Ja, 1982). Indeed, filial piety was seen to transcend even their responsibilities to their spouses and children, just as it conferred on eldest sons authority even greater than their own mothers' (Li, 1988b),[32] though they were obliged to provide for her in her old age (Lau, 1986). In turn, mothers' authority was limited, only exceeding that of her younger children and, later, her daughter-in-law (Shon & Ja, 1982).

Colman (1986) and Tamura and Lau (1992) indicate that relations among kin were shaped by formalized rules of conduct (Mandarin: *li*) characterized by reciprocal obligations, restraints, dependence and especially interpersonal sensitivity (Korean: *nunch'i*; Japanese: *ki*). In Colman's (1986) evocative phrase, Asians sacrificed "separateness to achieve connectedness." In accord with a Confucian perspective, interaction de-emphasized individual autonomy (seen as a form of selfishness) while accentuating helpfulness, kindness, sensitivity, consensus and harmony, known as *hwa hae* among Koreans (Shon & Ja, 1982; Yum, 1988). At the risk of disgracing the ancestors and bringing shame on the entire family (Tseng & Hsu, 1991), members were expected to defer to others, devalue their individual importance and avoid confrontation (Devore & Schlesinger, 1987; Johnson et al., 1974; Triandis et al., 1988).

These values are reflected both in interpersonal conduct and in language. Thus, both the Chinese and the Japanese languages are so structured as to emphasize indirectness (Colman, 1986; Hong, 1989). For example, Li (1987, cited in Duryea, 1992: 32) observes that "it is nearly impossible to say 'privacy' in the Chinese language so as to convey the full English flavor of personal freedom, individuality, and a sense of being shielded from undue outside influences." McGill (1987) agrees, adding that the subject of the sentence is often left grammatically vague or omitted altogether.[33] In turn, this means that selecting the correct form of address can be quite complex. As Schoonmaker (1989) comments, the "Japanese, Vietnamese, or Thais may have as many as thirteen ways to say "you." In these societies, one must know the age, status, and background of a person before selecting the appropriate form of address."[34]

As for interpersonal conduct, verbal politeness and the desire to please the other (especially in public) were rules shaping interaction (Tseng & Hsu, 1991). Thus, a smile or a nod need *not* have indicated mutual understanding; silence need *not* have indicated agreement; and interrupting or directly contradicting the other was carefully avoided. Nonverbal behavior too was very important. Body language, facial expression, spatial boundaries, physical contact and eye contact were all integral to Asian social interaction (Chin et al., 1993). For example, the avoidance of direct eye contact between persons of unequal status was a mark of respect, while body contact in greeting (such as hugs or kisses) was avoided (Duryea & Gundison, 1993; Schoonmaker, 1989).[35] [36] On similar relational grounds, certain personality attributes were highly valued. For example, among the Koreans, *kibun* and *chong* are both seen as critical attributes of persons rather than of behavior (Harris & Moran, 1991; Kim & Choi, 1994). While neither has an exact English equivalent, kibun refers loosely to inner feeling or mood; it is seen as important that a person have and maintain good kibun in his or her relations with others. Chong refers loosely to affection as a personal attribute, and is epitomized by "mother love" (*mo chong*). What both attributes share, and what is central to the Asian perspective, is the capacity to promote close, warm, harmonious interpersonal relations.

Conversely, conflict, seen as inevitable among Whites, was seen among Asians as negative, reflecting a shameful inability to maintain harmonious relations among members within their social network (LeResche, 1992). Again, this is evident in the language, with Duryea and Gundison (1993: 24) providing a contemporary example based on a recent Canadian study.

Initially, Chinese-speaking researchers reported difficulty in translating the word "conflict." Eventually, they settled on a word with moderate intensity, striking a balance between translations that connote catastrophic events and trivial annoyance. Even after they agreed upon an interpretation, researchers encountered difficulties with Chinese respondents, who preferred to view their experience through the prism of harmony rather than through an analytical framework which categorizes conflict.

This is not to suggest that Asians never disagree, but rather that they have evolved culturally prescribed ways of dealing with conflict. Perhaps the foremost was by denial or avoidance (Duryea & Gundison, 1993), since sacrificing one's own feelings or opinions and "swallowing the pain" was seen as both polite and contributing to relational harmony. Indeed, it is typical of this approach that what is *not* said is seen as just as important as what is said (Ting-Toomey, 1985), and with silence valued as an opportunity to contemplate what has been communicated (Axtell, 1985). Alternate approaches included indirect expression by means of nonverbal cues and stories (Doo, 1973; Lau, 1986); expressions of apology through actions rather than words, since the latter would involve an admission of error or fault (Duryea & Gundison, 1993); and the use of go-betweens (Schoonmaker, 1989) and mediators (Cohen, 1966; Doo, 1973; Wall, 1993; Wong, 1995) to achieve the compromise (Cantonese: *jang*) needed to restore harmony.

In a similar vein, Asians placed great emphasis on emotional control (Tseng & Wu, 1985), especially disapproving of the public expression of personal feelings, known as *kimochi* among the Japanese (Devore & Schlesinger, 1987; Duryea & Gundison, 1993).[37] Rather, personal feelings were kept to oneself,[38] just as problems were never discussed outside the family, for to "share one's shame" would involve a loss of "honor" or "face" (Chinese: *mentz*; Japanese: *haji*; Korean: *chaemyun*; Filipino: *hiya*),[39] both for the individual and, more importantly, for the family (Ho, 1976). Loss of face was associated with insensitive behavior by any family member that subjected the family to public criticism or embarrassment (Li, 1988b; Tsai et al., 1980). It was a central cultural value, with "[e]verything possible done to uphold a positive image of the family" (Duryea & Gundison, 1993: 25).[40] [41] However, should the source of conflict persist despite all efforts to restore harmony, it could become a source of unbearable tension, with members then liable to "blow up" under the pressure and resort to sudden and extreme violence (Duryea & Gundison, 1993).[42] Alternately, with so much riding on any action, it is not hard to understand why, among the Japanese, suicide (*seppuku*) was seen as an honorable solution to a shared but insoluble problem (Yamamoto, 1976).

Thus, Asians in general and the Japanese in particular were "pulled in two directions. The first is a very high-context, deeply involved, enveloping intimacy that begins at home in childhood but is extended far beyond the home. There is a deep need to be close, and it is only when they are close that they are comfortable. The other pole is as far away as one can get. In public there is great emphasis on self-control, distance, and hiding inner feelings." (Hall, 1976: 66-67; Kendis, 1989).

Finally, the above discussion has deliberately been framed in the past tense to raise doubts concerning the universal applicability of the above portrait. Most of the authors cited present their accounts in the present, thus implying their contemporary relevance. There is, however, reason to think this may be only partly accurate. In the United States, for example, Fugita and O'Brien (1991) indicate that, among the Japanese of California, there are few signs of the *iemoto*, since it is inconsistent with American norms of casual egalitarianism and further discouraged by the small size of many Japanese communities. Instead, it is easier to create horizontal peer relations within generations whose key expression is the voluntary community group centered on any number of common interests (for example, golf, horticulture, literature, square dancing and the like). They note too that most of the *tanomoshi* are gone, with the few remaining operating as social clubs more than credit associations. Similarly, Yu and Wu (1989) note generational changes in how native born Chinese conceptualize their filial obligations, while Huang and Uba (1992) provide evidence of increasing acceptance of premarital sex among native born Chinese college students. In Canada, Maykovich (1980), in a dated but still useful study, made a series of very similar observations. Thus, the Japanese of Toronto were widely dispersed and upwardly mobile. While a group orientation remained common, it was by no means universal, with many Japanese preferring to identify themselves as "Canadians" rather than "Japanese." While parents remained influential, adult children were more inclined to emphasize marital obligations than filial piety. The main language in the home, at least among Sansei (third generation) Japanese, was English.

These observations suggest that authors in the field have erred in failing to make distinctions on the basis of ethnic group, generation and immigration. Rather, Asian families across North America likely vary across a spectrum in their commitment to traditional norms (Lee, 1989; Takamishi, 1994). The above portrait will be most relevant to families at the traditional end of the spectrum: recent immigrants, elderly parents (some of whom may still not speak English) and families who find this approach philosophically appealing. However, in the face of assimilation pressure spread over generations, the majority of Asian families will likely have moved to the acculturated end of the spectrum. For these families, what might be described as the accoutrements of culture will have fallen away, including language, religion, dress codes, strict hierarchical divisions and food preferences, thus making them behaviorally indistinguishable from what would be found in average, White, middle-class families. What is left behind is quintessentially Asian in its emphasis on harmonious and consensual social relations, and strong self-identification with subgroup culture (Wetzel, 1988). This spectrum, then, will qualify all that follows.

LIFE CYCLE

The life cycle of the Asian family is shaped and elongated by twin concerns with achievement and mutual dependence (Japanese: *amae*). Following Fulmer's (1988) description of the "professional family," the phases of adolescence and young adulthood are expanded to meet the needs, first, of education and, later, of occupational or professional achievement (Kim, 1978; Kitano, 1976; Shon & Ja, 1982; Young, 1972). Such behavior illuminates Asian attitudes to time and work, sacrificing the present for the future (Shon & Ja, 1982) while enduring pain to ensure success (Morsbach, 1978). As noted above, Asians have been strikingly successful, both at the high school (Devore & Schlesinger, 1987) and the university levels (Hsia, 1988; McDowell, 1992).

However, in the context of the extended family, this accent on achievement is not without cost (Kim, 1993), with individual failure representing a tremendous loss of face for the entire family (Connor, 1974a, 1974b), mothers especially (Devore & Schlesinger, 1987). At the same time, childhood is elongated by a positive view of mutual dependence (Suzuki, 1980). Thus, Japanese and Korean mothers typically assume that children are born in a state of independence and must be drawn, first in the womb (Korean: *t'aekyo*; maternal prenatal care), and later through persuasion, reasoning, and maternal dew (intrinsic mother love), into dependence (Kim & Choi, 1994; Kitano, 1976). Accordingly, child passivity, submissiveness, dependence and obedience are encouraged (Sanua, 1985), with normal development seen to proceed from immature to mature dependence rather than independence, as would be expected among most Whites (Colman, 1986).

Among Japanese, mature dependence is thought to be achieved only in middle adulthood, associated with marriage and child bearing (Shon & Ja, 1982). Subsequently, life is oriented to work and parenting rather than marital intimacy (McGoldrick et al., 1989; Tseng & Hsu, 1991), while among the majority, old age brings with it the respect accorded high rank (Yu, 1984). Accordingly, as part of the kinship network, aging parents or other relatives need not fear abandonment. Involved either in paid employment (in a kin-owned establishment) or cared for in the home of an adult child (rather than an institution), their position within the family system is secure for life (McGoldrick, 1988). In some cases, however, old age may be associated with status loss (Duryea & Gundison, 1993), leaving them open to exploitation as babysitters or asked to forfeit their pension to support the family.

HUSBAND-WIFE RELATIONS

Historically, marriage had little or nothing to do with the feelings or the intentions of the respective spouses (McGoldrick et al., 1989; Morsbach, 1978). Rather, following (Vogel, 1967), aided by a go-between (Japanese: *baishakunin*) or a middleman (Japanese: *nakohdo*), it was an arrangement between families or clans to recruit a female into the male line, based on her family's rank, property and their absence of debt. Marriage for love was regarded as a selfish form of individualism. As a matter of public face, wedding ceremonies were typically a lavish and costly affair. However, in moving into her spouse's father's home, she confronted a life of drudgery under the thumb of her mother-in-law. Her only consolation was the special relationship she had with her children, especially her sons, based on *amae* (see above). In all other respects, her husband was dominant. For example, he had a unilateral right to sexual access, and he alone was free to have one or more extramarital partners.[43] Similarly, her responsibility was to produce a male heir; failing that, she could be abandoned and forced to return (in shame) to her mother's house. She had no legal right to own property, and only husbands could initiate divorce proceedings. While the death of her mother-in-law and/or her husband brought respite from labor and an increase in status, she was not expected to remarry. For some, the only escape was through suicide, perhaps with the hope of returning as a ghost to haunt her oppressive spouse.[44]

The ensuing half century has brought significant change. However, the extent to which spousal relations deviate from the above portrait depends in large measure on their position on the traditional-acculturated spectrum discussed above. Among traditional families, marriages are still semi-arranged. Among the acculturated majority, marriage for love is now the norm (Lau, 1986; Morsbach, 1978). The expression of such intimacy, however, is mitigated both by norms emphasizing emotional control and the salience of parenting. Thus, feelings of love and concern would more likely be expressed by caring for the other's physical needs, by good food and pleasant surroundings rather than by words (Tseng & Wu, 1985).[45] Similarly, wives seldom talk spontaneously or discuss their opinions or feelings with their husbands (Tseng & Hsu, 1991).

Such separateness is further encouraged by role segregation (Duryea & Gundison, 1993) which accords wives and husbands very different rights and responsibilities. Wives are in control of the home and associated household monies. Household activities remain her domain, with the generous assistance of other women in the kin system. Multiple parenting is thus commonplace, while babysitting by non-kin is strongly disapproved. In contrast, husbands are responsible for dealings with the outside world. They are not expected to help with household chores or child care. Those who fail to fulfil their material obligations (through unemployment or illness) risk shame and dishonor (Shon & Ja, 1982). Extramarital relations continue to be viewed indulgently for men while prohibited for women. While both parties can now initiate divorce (McGoldrick et al., 1989), divorce rates remain comparatively low (Cox, 1993; Sev'er, 1993). This relates to three processes: the centrality of family life as an organizing norm; the fact that divorce continues to be seen as a source of disgrace and dishonor, especially for women (Chin et al., 1993); and the restraining influence of extended kin (Lai & Yue, 1990).

In addition to child care, extended kin continue to be important in other areas. For example, for financial reasons, brides still often move in with the family of the groom (patrilocality), while mothers-in-law still carry much authority. Thus, that relationship can still be fraught with tension, sometimes mitigated by alliances between brides and their sisters-in-law (Lau, 1986). Even so, they and other extended kin would likely be involved with both spouses in dealing with any serious family problem (Lai & Yue, 1990), including serious marital difficulties. This not only reflects the esteem with which older, and thus higher status, family members are held, but also the reluctance of spouses to deal directly with such difficulties among themselves (Duryea & Gundison, 1993; Tseng & Hsu, 1991).

Finally, changes related to immigration and mobility have begun to undermine the traditional stability of Asian marriages. Among families newly arrived in North America, the traditionally subservient position of wives can be significantly altered by immigration (Duryea & Gundison, 1993; Muzny, 1989), with the one to arrive in North America first often in a dominant position, since they know better than their spouse how things work here.[46]

Among Asian families resident in North America over generations, the single most important change has been women's increased status by virtue of their involvement in higher education and their subsequent involvement in white-collar work (Aranas, 1983; McGoldrick et al., 1989). In the work context, contrary to traditional norms, women are expected to be effective and assertive. Their success in such efforts has brought them considerable economic freedom, but with double-edged consequences. On the one hand, in many Asian families, spousal relations have become much more egalitarian than would be expected among their traditional counterparts (Aranas, 1983; Devore & Schlesinger, 1987; Maykovich, 1980; Suzuki, 1980). On the other hand, changing standards have sparked spousal conflict, including increased rates of family violence and divorce (Aranas, 1983; McGoldrick et al., 1989; Muzny, 1989).[47]

PARENT-CHILD RELATIONS

In Asian families, fathers, mothers and children have different roles to play. Children's lives, in contrast to their White counterparts, are fully integrated with those of their parents and other adults in the kin network. In the words of Tseng and Wu (1985: 128), "[the child] is not the center of the social world but is only part of a social network of individuals who are intimate yet variously dominant." In practical terms, this means, for example, that there is likely to be few restrictions on children when they make noise in the presence of adults (Tseng & Hsu, 1991).

Koreans use the term *om bu ja mo*, strict father, benevolent mother, to suggest that fathers tend to be associated with discipline and rule enforcement (Kim & Choi, 1994), with the emphasis on emotional control, especially of aggressive behavior (Tseng & Wu, 1985). Consequently, fathers can often be rather distant from their children (Devore & Schlesinger, 1987; Maykovich, 1979; Shon & Ja, 1982; Sue & Morishima, 1982).

Finally, mothers are responsible for the bulk of child care, associated in this culture with a sense of deep accomplishment (Morsbach, 1978). The relationship between mothers and children is a very special one in at least *three* senses. First, given norms limiting the public expression of personal feelings, the relationship between mothers and their children is the only context in which the open expression of love is sanctioned. Further, it can represent a covert form of power, with mothers forming alliances with their children, especially their sons, against fathers.[48] Second, the dependence of children upon their mothers, especially that between mothers and eldest sons, can endure well past adolescence, in some cases lasting a lifetime. Third, the parent-child relationship can also be a focus of parental distress. Given approval of stoicism, even fatalism, in the face of adversity (Japanese: *shitagtanai*, water under the bridge; Filipino: *bahala na*, accept what comes and bear it with hope and patience, or, alternately, God wills it), admissions of adult distress are associated with a loss of face (Shon & Ja, 1982). Accordingly, child rather than adult behavior is much more likely to be seen as problematic.

This applies especially to traditional expectations of child academic success, obedience, and respect for adults. Both speak to the issue of family honor. For that reason, Asian families tend to place a good deal of emphasis on child discipline, including, among the Chinese and Indo-Chinese, approval of corporal punishment (Duryea & Gundison, 1993). This attitude extends to public schools which immigrant parents tend to see as less disciplined and structured than those "back home" (Duryea & Gundison, 1993). Indeed, more affluent families may prefer to send their children to private schools in the hope that they come closer to their educational ideal.

However, these efforts are often complicated by the children's exposure to the dominant culture, especially with its emphasis on autonomy and individualism (Fong, 1973; Muzny, 1989). For example, this may be the source of sibling conflict, as girls chaff at the traditional double standard wherein they are expected to help with domestic chores while boys are not (Duryea & Gundison, 1993). Similarly, while parents may stress the importance of hard work, their children may see work as onerous and something to be avoided. In addition, among immigrant families, the children's English proficiency may give them much greater power than they would traditionally possess (Duryea & Gundison, 1993). They therefore may feel much freer than they normally would to challenge parental authority, for example, by failing to show gratitude for their parent's sacrifices (Aranas, 1983; Devore & Schlesinger) or by refusing to learn the language of the group (Ho, 1992a). As Lau (1986) indicates, carried to extremes, such intergenerational conflict can have very serious consequences, exposing the family to public shame as their children run away from home and turn to delinquent activities (such as drug dealing, prostitution and/or petty theft) to support themselves (Trimble, 1993).[49]

Further, these sources of conflict extend into the school. There, it can place Asian youth in a bind, both "too Asian" for their peers while "too American" or "too Canadian" for their parents (Chao, 1992). For example, in a competitive system, their unjustifiable modesty and refusal to take credit for personal accomplishments may place them at a disadvantage (Triandis et al., 1988). The same may be true of their tendency to avoid conflict, thus refusing to complain despite just cause. In a similar vein, their tendency to form into groups, and to follow group norms, may unjustifiably lead them to be seen as a "gang," with its implications of extreme violence and antisocial behavior (Duryea & Gundison, 1993). Finally, their educational experience can provide yet another source of parent-child conflict. With a traditional emphasis on prosperity and financial support for the elderly, Asian parents may place intense pressure on their children to pursue a professional career in such areas as medicine, law, engineering, computer science or commerce, with double-edged consequences. On the one hand, parental support may be a key factor in explaining their academic sucess (Schneider et al., 1994). On the other hand, parental pressure may spark intergenerational conflict, parent-child estrangement and even psychiatric problems (Cheng et al., 1993; Kim, 1993). Especially explosive are situations in which children aspire to nonprofessional careers, for example, in the arts or the fine arts (Duryea & Gundison, 1993) which do not conform with their parent's cultural model of success (Kim, 1993).

PERSPECTIVE ON HELP-SEEKING

Finally, the Asian approaches to illness, distress and help-seeking are shaped by two interlocking belief systems. The first involves a humoral model of disease. Following Chao (1992) and Dana (1993), this posits that health requires a balance of good and bad (Chinese: *yin-yang*) or hot and cold (Vietnamese) forces or energies (Chinese: *chi*). Seen in combination with a vocabulary lacking terms for describing, labeling or communicating feelings (Dana, 1993), this model accords greater respectability to somatic complaints (cf. Kirmayer, 1984) while resisting recognition of psychological or psychiatric difficulties (Devore & Schlesinger, 1987; Lin et al., 1982). Indeed, based on a stark dichotomy between "normal" and "crazy" (Shon & Ja, 1982), those admitting to psychiatric disorder may be heavily stigmatized by their peers (Health & Welfare Canada, 1988; McInnis et al., 1990).

The humoral model of illness is complemented by a spiritual view of the mind. Thus, Tamura and Lau (1992) suggest that Asians tend to deal with problems by internalizing rather than externalizing them. This, they suggest, can be traced to the Buddhist belief that each person has a "true" voice, one that is always good. Distress or illness thus reflects failure to listen to that voice, often because of the loss of harmony in social relations (LeResche, 1992). This is also consistent with two observations by Hall (1976), namely that (a) the Chinese deal with minor problems by pretending they do not exist, for to acknowledge them would require some action, with potentially serious consequences; and (b) the Japanese make no distinction between active and inactive, so that what a White person would see as "just plain sitting," a Japanese person would see as doing something useful.

The upshot of these twin perspectives on illness involves two related forms of help-giving, active and passive. Active forms of help giving involve measures designed to restore balance or harmony, including the use of acupuncture, medicinal herbs, "coining" (massage using the edge of a coin or a spoon); moxibustion (burning a cone of herbs placed along acupuncture points); and "cupping," whereby a glass container, evacuated by heat is used to draw blood to the surface of the skin (Chao, 1992; Health & Welfare Canada, 1988; Sue & Morishima, 1982).[50] Passive or "quiet" forms of help giving (Reynolds, 1980) are also used, especially solitary meditation and contemplation (LeResche, 1992). As Hall (1976: 154) explains, "The study of Japanese spaces illustrates their habit of leading the individual to a spot where he can discover something for himself."

In this context, it will hardly be surprising that Asians tend to underuse formal mental health services (Lin et al., 1982; Murase et al., 1985; Yamamoto, 1982). Apart from the loss of face such a request would imply, many among the immigrant population are intensely distrustful of officials and bureaucracies of all sorts (Duryea & Gundison, 1993). Consequently, families may delay seeking treatment for so long that the condition has advanced to the point of psychosis (Sanua, 1985). When they do, eventually, seek mental health service, cultural biases among White service providers may significantly distort mental health assessment (Sue, 1981).

Asian clients tend to approach service providers rather differently than their White counterparts. The Japanese tend to view help givers as teachers

(*sensei*) and expect them to be active, even authoritative, while connecting
with and caring for the family, thus justifying family informality as if they
were family "insiders" (Tamura & Lau, 1992). In a related vein, the Chinese
and the Vietnamese regard help givers as "experts of the inner heart"
(Chinese: *xinlixuejia*; Vietnamese: *tam ly gia*), thus giving them enormous
latitude in service giving but, in return, expecting nurturance and care
(Chao, 1992).[51]

Consequently, subject to variations in subgroup expectations, help giving
with Asians, especially recent immigrants, should involve some combination
of the following (Acosta et al., 1982; Atkinson et al., 1978; Cerhan, 1990;
Chao, 1990; Duryea & Gundison, 1993; Health & Welfare Canada, 1988;
Ho, 1992; Ponce, 1974):[52]

> help givers should adopt a relatively authoritarian stance, based on their
> status as knowledgeable experts;
>
> help giving should be directive, while communication should be indirect with
> no effort made to hurry the process;
>
> harmony rather than independence or self-realization should be the goals
> of help giving, and no effort should be made to encourage or force the
> expression of feelings;
>
> discussion of topics such as sexuality or aggression should be avoided;
>
> help givers should display a thorough knowledge of the group in question,
> including its history, values, language and typical behavior patterns; and
>
> while family therapy is an acceptable service modality, it should focus on
> activity rather than insight.

Conversely, the application of standard forms of service has proven
ineffective (Mokuan, 1987; Okana, 1977; Tsui & Schultz, 1985), with Asians
more than Whites likely to drop out of service (Parker, 1988).

SUMMARY

This portrait of Asians in North America is organized around two sets
of similarities and differences. The first set concerns the comparison
between Asians and Whites. What is striking here is the extent to which
the two groups are similar. Many Asians, especially the Chinese and
Japanese, live in the same neighborhoods, speak the same language
(English), go to the same schools, date and intermarry, get the same
college degrees, have the same types of jobs and earn similar salaries. And
yet, in a quintessential sense, they remain very different from Whites, based
on a cluster of attributes which define Asian culture as allocentric in
character, including their self-identification as a people; their intense
sociality and community solidarity; their definition of the family; their

notions of harmony and "face"; their submission to authority, including a positive view of dependence; their extraordinary capacity for hard work; and their preference for long-term planning.

The second set concerns comparisons between and among Asian subgroups. Here, Asian allocentrism is pervasive across all subgroups and serves to define them as Asians. That said, their multiple subgroup differences are equally manifest. These range from traditional food and language preferences to religious and social traditions, demographic attributes, group histories, time in North America, reverence for education and even forms of greeting.

Like the Hispanics, among the Asians these differences intersect with generation and immigration. In most cases, new immigrants are disadvantaged compared to their second and later generation counterparts. Similarly, the forces of acculturation are such that members of more recent generations, such as the Yonsei among the Japanese, are more likely than those that came before them to eschew traditional Asian beliefs, values, customs and language, opting instead for a bicultural solution to the dilemma of cultural choice. The upshot is that generic statements about the "Asians" are invariably wrong in light of subgroup diversity and thus serve to obfuscate more than they clarify.

NOTES

1. South Asians include Indians, Pakistanis, Bangladeshis and Tibetans.

2. The Indochinese include people from Burma, Cambodia, Laos (including the H'mong people), Thailand and Vietnam.

3. Hacker (1992) reports that states having the highest proportion of Asians in 1990 included Hawaii (62%), California (10%), Washington (4%), New York (4%), Alaska (3.6%), New Jersey (3.5%) and Nevada (3.2%).

4. The Chinese alone, for example, encompass fifty-three distinct subgroups, with a combined total of six different written languages (Kong, 1985). Hall (1976) adds that Mandarin, the most widely used of the written languages, involves 214 radicals and four pronunciation tones, neither of which has any equivalent in English. This means that most Chinese words have multiple meanings, the correct meaning in a given context indicated by the tone used (Axtell, 1985). For example, the word for question also means horse, scold, sesame seed and mother. Similarly, while the Japanese have only one written language, they have three distinct spoken languages (Axtell, 1985).

5. Similarly, while pork is a staple of Chinese cooking, the Buddhist Malays do not touch it (Axtell, 1985).

6. Other subgroup differences can be noted (Duryea & Gundison, 1993), separating the mainland Chinese from the Taiwanese, and the Northern Vietnamese from their Central and Southern counterparts.

7. For histories of these peoples in North America, see Adachi (1991), Adelman (1982), Aranas (1983), Barth (1964), Dorais et al. (1987), Glenn (1986), Johnson (1979), Kim (1994), Kung (1962), Lee (1960), Lyman (1974), Ma (1979), Morton (1973), Nee & Nee (1972), Price (1974), Shih-Shan (1986), Steiner (1979), Sunahara (1981), Sung (1967), Takaki (1989), Takata (1983), Tchen (1988) and Wickberg et al. (1982).

8. For dated but still useful bibliographies, see Doi et al. (1981) and Morishima et al. (1979). For a bibliographic treatment of Canadian Filipinos, see Chen (1990).

9. Other Asian subgroups began arriving in North America one or more generations later (Endo, 1990), the Japanese in the 1880's, the Koreans in 1902 and the Filipinos in the 1920's.

10. While the smallest of the four, Toronto's Chinatown is distinctive in at least three ways (Thompson, 1989): it is growing at the fastest rate; it is seen as the most economically viable; and it has expanded into Chinatowns West and North, unlike New York or San Francisco where new immigrants must squeeze into old neighborhoods.

11. For studies of Chinatowns in smaller cities, see Baureiss and Driedger (1982), Fong (1993), and Weiss (1974).

12. Thompson (1989) notes that there were less than 2,000 Chinese in Toronto in 1951.

13. See also Duryea and Grundison (1993).

14. They have also been dubbed "the Astronauts," since many continue to commute between their businesses in Hong Kong and mainland China, and their families in North America, with concentrations of such commuters in Vancouver and the Toronto CMA.

15. Given their affluence, United States and Canada have gone out of their way to attract such immigrants. In 1986, for example, Canada established the Immigrant Investor Program, which gave preferential status to immigrants providing they made an investment of at least $250,000 in a government-approved project (Toronto Star, December 20, 1993: A2). These and other Hong Kong immigrants represent a significant capital flow to Canada, totalling an estimated $2.4 billion to Canada in 1988 alone (Lam, 1993).

16. The number and wealth of the Hong Kong Chinese in Vancouver is such that some have dubbed the city "Hongcouver" (Anderson, 1991: 249).

17. In 1986-87, 394,000 Asian undergraduates represented 3.6% of the total enrolment in the United States (Quality Education for Minorities, 1990). In the same school year, nearly 32,618 Asians graduated with a B.A., 3.2% of all students who did so. As for the Canadian context, a recent study by Statistics Canada (reported in the Toronto Star, 1995: June 14: A1, A11) found that among ethnic minority adults surveyed, 25% had one or more university degrees compared to 11% in the general population.

18. Thompson (1989) notes that, in Canada, foreign students are not permitted to attend public high school. The result has been the creation of a private high school system for foreign students whose parents can afford to pay the high rates.

19. The Filipinos are the exception.

20. This is the Latinized version of two Chinese characters meaning "Master K'ung," also known as Lun Yu, whose central tenent was, "What you do not want done to yourself do not do to others." (Wilson, 1982).

21. According to a Chinese aphorism, "Study is superior to all other walks of life" (Tseng & Wu, 1985: 201).

22. However, like all other generalizations one might advance with regard to the Asians, this one also requires subgroup qualification. Among the Japanese, for example, Shintoism and Buddhism, with values at some variance from Confucianism, have played an important role (Harris & Moran, 1991). Similarly, Buddhism, Christianity and Cho-ondo-gyo, as well as shamanism, have helped shape the Koreans (Harris & Moran, 1991).

23. Among the Japanese, four generations are recognized: *Issei* (first), *Nisei*

(second), *Sansei* (third) and *Yonsei* (fourth). There is some evidence that acculturation, especially among the Yonsei, may be associated with an increased risk of heart
disease (Marmot & Syme, 1976).

24. For a bibliography concerning immigrant women, see Cordasco (1985).

25. Conversely, the same study showed that almost half (43%) of all Southest
Asians surveyed were involved in service or manual labor compared to 16% of
Koreans and Japanese, 28% of Chinese, and 39% of Filipinos.

26. Parenthetically, occupational success among Asians in North America is
paralleled by economic success among Asian nations in the world. This has had two
related consequences: a variety of Asian corporations have established offices and
plants in North America and, in turn, have sent over Asians managers and their
families to run them. Thus, Sullivan (1992) reports that Japanese investment in North
America, involving some 2,600 firms, has brought with it 50,000 Japanese managers
and their families.

27. Cheng (1978) found that occupational success was associated with residential
mobility, away from old neighborhoods to the suburbs.

28. By contrast, there are relatively few self-employed Blacks (Light, 1979), and
those that exist may find themselves in fierce competition with their Korean
counterparts (Kim, 1987). Hacker (1992), for example, reported that in 1990, the
425,000 firms run by ethnic minorities represented 2.4% of all firms. Most minority-
run firms (85%) were family-run operations. Of these, many more were owned and
operated by Asians (Korean, 13.5%; Japanese, 11.1%; Chinese, 9%, Filipino, 3.6%,
South Asians, 6.6%; Vietnamese, 2.1%; total, 45.9%) than by either Blacks (3%) or
Hispanics (Cubanos, 8.3%; Latinos, 4.4%; Puertoriquenos, 2.9%; total, 15.6%).

29. There are several consequences of this propensity (Duryea & Gundison, 1993):
business dealings within the Chinese community are typically informal, based on
mutual trust and a shared sense of honor, and thus seldom involve a formal contract
or a lawyer; business disputes are seen as personal matters; and the Chinese are very
cautious in dealing with non-Chinese who do not subscribe to the same code of
honor.

30. Dana (1993) argues that this and several other aspects of Asian community
ultimately derive from the integration of three philosophies: Confucianism, with its
emphasis on balance, order and acceptance; Buddhism, with its emphasis on stoicism
and impassivity in the face of adversity and pain; and Taoism with its emphasis on
social harmony, respect for nature and the avoidance of confrontation.

31. The result, confusing in relation to North American traditions, is that mother
and child may have different surnames, with the last name traditionally given first
(Axtell, 1985). Naming traditions among the H'mong (of Laos) are still more complex
(Chao, 1990), with males receiving one name at birth and another when they marry.
The H'mong thus assume that any two people with the same last name must belong
to the same clan, and so have a claim on each other in accord with the courtesy or
hospitality bias common among Asians (Deutscher et al., 1993: 102; Jones, 1963).
Among Koreans, names involve three characters, one for the surname and two for
the given name (Harris & Moran, 1991). By custom, similar name are used by all
members of a given generation, thus locating a given individual in their family tree
(Harris & Moran, 1991), while making it difficult to distinguish between males and
females on the basis of their name alone (Axtell, 1985). To make matters still more
complex, which of a man's sons takes a "Mr." depends on his ordinal position in the
family (Axtell, 1985). While the Thais follow traditonal Asian practice in placing the
surname first, they put the "Mr." before their given name, and prefer to be so

addressed (Axtell, 1985). Among the Taiwanese, their history of contact with Christian missionaries has meant that they put the given name first, such that "Mr. Tommy Ho Chin" would be addressed as "Mr. Ho" (Axtell, 1985). Finally, in all of the above, Asians may follow traditional naming practices with other Asians but Western conventions when dealing with Whites (Axtell, 1985).

32. According to an old Chinese aphorism, "Women are supposed to obey not only their husbands, but also must obey their adult sons if their husbands pass away" (Tseng & Wu, 1985: 98).

33. While Hall (1969) makes the same observation, he adds a series of qualifications suggesting that the Japanese (at least in Japan) see the world very differently than Whites. For example, the Japanese tolerate "crowding" in public places, seldom want to be alone at home, like to sleep close together and don't mind people milling about them as they work, but they have strong feelings against sharing their home with strangers. Thus, they block out the outside world visually but use paper walls as acoustic screens. Whereas Whites place household furniture against the walls, the Japanese place theirs in the center of the room, to keep the walls clear. And, whereas Whites see space as empty, the Japanese give meaning to spaces, seeing them as essential in the creation of spatial experience (*ma*).

34. Harris and Moran (1991) argue that while this ambiguous language style allows the Japanese to recognize delicate nuances in states of mind and relationships, its lack of precision makes it clumsy for purposes of science and business.

35. Instead, the Japanese bow, the depth of the bow a function of the other's status, while the Thai perform a "*wai*," both hands together in a praying position on the chest, with the height of the hands a function of the other's status (Axtell, 1985). The Vietnamese are the exception, since they prefer to stand close together when conversing (Harris & Moran, 1991). In addition, smiling and nodding were understood more as indications of a polite effort to understand a stated view, and *not*, as would be the case among Whites, as evidence of agreement (Schoonmaker, 1989).

36. Schoonmaker (1989) also notes that exposing the soles of one's feet, say, by crossing one's leg over the other while seated, would be seen as a grave insult by orthodox Buddhists who normally sit in the lotus position, with the soles facing inward. For the same reason, orthodox Buddhists may refuse to walk under bridges or enter high rise buildings. On similar grounds, Japanese remove their shoes when entering a home or a temple, while the Thais never touch the head of another, since it is considered sacred (Axtell, 1985).

37. The exception concerns ritual occasions, such as funerals, when women were expected to cry loudly as a public demonstration of their grief (Tseng & Wu, 1985).

38. As Hall (1976) explains, this is not to suggest that affect is devalued in Asian cultures. On the contrary, affect has great salience in this culture, as long as its expression conforms to group norms.

39. Another possible consequence is that of incurring "bad luck" based on "bad deeds" in a former life (Duryea & Gundison, 1993).

40. Indeed, those who did not follow the basic rules of social exchange were thought "unpersons" (Harris & Moran, 1991: 419).

41. This extends to business dealings (Schoonmaker, 1989). The Japanese, for example, would rather lose a profitable deal than loose face. Similarly, they would never turn down a deal with a flat "no," since this would involve a lose of face. They would be more likely to change the subject or indicate their desire "to study the proposal in much detail." Concern with face also explains the use of go-betweens, since this would allow them to deny ever having taken a given position, thus avoiding

the loss of face associated with direct conflict.

42. Among the Vietnamese, yelling or speaking loudly is likely to invite violence (Duryea & Gundison, 1993). Indeed, once violence is joined, it is typically not thought necessary to separate the combatants. Harris and Moran (1991) make a similar observation about the Koreans while stressing how unusual such behavior would be.

43. In the Japanese tradition, such partners lived apart from the family. In the Chinese tradition, mistresses or concubines (and any offspring of such unions) lived with the family. Concubines (*casa chica*) have also had a respected place among many Filipinos (Harris & Moran, 1991).

44. Superstitious beliefs are a contemporary part of several Asian subgroups. Among the Hong Kong Chinese, for example, *joss*, means "good luck" but is more akin to a blessing (Axtell, 1985), the hope being that the person will be protected from bad luck. In addition, many Chinese continue to believe in *feng shui* (literally, "wind and water") a philosphy aimed at harmonizing man and nature (Real Estate Marketing Magazine [Toronto], September, 1994). In practice, it amounts to a series of superstitions in which, for example, the number four is thought unlucky (because in Cantonese the word sounds like the word for death), while the number eight is thought propitious (because the words sounds like the word for luck); west-facing doors, and houses in which front and back doors are aligned, are thought unlucky (because prosperity will flow in and then out again). While these views may sound fanciful, they have practical consequences, as White homeowners with houses numbered four have discovered to their displeasure; in areas frequented by Chinese buyers, such houses do not sell. The Thais provide another example, as they refuse to step on door sills (in the belief that kindly spirits dwell below), and they leave their windows closed at night to block the entry of evil spirits (Axtell, 1985). Many Koreans will refuse to use another's surname, in the shamanistic belief that to do so may call up evil spirits and bring bad luck (Harris & Moran, 1991); instead, they address the other by their position or title. Finally, many Filipinos also believe in spirits, ghosts and whitchcraft, including the evil eye (Malong, 1976), and they may use their appearance to explain being late for or missing an appointment (Harris & Moran, 1991).

45. However, just as funerals sanction open expressions of grief, so holidays and festivals sanction open expressions of joy. Among the Chinese, who, like the Jews, rely on the lunar calendar, such a joyous occasion would be the Chinese New Year, which annually falls anywhere between the middle of January and the middle of February (Axtell, 1985). Among the Japanese, *Chugen* (July 15) and *Toshidama* (January 1) would be similar occasions (Axtell, 1985).

46. Among the Vietnamese, additional sources of marital strain include conflict over sending money home to parents or parents-in-law and/or men's gambling debts (Duryea & Gundison, 1993).

47. Fugita and O'Brien (1991) report a divorce rate of 9.6% among Sansei (third generation) Japanese. Among Sansei who have intermarried, the divorce rate varied as a function of involvement in Japanese voluntary community associations: involved versus uninvolved intermarried couples had divorce rates of 5% and 23%, respectively. In a similar vein, Duryea and Gundison (1989), based solely on respondent reports, indicate that divorce is traditionally rare among the Chinese and Vietnamese. However, confronted with the rigors of immigration and the changed status of women and children, "family breakdown" has become commonplace among the latter in Canada.

48. Duryea and Gundison (1993) make reference to similar sorts of alliances between grandparents and typically one child in the former's bid to retain status in the family.

49. An alternate approach, also extreme, involves adolescent suicide (Garfinkel & Northrup, 1990).

50. Among the Indo-Chinese, use of spirit or folk healers remains commonplace (Conquergood et al., 1989; Health & Welfare Canada, 1988; Lemoine, 1986; McInnis et al., 1990; Muecke, 1983), although this varies by social class.

51. Chao (1992) sums up this view in the form of a Vietnamese saying: "*luong y nhu tu mau*," a good doctor is like a good mother.

52. For an annotated bibliography in this area, see Williams (1987).

6

The Jews

INTRODUCTION

For comparative purposes, the final ethnic group to be examined is that of the Jews. Jews comprise a heterogeneous group made up of Sephardic Jews from the Iberian Peninsula, Western Asia and North Africa; and the Ashkenazi Jews from Eastern and Central Europe (Heilman & Cohen, 1989; Taieb-Carlen, 1992). In North America (and in Israel for that matter), the latter represent about 75% of the total population (Herz & Rosen, 1982). The majority have been resident in North America for three or more generations.[1] [2] Furthermore, Ashkenazi Jews can be further distinguished in terms of their degree of religious orthodoxy (Brym et al., 1993), ranging from liberal (Reform) to conservative (Conservative) to orthodox (Orthodox and Ultra-Orthodox, such as the *Hasidim*).

In the United States, in 1990, Jews numbered about 4.7 million (Goldstein & Kosmin, 1992; cf. Waxman, 1992) or 1.9% of the general population (see Chapter 1, Table 1.1).[3] This proportion has remained extraordinarily stable, with Silberman (1985), for example, noting that Jews represented 2% of the American population in 1908. At present, Jews are heavily concentrated in the large cities on the Eastern seaboard: Boston, Philadelphia, Washington, D.C., Miami (Fowler, 1977), with about 35% of the total living in and around New York City.[4]

In Canada, in 1991, Jews numbered 246,000 or just under 1% of the general population (see Chapter 1, Table 1.1). While Jews are distributed across Canada (Medjuck, 1986), they are concentrated in Winnipeg, Montreal and Toronto (Tavuchis, 1989; Weinfeld et al., 1981), with more than half (54%) in the Toronto Census Metropolitan Area.[5] Of the latter, it has been estimated that about 26% are Sephardic (Taieb-Carlen, 1992).

The discussion that follows will concentrate on long resident Ashkenazi Jews, since they have received the most attention in the literature (Braverman, 1990; Devore & Schlesinger, 1987; Evans, 1973; Goldscheider,

1985; Herz & Rosen, 1982; Kadushin, 1974; Kallen, 1976; Maas, 1989; McGoldrick, 1982b, 1988; McGoldrick et al., 1989; Schneider, 1984; Silberman, 1985; Sklare, 1974; Tavuchis, 1989; Vigod, 1984; Zborowski, 1952; Zuk, 1978).[6] For quick reference, the profile of the Jews is summarized in Figure 6.1, below, with detailed description in the following text. Given substantial evidence of similarity (see below), no effort will be made to systematically distinguish between American and Canadian populations, save to note generic national differences examined above with respect to the Blacks.

MODAL SOCIAL CLASS

Two facets of the history of the Jews helps explain much of what is to follow in describing them: study and persecution. Study refers to a traditional reverence for intellectuality and educational pursuits (Abella, 1990; Vigod, 1984). Historically, the Jews of Eastern Europe (for example, in Russia, Poland, and the Ukraine) highly valued the pious, sedentary life of the scholar devoted to religious study (Stein, 1985), a vocation only open to men. This left the family in chronic poverty and the women with much training in the practical art of making do with very little (Zborowski & Herzog, 1952). In a similar vein, the Jews have traditionally sought the advice of men thought especially learned or wise (McGoldrick, 1982a, 1982b), a fact reflected in *Yiddish*[7] which is replete with honorific terms for such righteous men, for example, *tzaddik* (Herz & Rosen, 1982).

The modern outcome of this tradition has been a people who value education; complex verbal reasoning; direct emotional expression; logical and critical thought; openness to new ideas; problem-solving through discussion, analysis and inquiry; respect for "experts"; and the importance of insight and understanding. Conversely, they are likely to be suspicious of things physical (Devore & Schlesinger, 1987).

As for persecution, this refers to traditional adaptations to suffering. Historically, in Europe, Jews were not permitted to travel, own land, gain

---

Figure 6.1
Summary Profile of the Jews

Modal Social Class:	middle
Definition of the Family:	nuclear family
Life Cycle:	elongated, six phases, especially adolescence and early adulthood
Husband-Wife Relations:	egalitarian
Parent-Child Relations:	democratic, permissive, emphasis on child success
Perspective on Treatment	formal sources of help preferred

---

higher education[8] or to enter the professions, thus institutionalizing their chronic poverty. They were subject to periodic murderous attacks (*pogroms*) culminating in the holocaust associated with the Second World War (Epstein, 1979). This had several immediate consequences (Benkin, 1978). Forced into ghettoes, they came to think of themselves as "outsiders." The objects of hatred, they became unusually self-reliant, especially in terms of forming and operating voluntary, self-help organizations. Excluded from the mainstream economy, they became experts in the few areas open to them, especially business and finance. While the latter required routine dealings with non-Jews (*goys*), they preferred to buy and sell from each other. And, toward the end of the nineteenth century, they were highly motivated to escape to North America (among other destinations) through emigration.

In North America, during the first half of this century, the Jews confronted conditions that, while less extreme, were all too familiar, including virulent anti-Semitism (Abella, 1990; Abella & Troper, 1991; Dawidowicz, 1975; Herz & Rosen, 1982). Their response was to apply the same solutions that had helped them survive in Europe: an emphasis on self-employment (Goldscheider & Kobrin, 1980; Perlman, 1983) within the context of an ethnic enclave (Rischin, 1962); reliance on voluntary, self-help organizations (Benkin, 1978; Rosentaub & Taebel, 1980; Turner & Bonacich, 1980); a propensity to buy and sell from each other (Wirth, 1928; Bonacich, 1973) within an urban ghetto (Gendrot & Turner, 1983); and, a sense of what Rose (1959) calls "dual cultural membership" (Fowler, 1977), that is, skills allowing comfortable interaction with either Jews or non-Jews.

In considering recent events, it will be useful to distinguish between general and specific outcomes. Among the general consequences are a people who fear persecution; deal with problems by intensifying closeness and interaction; are extremely flexible and adaptive; see suffering as inevitable (and thus to be shared and born with pride rather than overcome); identify with the poor; sustain a belief in philanthropy and good works, *tzedaka* (Sklare, 1972), seen as a religious obligation and a blessing (*mitzvah*); feel a driving need to achieve material success (Fernando, 1986; Silverman, 1989); and place inordinate emphasis on food (Braverman, 1990; Tuchman & Levine, 1993).[9]

More specific outcomes include:

> a comparatively high level of educational achievement (Chiswick, 1992; Fetgin, 1995; Kamen, 1985; Shamai, 1992). Silberman (1985), for example, estimated, and Goldstein and Kosmin (1992) have recently confirmed, that 60% of Jews in the United States, both men and women, have graduated from college or university. This places them higher than Whites, Asians or Caribbean Blacks, and much higher than either Blacks or Hispanics.

a comparatively high level of involvement in the professions (Braverman, 1990; Breton et al., 1990; McGoldrick et al., 1989; Silverman, 1989; Tavuchis, 1989).[10] The contribution of Jewish professionals has been significant. In examining a list of the 200 men and women constituting America's "intellectual elite," including academics, journalists, artists, writers and the like, Kadushin (1974) found that half were Jews. This places them higher than Whites, Asians or Caribbean Blacks, and much higher than either the Blacks or the Hispanics.

a comparatively high level of residential segregation (Breton et al., 1990; Silberman, 1985), that is, Jews like to live near each other. This places them higher than either Whites, Blacks, Caribbean Blacks or Hispanics, and much higher than Asians.

a comparatively moderate rate (about 25%) of intermarriage (Kalbach, 1983; McGoldrick, 1982a; Silberman, 1985; cf. Goldstein & Kosmin, 1992),[11] that is, higher than either Blacks, Caribbean Blacks or Hispanics, but lower than Asians.

a comparatively high level of ethnic self-identification (Kallen, 1976; Silberman, 1985). Thus, like the Chinese and the Japanese, the Jews take great pride in their shared "peoplehood." However, based on evidence from Breton et al. (1990), unlike the Japanese, ethnic identification among the Jews has not declined across generations (see below).

a comparatively low fertility rate, with 2.7 the average family size in 1990 (Braverman, 1990; Goldstein & Kosmin, 1992; Halli et al., 1990; Simmons & Turner, 1986; Tavuchis, 1989). Bearing in mind class and religious differences (see below), this places them on a par with Asians, lower than Blacks or Caribbean Blacks, and much lower than Hispanics.

relative freedom from persecution (Silberman, 1985). While Jews remain vigilant for signs of a resurgence of anti-Semitism, by and large, they have, compared to the other groups in question, moved with remarkable speed into the mainstream (Schneider, 1984).[12] Ironically, such relative freedom has created a dilemma (Silberman, 1985), making it easier to abandon Jewishness while reducing the temptation to try. As noted above, the overwhelming majority of Jews choose to remain Jews (Weissler, 1989). Indeed, even among those who intermarry, a significant proportion of their non-Jewish spouses convert to Judaism and agree to raise their children as Jews (Silberman, 1985), a fact that can become quite problematic should they later divorce (see below).

finally, in keeping with their occupational success, comparatively high average incomes (Breton et al., 1990; Chiswick, 1992; Heilman & Cohen, 1989; Silberman, 1985; Silverman, 1989; Tavuchis, 1989), that is, on a par with or higher than that of Whites, Asians and Caribbean Blacks, and much higher than that of Blacks or Hispanics.[13]

In light of the above, it seems safe to conclude that the majority of Jews fall into the middle class.

DEFINITION OF THE FAMILY

Like the Hispanics, the Jews are characterized by familism which emphasizes the central importance of family life (Zuk, 1978). Marriage, for example, is seen as a duty (Birnbaum, 1975) while celibacy is condemned (Herz & Rosen, 1982). Husbands are expected to be good spouses, fathers and providers, while wives are expected to be good spouses as well as the mother of intelligent children. Thus, unlike any of the groups examined thus far, the Jewish focus is on the nuclear rather than the extended family.

This is not to suggest that the extended family is unimportant, just not central. Indeed, regular contact, by telephone and in person, is commonplace (Devore & Schlesinger, 1987). It is also linked to a recent fact novel in Jewish history, namely, women's opportunity for personal success (Koltun, 1976).[14] Traditionally, women's success has invariably been vicarious, her social status derived from her husband's, her success that of her children's, whether through their daughter's marriage or their son's occupation (Herz & Rosen, 1982). More recently, education and a changing labor market has afforded Jewish women an opportunity for personal success, thus, for the first time creating the real possibility of a conflict between family life and career (Koltun, 1976; Schneider, 1984).

LIFE CYCLE

Following Fulmer (1988), the Jews are a classic example of the elongated life cycle typical of the professional family. Even at an early age, parents, especially mothers, are deeply invested in child academic achievement and the maximization of whatever aptitudes and talents they display (Sanua, 1978). To these ends, they are ready to make whatever sacrifices are necessary to translate these talents into concrete achievements. Later, the *bar mitzvah* (for boys, as they reach the age of thirteen) or the *bas mitzvah* (for girls, as they reach the age of twelve) are unique rituals that reflect the value Jews place on intellectual development (McGoldrick, 1988).

Next, higher education coupled with graduate or professional school (see above) are typically taken for granted (Herz & Rosen, 1982), thus delaying marriage and childbearing. In this context, leaving home may be considerably delayed as well, although legitimized by the requirements of achievement (McGoldrick, 1988). As McGoldrick (1988) suggests, child leaving may be characterized by "ambivalent closeness," that is, distance mixed with guilt at going and coupled with the expectation of ongoing, intimate interaction with parents.

Later still, parenting is complicated by the rigors of consolidating a professional career and being involved in the larger community, especially in voluntary, self-help organizations (Silberman, 1985). Finally, following an empty nest period, old age may be characterized by caregiving by an adult child. However, unlike the other groups examined above, Jews see institutional care as an acceptable solution (McGoldrick, 1988), a fact exemplified by an extensive network of community-funded charities, and residential and nursing homes (Devore & Schlesinger, 1987). While a reflection of community norms concerning aging and giving, that network is also the result of effective group cooperation, especially among Jewish women (McGoldrick et al., 1989).

HUSBAND-WIFE RELATIONS

The character of husband-wife relations turns on the family's position on the spectrum of religious belief.

Among the Orthodox (Bulka, 1986; Return to the Source, 1984), all adults are expected to marry, with marriage and family life organized in accord with Jewish law (*halakhah*) and with the goal of achieving marital satisfaction (*shalom bayit*). Arranged marriage, often with the aid of a marriage broker (*shadkhan*), is still quite common. The marriage ceremony itself, foreshadowing what is to follow, involves nearly complete gender segregation. In turn, married life is shaped by strict adherence to an array of prescriptions or commandments (*taryag mitzos*), 613 in all, drawn either from the first five books of the Old Testament (the *Torah*) or the accumulated commentaries about the Torah (the *Talmud*),[15] which regulate virtually all aspects of life, including dress, diet, religious observance, community relations and married life.[16] Men grow beards and earlocks (*payess*), wear skullcaps (*yarmulkes*), natural fibers (*sha'atnez*) and special tasseled undershirts (*tzitzits*). Women, to be unattractive to other men, wear extremely modest clothing, no makeup, shave their heads and wear wigs; monthly they go to a ritual bath (*mikveh*). Dietary laws (*kashrut, kosher*) dictate that milk and meat never be mixed, while forbidding the consumption of some foods seen as unclean (*trayf*), especially pork. Religious observance not only includes a variety of festivals (*yomtovim*), but organizes daily life, with prayer required three times daily.[17] Further, prayer on the sabbath (*shabbat*), which extends from Friday sundown to Saturday sundown, is not only segregated by gender, but forbids thirty-nine kinds of work. Good works and charity may entail donating up to 10% or more (*maaser*) of a family's annual income.

Finally, married life is characterized by role segregation, with religious tradition specifying by written contract (*ketuvah*) the rights and obligations of each spouse. For example, sexual satisfaction is seen as the wife's right and the husband's duty (Guttentag & Secord, 1983). Consequently, the frequency of sexual relations is regulated. Sexual relations are forbidden while the wife is menstruating (approximately five days) and for seven days thereafter. During this time, the husband is obliged to remain abstinent, being forbidden either masturbation or infidelity. Thereafter, however, couples are encouraged to have sex frequently. This has two consequences: it maximizes the likelihood that the wife will become pregnant, and significantly increases the likelihood of bearing a male as opposed to a female child.[18] Further, given that birth control is strictly forbidden, the likely result is not a family with six to twelve or more children, but also one with more boys than girls. Indeed, Guttentag and Secord (1983) report that a sex ratio of 130 or higher (130 boys for every 100 girls) is typical among orthodox communities.[19] They go on to argue that sexual practices, sex ratio and community attitudes and beliefs form a complex feedback loop. Thus, the high sex ratio in such communities helps explain the patriarchal character of the culture (Baum et al., 1975). Authority concerning community and religious matters accrues to men who, as husbands, are expected to be faithful and prosperous, and, as fathers, to help with discipline and instruction. Conversely, authority concerning most domestic matters (see below) accrues to women who, as wives, are expected to be patient and submissive, and, as mothers, to be self-sacrificing and devoted to child care and housekeeping. Both men and women, however, will favor male children, an attitude that is supported by their sexual practices, which helps give rise to a high sex ratio, thus serving to perpetuate such beliefs. Given these specialized requirements, orthodox families often form into small, relatively segregated, homogeneous communities.

At the other end of the spectrum, Reform families are, in many ways, indistinguishable from what is typical among dual career families in the dominant culture. Marriage is seen as extremely important, with much effort to ensure good, stable marriages between daughters and successful, prosperous husbands (Herz & Rosen, 1982). Marriage is based on love, with relations among the spouses democratic and egalitarian, and with both agreeing on the primacy of family life (McGoldrick, 1988). As with most professional families, birth control is affirmed (Silberman, 1985), with families, as noted above, typically small. Both parents share child care and housekeeping tasks, although the balance still often tilts in favor of women who must juggle family and career responsibilities.[20] Finally, not only is the marriage rate high, but the divorce rate is correspondingly low (Herz & Rosen, 1982),[21] that is, lower than either Whites or Blacks (Vigod, 1984; Sanua, 1978), and on a par with Hispanics and Asians.

However, even in divorce, Orthodox and Reform Jewish families can be distinguished (Irving & Benjamin, 1992; Syrtash, 1992). While both groups necessarily seek divorce through the civil courts, only the Orthodox also seek divorce through the Rabbinical Court (*Beth Din*). Since under Jewish law, marriage is entered into voluntarily and without coercion, it can only be dissolved in the same way, indicated by the giving and receiving of formal notice of consent (*get*). However, here the spouses are not equal, for only husbands can give a get, while only wives can receive one. This has four consequences. First, it speaks to child custody. Under the age of six, male children are traditionally given into the custody of their fathers while female children go to their mothers; the case of older children is decided individually, on the basis of child "best interest." Next, it addresses child support. Under Jewish law, fathers are obliged to support their daughter(s) to age eighteen (even should his former wife remarry) and his son(s) to the age of six; after six, should his son(s) be given into the custody of their mother, the responsibility for their support becomes hers. Third, in couples whose marriage was the product of religious intermarriage, typically between a Christian and a Jew, it can create serious problems around child education and upbringing. In such cases, the Christian partner will have converted to Judaism. On divorce, some revert back to Christianity. The court is thus confronted by a couple one of whom insists that the child(ren) be raised as Orthodox Jews, while the other is equally adamant that they be raised as Christians. Finally, it creates a situation unique among Orthodox Jews, for a husband may refuse to give his wife a get. This transforms her into an *agunah*, a chained woman, one who does not live with her husband, receives no support from him, but cannot be divorced from him, and so is forbidden to remarry or even to live with another man. Should she do so anyway, she risks being branded an adultress while any children of the union would be seen as bastards who, as adults, may only marry others who are the product of a similarly illicit relationship.

PARENT-CHILD RELATIONS

As with marriage, parent-child relations depends on the level of religious commitment.

Among Orthodox families, parental devotion and care, like child bearing, is seen as a religious obligation (Guttentag & Secord, 1983). In combination with religious practices, such as hand washing before and after every meal and a general concern for health (see below), such devotion has resulted in a disproportionately low rate of infant mortality among Orthodox Jews. In turn, this has contributed to the high sex ratio, noted above, since it means male infants survive that would otherwise have died.

Further, life in a small, closely-knit orthodox community has its advantages. One of these concerns shared child care, although only among the women. Parental authority, however, is distributed along gender lines. For example, the training, instruction and discipline of boys is left almost exclusively to fathers, who rely solely on reason. Indeed, socialization directed toward fostering intellectual achievement, autonomy and religious faith is very much organized along gender lines. Boys and girls, for example, follow parallel tracks, since they are sent to similar but different private schools. Schools for boys[22] meet all state educational requirements but attend equally to language and religious instruction, making for a very demanding educational course (Helmreich, 1986). Schools for girls are similar but stress skills related to female roles in the home (*yiddishkeit*).

In contrast, as noted above, among Reform families, child care is shared by mothers and fathers but likely restricted to them; outside help by kin or paid babysitters is a function of individual circumstances as opposed to community norms. Child socialization stresses intellectual achievement, independence, emotional development and social skills (McGoldrick, 1988). Moreover, compared to their Black or Hispanic counterparts, Jewish children are allowed so much more latitude that they might appear spoiled, known as *zelosen* (Blau, 1974). As Silberman (1985: 138), explains "Jewish parents traditionally have seen their children as extensions of themselves rather than separate, still less subordinate, creatures; children are their parents' *nachas*--a hard to translate term that means that children provide their parents with honor and fulfillment as well as with joy." (emphasis added). He quickly adds, however, that indulgence is linked to high expectations and rigorous standards in keeping with demanding and ambitious parents; thus, no one is spared, neither children nor parents (Braverman, 1990; Blau, 1974).[23]

This is exemplified in education. Children are typically educated in the public school system, although they may receive supplementary instruction in languages and religion after school hours (Devore & Schlesinger, 1987). Academic success is emphasized; parents are highly supportive of their children's academic efforts (Chiswick, 1988; Coleman, 1988; Muller, 1993), and react quickly to any indication of emotional disturbance or grades falling below an "A" (McGoldrick, 1988). Fetgin (1995) argues that it is the combination of parental resources, parental support, private schooling and child effort that accounts for the academic excellence characteristic of Jewish children (Gross, 1967). Alternately, such pressure to achieve can be a major source of parent-child conflict (Radetsky et al., 1984).

At the same time, parenting is often permissive and democratic, with discipline based on reasoning rather than corporal punishment, and with cross-generational boundaries much more open than in the other groups examined. For example, children are typically free to challenge parental beliefs and are often included in family efforts at problem-solving (Herz & Rosen, 1982). Parents are also receptive to their children's interests and encourage them to bring their friends into the family home (McGoldrick, 1988). This process can lead to identity diffusion and thus may become another source of cross-generational conflict (Fernando, 1986). Until very recently, even in such families, boys had special status, burdened with the responsibility of being successful in the world, therefore ensuring the transmission of Jewish values and traditions (Silberman, 1985). Ironically, the later price of their success may be a feeling of relative impotence and lack of appreciation in the face of a powerful wife and demanding children (Herz & Rosen, 1982). In contrast, somewhat like Blacks and Hispanics, relations between mothers and adult daughters are unusually close and intimate, and typically free of generational restrictions (McGoldrick et al., 1989; Simmons & Turner, 1986).

PERSPECTIVE ON HELP-SEEKING

Finally, unlike the ethnic groups examined above, Jews do not equate illness with weakness. Rather, with hypochondria quite common (Zborowski, 1952; McGoldrick et al., 1989), they are extremely sensitive to any signs of illness, quick to seek medical treatment and voluble about their pain (Greenblum, 1974; Sanua, 1985). Similarly, while relatively tolerant of deviant thinking and emotionality (Wylan & Mintz, 1976), they tend to view psychotherapy positively and to seek service early in the course of psychological disturbance (Srole et al., 1962). Consequently, compared to other groups, they display a much higher rate of outpatient treatment and a much lower rate of serious impairment (Sanua, 1985; Silberman, 1985).

As noted above, problems with children are typically the basis of their help-seeking efforts, especially with regard to intergenerational conflict and parental concern over either academic failure and/or home-leaving (Herz & Rosen, 1982). Once receiving service, their concern with logic and understanding may immobilize them, while family enmeshment may block change. Conversely, these concerns mean that Jews value talking therapies oriented toward insight. Typically bright and verbally sophisticated, they tend to use anger, criticism, argument, self-deprecating humor and the direct expression of feelings as ways of dealing with problems. Thus, they are likely to recognize complex levels of meaning (McGoldrick, 1982a) and favor complex solutions to presenting problems (Herz & Rosen, 1982).

SUMMARY

This portrait of Jews in North America is organized around two sets of similarities and differences. The first set concerns comparison between Jews and the other ethnic minority groups examined in previous chapters, that is, the Blacks, the Caribbean Blacks, the Hispanics and the Asians. What is striking here is the extent to which the Jews stand part way between the Whites and the other groups in question, that is, similar to them in some respects while quite different in other ways. Hence, Jews are similar to other ethnic minority groups, and different from Whites, by their emphasis on the central importance of marriage and the family, and with it the importance of close family ties and of child socialization. Further, Jews remain continuously vigilant of discrimination and persecution; retain a strong and abiding sense of "peoplehood" and high levels of voluntary residential segregation; have typically opted for a bicultural solution to the problem of choice; often loudly approve of affective expression; and, despite entry into the mainstream, remain inordinately reliant on self-help efforts that emerge from within the community.

In contrast, there are various ways in which they are manifestly different from ethnic minority groups, and thus similar to Whites. Perhaps most central, Jews, by their focus on the nuclear rather than the extended family, are clearly idiocentric instead of allocentric. Further, they support norms of egalitarian spousal relations, democratic parenting styles and espouse very different notions of illness and the role of service professionals, including care of the elderly outside of the home. Finally, like Whites and Asians, they have demonstrated exceptional academic and occupational success.

The second set concerns comparisons between and among Ashkenazi Jewish subgroups, based on their degree of religious orthodoxy. Here, all groups share a core set of values and behaviors which identify them as Jews, especially a shared sense of ethnic self-identification. However, in most others ways, subgroups stand apart from each other, not only in terms of religious devotion and practice, but also in the norms and behaviors attached to their level of beliefs, from food preferences, dress codes and marital styles, to sexual practices and child socialization. Once again, such diversity should enjoin great caution in making generalizations that would almost invariably require careful qualification. Even more importantly, this account of the Jews has served well to highlight the extraordinary extent to which this is true of *all* the groups examined herein. In turn, this implies that any effort to respond to the diverse needs of these groups must *necessarily* encompass *both* the similarities as well as the differences.

NOTES

1. One of the first Jewish communities in North America was established in Quebec City in 1759, while the oldest Jewish congregations in Canada was establised in Montreal in 1768 at the Spanish and Portuguese Synagogue.

2. While this is true of most Jews, there has been a recent wave of Israeli and Russian Jewish immigrants (Herz & Rosen, 1982).

3. Whereas Statistics Canada recognizes "Jewish" as a census category, this is not true of the United States census bureau, which is prohibited by law from collecting data about religious groups. Accordingly, any population estimates reported in the United States literature should be regarded as approximations only. McGoldrick (1993), for example, reported that there are 5.5 million Jews in the United States (half the world's Jewish population), while Waxman (1992) puts the figure closer to seven million. I have treated Goldstein and Kosmin's (1992) estimate as definitive, as it was based on the 1990 National Jewish Population Survey. The latter was initiated in 1971 with private funding provided by the Council of Jewish Federations (Silberman, 1985), a voluntary, self-help organization.

4. Goldstein and Kosmin (1992) found that 51% of Jews in the United States live in the Northeast, 20% in the South, 18% in the West, and 11% in the Midwest. In addition, 76% lived in urban centers.

5. Based on McGill University's "Consortium for Ethnicity and Strategic Social Planning," in 1991 there were 101,210 Jews living in Montreal and 162,605 living in Toronto, representing 3.3% and 4.1%, respectively, of the populations of those cities (cited in the Montreal Gazette, 1995, August 22: A14). Any discrepancy between these figures and those cited in Chapter 1, Table 1.1, derive from my reliance on single origin responses only.

6. Bibliographies concerning the Jews have been compiled by ABC-Clio (1983), Kaganoff (1990-1991) and Schlesinger (1971, 1987). For the early history of the Jews, see Holder (1986) and Goldwurm (1982). For histories of the Jewish experience in North America, see Abella (1990), Abella and Troper (1991), Dawidowicz (1975),

Kahn (1987), Paris (1980), Rischin (1987), Robinson et al., (1990) and Weinberg (1988). For an economic history of the Jews, see Perlman (1983).

7. Yiddish, derived from German, was the traditional language of the Ashkenazim; the mother tongue of many older Jews, its use is becoming increasingly rare among members of the most recent generation, thus rendering inaccessible much Jewish literature. Its counterpart among the Sephardim is Ladino, derived from Spanish. Both groups use Hebrew as the language of religious expression and study.

8. At that time, when all but the clergy and the nobility could neither read nor write, education was universal among Jewish boys over five years of age.

9. This preference provides a window on intercultural relations. Tuchman and Levine (1993), acting on a hunch, examined New York City by matching the movement of Jews against the proliferation of Chinese restaurants. It turned out the two were highly correlated.

10. Given their earlier emphasis on self-employment, Evans (1973: 9) captures the irony of this shift in preference when he says "The story of the Jews is the story of fathers who built businesses to give to their sons who didn't want them."

11. Among the orthodox, intermarriage is typically seen as so traumatic as to result in an emotional cutoff between the parents and the child in question (Gordon, 1964). In extreme cases, orthodox parents may even "sit shiva," the seven-day mourning ritual for the dead.

12. Conversely, McGoldrick et al. (1989) notes that in some cases Jews have responded to discrimination with self-loathing.

13. In 1990, average income among American Jews was $37,800 (Goldstein & Kosmin, 1992).

14. Ironically, such success can be accompanied by depression and anxiety, major reasons why Jewish women have sought out therapy in unprecedented numbers (Siegel & Cole, 1991).

15. This is a compilation of sixty-three volumes completed prior to the 6th century.

16. This includes the frequent but highly ritualized use of alcohol, a practice that Snyder (1958) argues, accounts for the comparatively low rate of alcoholism among Jews.

17. Shacharis is the morning prayer, while minchah is conducted in the afternoon, and maariv in the evening. Prayer is done facing East, towards Israel (*Eretz Yisrael*). It also requires the presence of not less than twelve males (*minyan*) each of whom wears phylacteries (*tefilin*).

18. Guttentag and Secord (1983) note that, after a period of abstinence, seminal fluid will contain 57% Y or male sperm. Similarly, they note that a day or two prior to ovulation, a women's cervical mucus will tend to favor the passage of male sperm.

19. By contrast, in 1990, gender parity was the rules among Jews in general, with 104.9 males for every 100 females (Goldstein & Kosmin, 1992).

20. Relative freedom from discrimination coupled with relative affluence has meant not only an increase in intermarriage (see above), but also a steady increase in the ranks of liberal as opposed to orthodox Jews. This has lead some Jewish scholars to worry that Jews, in any meaningful sense, would eventually cease to exist (Waxman, 1992). The debate continues. On the one hand, Silberman (1985) notes that Jewish immigrants to North America were typically relatively secular and that most Jews continue to identify with Jewish values. Conversely, Hansen's law of generations states, "What the son wishes to forget the grandson wishes to remember." (quoted in Buenker & Ratner, 1992: 241). Thus, on the other hand, there appears to have been a recent revival of interest in orthodox Judaism (*ba'al teshuvah* or *hozrei*

biteshuva), especially among women (Danziger, 1989; Davidman, 1991; Ellenson, 1990; Kaufman, 1991; Waxman, 1992).

21. In 1990, 9% of Jews in the United States had been divorced, compared to a national lifetime probability of divorce of about 50% (Irving & Benjamin, 1995: Chapter 2). In contrast, among Orthodox Jews, divorce is rare.

22. Private schools extend from kindergarten (*heder*) to primary school (*yeshiva*) to high school (*mesivta*).

23. These expectations extend to food, with Jewish parents inordinately proud of children who are "good eaters" (Braverman, 1990).

PART III

Transforming the University

7

The University in Context

INTRODUCTION

These profiles of Blacks, Caribbean Blacks, Hispanics, Asians and Jews make abundantly clear that very diverse responses exist for such universal challenges as birth, child rearing, marriage, work and education (see Figure 7.1). Consequently, in some respects these groups exhibit commonalities, including the universal experience of oppression, while in other respects they appear very different. Such similarities and differences have their further expression across ethnic minority subgroups, fractured still further by the added complexities of immigration and generation, with diversity across subgroups in their preferred adaptation to ongoing assimilation pressure.

In turn, these sources of divergence hold profound implications for the implementation of a policy of cultural diversity and educational equity whose ultimate thrust is the fundamental transformation of higher education as we have known it over at least the past half century (La Belle & Ward, 1994). However, before such change can be meaningfully addressed, several contextual issues must first be handled. That is the task of this chapter, while the next chapter will be concerned with the complexities of implementing policies directed toward transforming the university in accord with the aims of cultural diversity (in the United States) and educational equity (in Canada).

MATTERS OF CONTEXT

The challenge of cultural diversity and educational equity involves *four* related issues: the bases of support for these policies; the current status of diversity and equity policy; the links between diversity policy and the core categories used to construct the above profiles; and the nature of the universities as a complex ecological systems as crucial to the implementation of cultural diversity policy.

Figure 7.1
Comparison of Five Ethnic Groups

Attribute	Black	Caribbean Black	Hispanic	Asian	Jew
Family:					
Social Class	Lower	Middle	Lower	Middle	Middle
Family Defined	Extend	Nuclear	Extend	Extend	Nuclear
Life Cycle	Compr.	Elong.	Compr.	Elong.	Elong.
Marital Relations	Mat.	Mat.	Pat.	Pat.	Egalitarian
Conflict Style	Direct	Direct	Indirect	Indirect	Direct
P-C Relations	Auto.	Auto.	Auto.	Auto.	Democratic
Family Size	High	Low	High	Low	Low
English Proficiency	NA	NA	Low	Low	NA
Marriage Age	Young	Older	Young	Older	Older
Child Lending	Yes	Yes	Yes	No	No
Intermarriage	Low	Mod.	Low	High	Mod.
Divorce Rate	High	NK	Low	Low	Low
Teen Parent Rate	High	Low	Low	Low	Low
Sex Parity	No	Yes	Yes	Yes	Yes
Work:					
Income Parity	No	Yes	No	Yes	Yes
Unemployment Rate	High	Low	High	Low	Low
Work Type	Skilled	Pro.	Skilled	Pro.	Pro.

Figure 7.1, continued

Attribute	Black	Caribbean Black	Hispanic	Asian	Jew
Self-Employment Rate	Low	Mod.	Low	High	Mod.
Maternal Work	High	High	High	High	Mod.
Higher Education:					
Enrollment Rate	Low	NK	Low	High	High
Success Rate	Low	NK	Low	High	High
Attrition Rate	High	NK	High	Low	Low
Other:					
Self-Help	Yes	Yes	Yes	Yes	Yes
Spirituality	High	High	High	Mod.	Low
Self-Identification	High	Mod.	High	High	High
Time Sense	P-time	P-time	P-time	P-time	M-time
Residential Seg.	High	Mod.	High	Low	High
Help-Seeking	Inform.	Inform.	Inform.	Inform.	Formal

NOTE: Compr.=compressed; Elong.=elongated; Mat.=matrifocal/matriarchal; Pat.=patriarchal; P-C Relations=Parent-Child Relations; Auto.=autocratic; Mod.=moderate; P-time=polychronic time; M=time=monochronic time; NA=not applicable; NK=not known.; Pro.=professional; Residential Seg.=Residential Segregation; Inform.=Informal.

BASES OF SUPPORT FOR CULTURAL DIVERSITY AND EDUCATIONAL EQUITY

Whether in the United States or Canada, policies concerned with cultural diversity and educational equity propose similar visions of the university as a learning community (Bensimon, 1994; Bowser et al., 1993; Green, 1988; Hill, 1991; Odell & Mock, 1989; SESG, 1992; Stage & in which people of all cultures and classes have equal access to higher education; have an equal voice in shaping institutional aims and practices; and engage, as equals, in what Hill (1991: 42) calls a "conversation of respect" in which their divergent views make for a rich educational experience for all.

That said, support for these policies derives from quite different sources in the United States and Canada. In the United States, the recent push favoring cultural diversity originates primarily from *within* institutions of higher education. This is not to deny the salient influence of external forces. On the contrary, as noted in Chapter 1, social justice movements (for example, civil rights, employment equity and feminist), various federal and state statutes, policies and regulations,[1] and various specific organizations[2] have all sought to promote institutional support of diversity.[3] However, with few exceptions (La Belle & Ward, 1994; Nieto, 1992; Orlans, 1992; Rowe, 1993), the available literature makes scant mention of these sources of pressure, suggesting that writers in this area have internalized the notion of diversity, giving the appearance that support for diversity now originates within such institutions. Accordingly, institutional rationales for that support include demographics, accountability and, more distantly, social justice (Brown, 1991; Cardoza, 1986; Cheatham, 1991; D'Souza, 1991; National Commission on Testing & Public Policy, 1990; Nettles, 1988, 1990; Sleeter & Grant, 1988; Smith, 1989, 1990, 1994; Westbrook & Sedlacek, 1991; Wright, 1987).

Repeatedly, authors in the field note the inexorable effects of the rate of population growth among the groups profiled above. If they have not already done so (La Belle & Ward, 1994), by the turn of the century or soon after, the minority groups of today will, collectively, become the majority of tomorrow (Riche, 1991). Thus, universities will soon be challenged by a rising proportion of students from the profiled groups, whether they want to be or not. This leads proponents to argue that it is in our collective interest, and that of their future students, to prepare for that shift now. Cardoza (1986) had precisely this in mind when he entitled his article, "Colleges Alerted: Pay Attention to Minorities or Risk Future Survival."

Concern with changing demographics is coupled with a devastating critique of the way universities have treated students from the profiled groups. As detailed above, they have not fared well. Indeed, apart from difficulties in achievement (Allen, 1988; Fleming, 1984), there is evidence that campus racism is actually rising (Altbach & Lomotey, 1991; Dalton, 1991; Siggelkow, 1991; Stage & Hamrick, 1994). Such processes have been directly in conflict with increasing government demands for accountability and quality in higher education (Benjamin, 1994; Borden & Banta, 1994). Consequently, in many instances state funding support has been tied directly to evidence of change in these areas (Ehrenberg & Murphy, 1993).

Those institutions dependent on funds have thus been highly motivated to change.

Finally, some have argued that cultural diversity policy is fundamentally a matter of social justice or "natural" law (Madison, 1992). All of the profiled groups, especially the Blacks and the Hispanics, have been and continue to be treated unfairly in higher education, and that, so the argument goes, needs to change, finally and permanently.

Ironically, the social justice argument is first rather than last among proponents of educational equity in Canada. With the profiled groups representing a much lower proportion of the population in Canada than the United States, there is much less impetus for these policies among Canadian institutions of higher education. The recent Smith Commission (1991) report is a case in point. Mandated to survey higher education in Canada, its recommendations were based on 200 presentations, 250 briefs and an extensive review of the literature. Yet there is mention neither of cultural diversity nor educational equity anywhere in its pages. True, certain groups are singled out for attention regarding university access, but this includes direct mention of none of the profiled groups.[4]

Where then does the impetus for educational equity originate? Based on recent overviews of the Canadian scene (Kallen, 1995; Student-Environment Study Group, 1992), it appears to originate *outside* institutions of higher education, with pressure emanating from protest movements among Francophones in Quebec and natives and Inuit across Canada (Kallen, 1995); changing statutes[5] and provincial affirmative action programs; and shifts in public opinion. The latter especially have caught the eyes of provincial politicians, including, for example, a series of highly publicized police shootings of Blacks in Toronto and a controversial exhibit at the Royal Ontario Museum in Toronto. Both occasioned much public debate, and the push for change in various areas affecting profiled groups, among them higher education. Thus, in Canada, educational equity appears grounded in a relatively broad concern for social justice. Therefore, motivation to pursue this policy is likely to be rather less robust and more variable than its counterpart in the United States. While there are a handful of exceptions across the country (such as Queen's University), the majority are institutions (such as Dalhousie University, University of Toronto, York University) that already have a relatively high proportion of profile group students.

PROGRAMMING FOR DIVERSITY AND EQUITY: STATUS REPORT

That being so, the current status of programming for diversity and equity is my next concern. In the United States, I think it fair to say that the current status of cultural diversity policy is decidedly mixed.

On the one hand, the evidence of change is incontrovertible. Levine and Cureton (1992), for example, argue that American higher education is now undergoing a "quiet revolution." This view was based on a 1991 survey of 196 colleges and universities which showed, among other things, that: 34% had adopted a multicultural general education requirement; 33% or more offered courses in ethnic and/or gender studies; 54% had introduced multiculturalism into their course offerings; 36% were actively recruiting ethnic minority faculty, while 22% were doing so using passive mechanisms; 50% had a multicultural advising program; and 35% had establisehd multicultural centers or institutes. Along similar lines, Adams (1992) noted that 35%-50% of all colleges and universities have already engaged in some diversity programming, while Jones et al. (1991) reported, based on a survey of 146 institutions, that 89% indicated some active involvement with the issue. Further, Ehrenberg and Murphy (1993) contend that "need-blind" admission policies coupled with "need-based" financial aid have meant that highly selective private universities, such as Cornell University, have a more diverse student body now than they have ever had in the past. Indeed, Astin (1993) found that on campuses with a diversity emphasis, students had a greater awareness of and commitment to racial understanding and were generally more satisfied with their experience at college. Finally, program compendia (Mintz, 1993) and "how-to" books (Downing et al., 1993; Kramer & Weiner, 1994; Sims, 1994; Terrell, 1992) rich with programming ideas have begun to appear on the market.[6]

These developments explain Smith's (1990: 62) observation that "[m]ore and more institutions are beginning to articulate a commitment to educate all students for a pluralistic world and to create environments that can embrace diversity." For most educators, Stockdill et al. (1992: 23) argue diversity "mean[s] full and complete integration of all races and cultures into curricular content, instructional processes, and all interactions related to schools." Wong (1991: 53) puts it somewhat differently, saying that "[proponents of diversity] seek not a community of the lowest common denominator, where differences are tolerated and sometimes sullenly accepted, but a community of the highest common denominator, where difference is an enriching resource that leads to a fuller understanding of what is universally true."

Given this goal, diversity policy has meant and/or should mean:

> consensus decision-making, with the meaningful involvement of all stakeholders assured (La Belle & Ward, 1994; Stockdill et al, 1992; Tierney, 1993);
>
> conscientious recruitment of students from profiled groups, coupled with retention programming (Brown, 1991), including academic and social support, intensive advising, and careful tracking (both of grades and student satisfaction) to graduation (Crosson, 1988; Smith, 1990);
>
> innovative financial aid programs (Brown, 1991; Ross-Gordon et al., 1990);

creation of a transcultural environment, intended to make the community an attractive, welcoming and secure one for students from profiled groups (Brown, 1991), thus promoting mutual understanding among all groups;

training to ensure that all faculty and student affairs personnel are sensitive to transcultural issues (Brown, 1991; McEwen & Roper, 1994), especially as regards respect for differences (Jones et al., 1991);

aggressive efforts to recruit, retain and promote faculty from profiled groups (Bowser et al., 1993; Moses, 1989, 1991, 1994; Smith, 1990; Spann, 1988);

systematic coordination between high school and university so that entering students have realistic expectations on arrival in university (Brown, 1991);

pervasive diversification of the core curriculum to reflect a transcultural, inclusive context; the availability (in some cases on a mandatory basis) of transcultural course offerings; and a flexible repertoire of teaching practices (Adams, 1992; Banks, 1991; Gaff, 1992; Gay, 1988; Moses, 1994; Nieto, 1992; Ross-Gordon et al., 1990; Smith, 1990; Spann, 1988; Suzuki, 1984);

changes in testing procedures so that they are fair, given the experience of students in profiled groups, and the use of testing to emphasize the enhancement of development, talent and productivity (La Belle & Ward, 1994; Looney, 1990; McDowell, 1992; National Commission on Testing & Public Policy, 1990);

construction of new, culturally sensitive models of student development (Helms, 1984; Jones, 1990; Manning, 1994; McEwen et al., 1990) while eliminating the use of traditional negative labels (such as "disadvantaged") to describe profile group students (Shang & Moore, 1990); and

strong leadership by the board of governors and other administrative leaders reflecting their commitment to cultural diversity policy (Brown, 1991), with diversity to be included in institutional mission statements (Smith et al., 1994) and with all staff to become "culture brokers" in support of this policy (Stage & Manning, 1992). Such support implies a shift, with student success seen less a function of student attributes and more a matter of institutional practices (Smith, 1990; Stage & Hamrick, 1994).

On the other hand, there is considerable evidence that full realization of these goals remains farther into the future. Consequently, a number of sources urge institutions in higher education to "mov[e] from rhetoric to results" (Sagaria & Johnsrud, 1991; DeVaney & Hughey, 1992; Hill, 1991). That is, in many cases, diversity programming is under development and does not exist in any concrete sense. It is therefore quite unclear whether the substantial literature now available is describing what *should* exist rather than what *does* exist. Stockdill et al. (1992: 23), for example, make clear that for some people, diversity means substantially less than full integration, including "special units of study, displays of artifacts, multicultural fairs, and shaded faces in textbooks." Similarly, Stage and Manning (1992) argue that diversity programming is often piecemeal and consequently quite ineffective. While La Belle and Ward (1994) approve of ethnic studies programs, they also note (p. 178) that on these campuses most students have no contact with or knowledge of the groups being studied. Stage and Hamrick (1994: 331) note that diversity policy may not involve an integrated strategy, but rather is reactive, directed toward individual transgressions, thus "ignoring [institutional] characteristics within itself that tacitly foster such behaviors."[7] Similarly, Ehrenberg and Murphy (1993) note the disruptive effects of external forces; while extolling the virtues of "need-blind" admission polices in private institutions, they note too that such policies have been so expensive that, coupled with ongoing antitrust investigations, they have "begun to die" (p. 66). Olivas (1993) and Thelin (1992) document the ongoing attack on affirmative action policies, especially among faculty concerned about academic freedom (Wong, 1991), while Spann (1988) observes that resistance to hiring ethnic minority faculty can be substantial. Others document the hardships of ethnic minority faculty who agree to teach at predomiantly White colleges (Bernal, 1994; Bowser et al., 1993; Davis, 1994; Gainen & Boice, 1993; Rowe, 1993). Further, Jones et al. (1991) found that only 40% of the universities they examined regarded the academic department as important in advancing the objectives of diversity. Hence, Moses (1994) argues, faculty typically play only a token role in diversity-related change, while Stage and Hamrick (1994: 332) observe that a piecemeal approach to diversity may allow "a small proportion of institutional constituents (e.g., appointed or volunteer faculty, staff and students) to commit significant time, sacrifice, and energy while the rest of the institution is permitted to observe such efforts from a distance." Smith et al. (1994) note that most diversity research to date has simply focused on a campus census. As Baizerman and Compton (1992: 13) explain, it should mean much more, since "[e]valuation, *in its very process*, and as a moral enterprise, can sensitize individuals to their moral right to have and use their voices and to join in constructing a discourse about their worlds." (emphasis in original). McEwen and Roper (1994) comment on how poorly prepared most student affairs professionals are for the diverse campus. Westbrook and Sedlacek (1991: 21) agree, arguing that, "[h]igher education personnel need to be sensitive to the interactional needs of groups of nontraditional students, but more than that, they need a set of strategies that will enable them to establish rapport with any individuals that are potentially different from themselves in interpersonal interactional styles." Finally, Wong (1991: 51) acknowledges that, "[d]iversity divides, it fragments, it attacks tradition, it will often undermine a common sense of purpose." Thus, at least in its initial stages, diversity policy, directed toward "building communities of difference" (Tierney, 1993), may instead generate conflict, bitterness and division; only with persistence are the results of such efforts likely to bear fruit (see below).

In short, in the United States, despite much controversy and opposition, diversity programming appears well-advanced, though advocates all agree that we are a long way from realizing the full transformative potential of cultural diversity policy (Barr & Strong, 1989; Bernal, 1994; DeVaney & Hughey, 1992; Stage & Hamrick, 1994).

Turning to the Canadian scene, the piecemeal approaches that Stage and Manning (1992) eschew characterize most Canadian efforts at educational equity. As noted in the Student-Environment Study Group (1992), while various official bodies approve the policy, few programs actually exist, so that it is at present more chimera than reality. For example, Dalhousie University (Halifax, Nove Scotia) has created several programs geared to natives and African Canadian Blacks, including: a transition year program; an academic support program for students in law, medicine and dentistry; a student services center; and several supplementary staff positions in advising and counseling. Its policy also favors hiring faculty with transcultural expertise and, in turn, supports curricula that are sensitive to transcultural reality. The University of Guelph (Guelph, Ontario) has recently begun moving in the same direction. It has already adopted policies regarding employment equity and sexual and gender harassment; policies regarding human rights and racism are currently under development and exist on an interim basis only. Various universities have special "studies" programs in areas concerned with women, Black history and ethnicity. Carleton University (Ottawa, Ontario) has approved equity-based special programs, although such programs remain at the planning stage. Similar initiatives are under way at the Universities of Queen's (Kingston, Ontario), Toronto and York (both Toronto, Ontario). In short, whatever criticism may be leveled at diversity initiatives in the United States, similar initiatives in Canada are rather less advanced.

LINK WITH CORE CATEGORIES

Given support for cultural diversity and educational equity, I turn next to a substantive issue, namely, the link between these policies and the core categories around which the group profiles were constructed. Their utility derives from a contrast between traditional policy concerns with matters on campus and the experiential reality of the students who increasingly populate those campuses.

Only brief review of the sources cited in the preceding section will show almost no substantive content regarding the profiled groups in question. Rather, frequent mention is made of respect for "differences" between students from White and profiled groups. Indeed, we are repeatedly told that such policies mean respecting and valuing differences and engaging in meaningful dialogue (Hill, 1991; Woolbright, 1989), but nowhere are these differences or the barriers they create for dialogue ever spelled out in detail. Cultural diversity and educational equity, then, have a distinctly

¹ generic feel. This reflects a traditional approach to policy change which has largely been geared inward. It has treated the campus as the extent of the world, and thus been concerned with matters which directly derive from or which impact upon that world.

As various empirical studies have shown (Benjamin, 1990; Benjamin & Hollings, 1995; Moses, 1990), however, the clean separation between processes on and off campus thus implied are simply convenient fictions. Students carry their cultures in their heads; hence, they are indifferent to these artificial boundaries. It follows that in translating diversity and equity policies from philosophy into practice, the importance of knowing who these students are, and what beliefs and practices are likely to shape their experience on campus, cannot be overstated. The *six* core categories are intended to speak to that need.

Social class speaks to a range of campus-related issues, including such matters as access, financing, academic preparedness, self-esteem, nutrition and health, expectations, language use, social relationship conventions, skills related to transition and adaptation, coping with stress and so on. *Family definition* speaks to ongoing parental involvement, values related to work, sense of time and space, the place of religion, values related to individualism and autonomy and so on. *Spousal relations* speak again to social relationship conventions as well as to notions of femininity and masculinity, the salience of marriage (including intermarriage), fidelity, the role of children, conflict management and so on. *Life cycle* conventions speak to the role of education, social expectations of adult conduct, stage-related dress codes, the role and identity of transitional events and rituals and so on. *Parent-child relations* speak to the role of authority, of appropriate responses to instruction, to food preferences, the definition of nurturance and support, of rules and consequences and so on. And, *help-seeking* speaks to definitions of health and well-being, of illness and its consequences, of the role of formal institutions, the definition of "helper," of appropriate conduct when seeking help and so on. In short, core categories illuminate those very beliefs and practices that, to a large extent, shape student experience on campus, especially among entering students.

UNIVERSITY AS COMPLEX ECOLOGICAL SYSTEM

What the above discussion makes clear is that implementing a policy of cultural diversity and educational equity is no simple undertaking. Philosophical debate aside (Hill, 1991), the main reason for this is that universities are very complex organizations. It follows that any discussion about implementing such a policy must start with a fundamental understanding of how such organizations work. Most advocates of diversity appear to have sophisticated, first-hand knowledge of such matters, and it shows in the character of the models they have advanced (Bensimon, 1994; Hill, 1991; La Belle & Ward, 1994; Manning, 1994; Manning & Coleman-Boatwright, 1991; Smith et al., 1994; Stage & Hamrick, 1994; Stage &

Manning, 1992). However, these views of the university have taken the form of a loose working model, informing rather than shaping policy and planning, and implicit rather than systematic. Hill (1991), for example, debunks various myths which he suggests act as barriers to the implementation diversity policy. LaBelle and Ward (1994) identify a variety of problems associated with diversity policy and suggest a range of practical solutions. Manning (1994) reviews various multicultural theories and discusses their implications for practice. Stage and Manning (1992) argue persuasively that administrators, managers and faculty should all act as "cultural brokers" in the interests of promoting diversity policy, while Stage and Hamrick (1994) argue that diversity policy requires that institutions be proactive, multicultural and concrete. In short, while these authors advocate vigorously for diversity policy and advance a variety of pragmatic suggestions toward that end, they begin with an implicit, rather sketchy model of the university as a complex organization.

An alternative approach, to be advanced here, involves a formal model that is slowing gaining currency in higher education, namely, that of systems theory (Benjamin, 1983, 1994; Bronfenbrenner, 1989; Steenbarger, 1991) which conceptualizes institutions such as universities as complex ecological systems (Birnbaum, 1988; Weinstein, 1993). Full explication of this model is beyond the purview of this text. However, brief summary of three ideas central to the model will prove useful for later discussion: *wholeness, feedback* and *level.* In exploring these notions, below, I will focus especially on what they have to tell us about inducing change in complex systems, a key consideration in the introduction of policies concerning cultural diversity and educational equity.

An adage well-known among systems theorists is that "the system is more complex than the sum of its parts." Put more simply, this means *three* things.

First, as an organization, the university is a complex *whole* or system. That is, it is (a) composed of a variety of units (b) that operate in a semi-autonomous fashion to meet unit goals, yet (c) regularly interact (d) in a coordinated way (e) to achieve common system goals. What makes such systems discrete and coherent is that interaction among their components is organized, that is, (typically) hierarchical in form and, repetitive in action. In short, the continued existence of the "university" as a functioning whole requires the cooperative involvement of all of these components; each is thus asked to relinquish some of its autonomy in the interests of achieving goals common to them all. In practice, the actual degree of cooperation is likely to vary. Units within university systems tend to be only "weakly coupled" (Weick, 1969), another way of saying that individual units behave in a semi-autonomous fashion in pursuit of a plurality of unit goals. In turn, these goals will diverge to varying degrees from a range of wider system goals. Interaction among units thus requires ongoing and sometimes rancorous negotiation among and between units, often over control of scarce resources and/or over priorities in relation to competing goals.

This makes clear, first, that the behavior of any given unit, whether that refers to a group of people of varying size or a set of groups, can *only* be understood in the context of their relations with other units. Second, that the primary product of their interaction, student education, is far more complex than the contribution or conduct of any given unit. And, third, that such complexity renders problematic any effort at intervention, however simple or innocuous it may appear. In the words of Thomas (1979: 110), speaking about environmental ecosystems but equally applicable here, "[y]ou cannot meddle with one part of a complex system from the outside without the almost certain risk of setting off some disastrous events that you hadn't counted on in other, remote parts."

Next, once systems have formed, that is, once the interaction among the units which make it up have become regular and coherent, their characteristic patterns of behavior tend to remain highly stable, despite changes in either internal personnel and/or the external environment. Indeed, universities are an especially good example of "ultrastable systems," for by their nature, stability must be maintained despite continuous change. Student careers are necessarily time-limited. Presidents are only appointed on a short-term basis, and faculty, while they may appear to be there "forever," do change jobs, retire or die. Thus, universities are relatively effective in socializing new personnel into "the way things are done here," that is, those organized ways of relating that characterize interaction among units noted above.

In formal terms, these processes are subsumed under the term *feedback*. What this means in systemic terms is that the consequences or outcomes of any interaction sequence shape future moves in that sequence, thus promoting either stability or change, depending on circumstances. Under ordinary conditions, norms implicitly govern the extent to which behavior may vary randomly. As long as behavior remains within the acceptable range, all proceeds smoothly. Should behavior stray close to or beyond those limits, however, feedback acts to dampen any such deviation and may involve behavior ranging from a brief memo or a friendly chat, to supervisory intervention and/or formal sanctions.

Under other conditions, the opposite may occur, with feedback amplifying deviation from acceptable norms. In one scenario, this may involve orderly change or transition. Recessionary economics have dramatically altered the resources available to many colleges and universities, forcing them to rethink their plans and priorities. Similar effects have resulted from legislative changes and recent state demands for increased institutional accountability as well as increased diversity in the student population (La Belle & Ward, 1994). All of these changes create widening discrepancy between conventional practices and external and/or internal demand. Some institutions have responded with elaborate strategic planning exercises, while all have been forced to acknowledge that prevailing norms no longer apply. Many have discovered that developing new rules of conduct is neither easy nor pleasant.

In another scenario, deviation-ampifying feedback induces a disorderly process of change. Under conditions of misunderstanding and/or conflict, routine efforts to dampen deviation may have the opposite effect. Misunderstandings grow, conflict escalates and past resentments resurface, as, in systems terms, a "runaway" begins. This can take a variety of forms, from student protests and staff work stoppages to judicial hearings and civils suits to full-blown riots accompanied by violence. Despite these disruptions of routine practice, the system may still return to the status quo ante, or it may do so while sowing the seeds of future disruption. However, what is most likely to emerge is a system organized differently than it was before, with modified patterns of interaction and changed norms concerning the range of acceptable conduct.

Further, in practice, tendencies toward stability and change seldom occur in orderly sequence. Rather, they overlap, the complex balance between them determining the immediate consequences. Over a long enough time span, however, complex systems will necessarily favor stability, the revolution of today being inexorably transformed into the routine of tomorrow.

Note further, that even apparently tiny changes in the present, can, magnified through the interaction between feedback and time, produce enormous long-term change. This gets us back to the original adage that initiated this discussion. Patterns which characterize the system as a whole may be quite different from those among lower-order components, such as divisions or departments or programs, from which the higher-order patterns were ultimately derived. For the whole, it seems, is both more complex and differently organized than its constituent components; what works at one level will not work, or not work as well, at any other level.

In turn, this way of thinking about complex systems supports several inferences concerning change. One is that the dynamic stability that characterizes university systems renders highly problematic any deliberate effort to induce change, as might be associated with diversity policy, or as some have discovered, with regard to strategic planning. Certainly that was the experience of Lawrence Weinstein, former president of the University of Wisconsin, who likened his efforts to that of "moving a battleship with your bare hands" (Weinstein, 1993). Another concerns the differential impact of such efforts across *levels* (see below). Thus, as Richardson and Skinner (1991) suggest with respect to cultural diversity, cooperation and effective functioning at the highest level may only be achieved in the long run at the cost of considerable initial conflict at lower levels over the short run. A third is that this view calls in question conventional models of change, namely, that it must either be initiated from the top down or from the bottom up. For ultrastable systems, such as universities, effective change over the short run may only occur when it originates from more than one level at the same time, thus indicating the existence of a critical mass of policy advocates large enough to induce relatively sudden system transformation (see below).

Finally, the hierarchical form universities usually take derives from the fact that complex systems operate at multiple levels. Each level has a dual character. In one sense, each is a system in its own right, since each level involves multiple components at "lower" levels. In another sense, each level (except the highest) is simply one among a variety of components in a larger system "above" it. For example, the Faculty of Arts involves lower-order components, such as groups of departments concerned with social sciences, humanities, fine arts and the like. Finer divisions might distinguish between the departments of sociology, history and art, and the even smaller subsections or committees into which they too might be further subdivided.

As one goes *down* these levels, note that the organization of the components becomes increasingly less complex, for although the number of people representing these various units collectively increases, their specific responsibilities become more specialized and thus restricted. However, at the same time, each level is only a component in a larger, more inclusive level that exists above it in the hierarchy. Therefore, that same Faculty of Arts stands with other Faculties (of Sciences, Professional Schools, and the like) to represent academic matters and, in turn, is only one of a series of higher-order components, some of which have already been listed. And, as before, as one goes *up* these levels, the organization of these components becomes more complex, for while it subsumes fewer and fewer people, their responsibilities become increasingly generic and inclusive. Finally, note that the terms "down" and "up" or "higher" and "lower" are necessarily both relative and metaphoric. Thus, university presidents are normally about the same height as the average student. What makes the former "higher" than the latter is that they stand at opposite ends of an organizational hierarchy that accords one more status than the other.

With this caveat in mind, and following Bronfenbrenner (1989), one way of thinking about the university as a complex system is to distinguish between four levels based on the system's hierarchical structure: *suprasystem, macrosystem, mesosystem* and *microsystem*.

The suprasystem level will be used here to refer to the university per se, that is, to the system as a whole, at its most inclusive.

The macrosystem level will be used here to refer to the assemblage of administrative units, including the office of the president, the board of governors, senior administrators and managers of operational units, such as those which provide student services. Note that units at the macrosystem level "face" in two directions. On the one hand, they are the university's major link with the outside world, having responsibility for matters both political and fiscal. On the other hand, they face inward, striving to formulate institutional policy in response to managerial and operational inputs.

The mesosystem level will be used here to refer to the professorate, including the elaborate structure of Faculties, departments and committees in which faculty normally operate. Note that units at the mesosystem level have a more limited mandate, namely, to implement institutional policies regarding teaching, learning and research, and particularly to ensure that such policies meet approved standards of quality while staying within restricted fiscal guidelines. Paradoxically, units at the mesosystem level also face in two directions. They face upward in the institutional hierarchy, since they depend on the administration for much of their funding. However, they also face outward, since they alone deal directly with student clients; they act as the university's primary means of discovering what students want, thereby gaining knowledge critical to the institution's survival. They also face outward in regard to their research efforts, including their perpetual efforts to obtain external funding which contributes not only to the institution's fiscal status but also to its reputational status. Both sorts of activities give these units more power than one would expect of such units in business, hence their semi-autonomous position in the university.

Finally, the microsystem level will be used here to refer to the under-graduate student body, including those in various faculties and programs as well as those in organized groups. Without being overly cynical, students primarily strive to survive the system and to succeed on its terms, that is, to graduate in a reasonable time and with grades that will accord them a favorable status, as they pursue further education or vocations. Units at the microsystem level also face in two directions. They face upward in the hierarchy, as they are dependent on faculty for the marks that are the primary index of status in the university's reward system. They also face upward to the administration and various operational units on whom they depend for the rules, regulations, procedures, services and resources which collectively regulate much of their on-campus lives. However, they, like units at the macrosystem level, also face outward. In relating to parents, relatives and others, they come to embody the university's reputation and thus its standing in the community, both academic and nonacademic. In time, they will also become the university's alumni and will come to have some say in its fiscal well-being and, to some extent, its policies. On both grounds, students collectively have rather more power than is usually accorded them, and certainly more than they themselves typically recognize.

This notion of the university as a multi-leveled complex system supports further inferences regarding change. First, note that units at different levels are indeed different from each other and distinct in their composition, personnel and goals. Accordingly, units at any given level may have a clear sense of their own mandate and methods, but they may be much less clear and perhaps less sympathetic to the mandate and methods of units at any other level. This makes for problematic communication across levels, as a given policy is likely to mean different things to units at different levels and at different times. Given that "the university oozes with uncoded messages about centrality and marginality" (Hill, 1991: 44), variation across levels is likely to mean that support for policies, such as diversity, will similarly vary, being seen by some as central and important while regarded by others as marginal and irrelevant. By the same token, achieving cross-level consensus is likely to represent a significant challenge. Second, while units at each level may act *as if* they are autonomous, in fact units across levels are interdependent, since each literally cannot exist without the other. This means that a change in units at one level will necessarily affect units at other levels with which they interact. Depending on the cir-cumstances of their relationship, the effects will be one of two sorts: change in one unit will induce similar change in the other unit; alternately, the response of one unit to change in the other will block change in the first unit. The latter can be explained in terms of a change in "sign." Policy-based behavior, such as that associated with cultural diversity, that serves to amplify deviation from acceptable norms at one level, that is, "positive" feedback, may have the opposite effect at another level, dampening deviation ("negative" feedback) and thus "resisting" change. Depending on the nature of the discrepancy between them, the results may be explosive or they may simply exacerbate ongoing cross-level tension or conflict. Finally, given difficulties of communication and changes in sign across levels, system transformation will take time, with results that can only be predicted on a probabilistic basis. This results from system complexity, which renders causal predictions futile. Above, I have noted the possibility of "sudden" transformation. This does indeed occur, but is misleading if the word "sudden" is taken to mean that it appears de novo, unrelated to the past history of interaction. In fact, such processes are more likely to represent a threshold effect, processes progressing over time to a point when "suddenly" a revolutionary transformation appears to occur. Such changes in sign can occur with remarkable speed; the progressive processes leading to the threshold do not.

However intricate this four-level model may appear, it remains an extremely simplified way of characterizing complex systems such as univer-sities. Elsewhere (Benjamin, 1988b) this approach has demonstrated tremendous heuristic value in appreciating residence life systems. In the next chapter, coupled with the group profiles, the same approach will be applied to the implementation of cultural diversity policy.

SUMMARY

Cultural diversity policy did not arrive de novo in the North America in the late 1980's. Rather, it was the culmination of several related tendencies long underway and involving changes external to higher education, including changes in demography, statutes, regulations and public sentiments. Bowing to such pressure, universities and colleges have begun to change in ways consistent with cultural diversity policy, by broadening access, changing curricula, recruiting ethnic minority faculty, establishing multiculture services and the like. That said, progress in these directions has been anything but even or smooth. Some institutions have made significant progress, others have begun the process, while for still others, diversity remains a rhetorical reality only. Even so, it seems plain that the issue has a good deal more urgency in the United States than in Canada, and so is further along in the former than the latter. In both contexts, however, existing efforts fall far short of realizing the policy's full transformative potential.

Toward that end, the group profiles detailed in previous chapters appear highly relevant to the goals of diversity, describing values, attitudes, expectations, feelings and behaviors intimately related to life on campus. At the same time, these profiles highlight the extent of the challenge represented by diversity policy. While profiled groups show generic similarities, they also reveal stark differences. These complexities are exacerbated by additional similarites and differences across ethnic minority subgroups.

Finally, any effort at implementation must confront head-on the enormous complexity of universities as ecological systems. While advocates of cultural diversity are certainly aware of this complexity and have been influenced by it, none have advanced a systematic model of the university useful in shaping diversity policy. Such a model is advanced here in which universities are conceptualized as complex, multi-leveled ecological systems whose operation is organized on the basis of wholeness, feedback and level. The model thus characterizes university systems as involving four levels, each with distinctive properties.

NOTES

1. Examples include the Civil Rights Act (1964), the Elementary and Secondary Education Act (1965), the Ethnic Heritage Studies Act (1972) and the Bilingual Education Act (1974).

2. Examples include the Office of Minorities in Education, the Commission on Multicultural Education (Baptiste et al., 1980; Gollnick et al., 1981), the National Association of International Educators (Althen, 1994), and the National Association of Student Personnel Administrators (Terrell, 1992).

3. For a more complete history of cultural diversity in the United States, going back to the nineteenth century, see La Belle and Ward (1994: Part 1).

4. Specifically, mention is made of the poor, native peoples, the disabled, women (in certain fields) and French-speaking people (outside of Quebec).

5. Examples of federal statutes include the Canada Multiculturalism Act (1988) and the Canadian Charter of Rights of Freedoms (1982).

6. In higher education, related texts include Bensimon (1994), Ross-Gordon et al. (1990), Saunders (1982), and Sikkema & Niyekana (1987). Useful material is also

available directed at primary and/or secondary levels, including Garcia (1982), Johnson and Smith (1993), McLeod (1980), Moodley (1992), Morris (1989) and Wurzer (1988).

7. La Belle and Ward (1994: 182), for example, indicate that despite hate-speech codes on many campuses, offenders are rarely expelled or suspended and are more likely to be required to provide community service or take sensitivity or multicultural workshops.

8

Cultural Diversity and Educational Equity as Engines of Change

INTRODUCTION

The discussion of context in Chapter 7 was necessary but has taken us rather far from issues of diversity. In what follows, I return to the group profiles and their implications for policy concerning cultural diversity and educational equity. This will be divided into *three* parts, based on the preceding discussion of levels. The suprasystem level will be the initial focus of concern, to enumerate a series of general first principles. The remaining levels will then be addressed in regard to a series of specific policy implications. Finally, these policy implications will be re-examined through the lens of the ecological model of the university developed in Chapter 7.

Throughout, I will take as given that cultural diversity and educational equity in higher education is consistent with social justice, and that pursuit of such policies is justified, worthwhile and in the long-term best interests of all participants in higher education. To balance this positive framing of diversity, throughout I will also be at some pains to note various points of tension or conflict likely to be generated or exacerbated by the introduction of policies of cultural diversity and educational equity.

SUPRASYSTEM LEVEL: FIRST PRINCIPLES

With few exceptions (Manning & Coleman-Boatwright, 1991; Stage & Manning, 1992), the literature concerning cultural diversity consists of a long list of specific actions and policies that have been or should be enacted. Nowhere is there a model that indicates the connection between objectives and actions, and which locates specific policies as part of a larger picture whose thrust is the transformation of traditional colleges and universities. Below, I begin to construct such a model. This takes the form of a series of *eight* first principles, each of which is listed and then briefly discussed. Taken together, they paint in rather broad strokes the larger picture whose existence is a prerequisite to any specific policies or actions.

1. Diversity Will Apply Across Every Level of the System

Policies concerning cultural diversity and educational equity have the potential to change or transform the entire university system. No level will be unaffected, and none will be untouched or uninvolved in such efforts.

Smith et al. (1994) advance this argument on the grounds that such involvement is both necessary and desirable. I agree, but on ecosystemic grounds. As suggested in Chapter 7, in complex systems all level of the system interact, either directly or indirectly. Over time, a major change in any one component will impact on all other components. These can react in only one of two ways: they can seek to nullify it or they can, in turn, be changed by it. As long as the change is restricted to one component, the former is possible, though by no means certain; as we have seen, even small changes can have large systemic repercussions. Should it apply to multiple elements, then the latter outcome is more likely, though again not certain. This implies, on theoretical grounds, that the more elements initially involved in diversity, the more likely and the more quickly its effects will spread across the entire system.

2. Diversity Must Be Intentional

In the area of transcultural personal counseling, Ivey (1987) stress the importance of cultural intentionality (Ivey et al., 1993). By that he means an intentional effort to understand self and others, and thus carefully plan interventions that will be helpful. Similar reasoning applies to diversity. This implies three types of knowledge and awareness.

First, it implies knowledge of self (La Belle & Ward, 1994). As suggested in the introduction, we all necessarily hold various assumptions about ourselves and the nature of the world. These biases, for that is what they are, are typically unconscious and thus orient us to favor certain choices over others, certain people over others and certain practices over others. Such biases serve us well as long as we deal with others who hold similar biases. However to the extent that we deal with others different from ourselves, our biases can create problems, blinding us to opportunities, options, structures and, in extreme form, they can yield behavior perceived by others as racist. Cultural intentionality requires that we avoid such unintentional pitfalls by being consciously aware of our own biases and changing those that are likely to be problematic for diversity. This applies to individuals across all levels of university systems, from the president and the top administrators, to middle-level managers, to faculty and profesional staff, to students. Indeed, such self-awareness may be seen as a key component of the institution's student development efforts. Currently, there are a variety of programs available that can be helpful in this effort (Katz, 1978; Lee & Richardson, 1991; Pedersen, 1988).

Next, similar self-knowledge is necessary at the level of the institution. I refer here to a process somewhat like what Wilcox and Ebbs (1992) call the "values audit." As they use the term, they mean a survey of beliefs and practices that may potentially act as a barrier to diversity. For example, Spann (1988) notes a series of myths, the acceptance of which will likely deter an institution from even attempting to recruit profile group faculty members. Such myths include the belief that profile group faculty are likely not the best qualified for the job or that they likely would not want to move to the institution in question. The point of such an audit would be to develop institutional self-awareness so that such barriers can be consciously eliminated, whether conceptual, structural or physical.

Finally, implementation of cultural diversity policy would benefit enormously if shaped by substantive knowledge of the groups in question. This text has been prepared precisely because this sort of knowledge is not available in the higher education literature; it is widely scattered in other literatures and across disciplines, thus hard to come by in a coherent, succinct form.

3. Diversity Must Be Concerned With the Proportion of Profile Group Students

Smith (1989, 1990) argues that diversity must involve a critical mass or minimum number of profile group students on campus. This is based on the massive alienation which characterizes the experience of most African American Blacks on predominantly White campus in the United States. If Black students are to be retained, he argues, they must be present in sufficient numbers to allow for mutual support.

While I agree with Smith's conclusion, I do so on different bases. As seen above, in four of the five groups profiled, the extended family in some form is central to group organization. Intense sociality is especially prominent among Hispanics and Asians. This is so much the case that Gary Hanson at the University of Texas (Austin) notes that each year a handful of Hispanic students, typically women, experience homesickness of such severity as to require temporary hospitalization (reported in Benjamin, 1994). Thus, even if university campuses are entirely welcoming to profile group students, on cultural grounds a minimum number of such students would still be required for adequate group functioning.

Such numbers are consistent too with the discussion in Chapter 7 of change across levels. It is important that proponents of diversity exist at the macrosystem level (see below). Seen in context, however, the power of units at that level to unilaterally impose change from above is likely to be quite limited, since it ignores the substantial power of units at the mesosystem and the microsystem levels to effectively resist change. Thus, it is just as important that advocates of diversity simultaneously exist at the microsystem level. Given the system's ultrastability, pressure from both ends of the system may be necessary to facilitate the sort of transformation implied by diversity.

As to what that proportion should be, Smith (1989, 1990) suggests that the proportion of any given group on campus should roughly match their representation in the general population. It remains unclear, however, whether this refers to the local, state or provincial or national context. As seen above, profiled groups are not homogeneously distributed across the United States or Canada. In the United States, for example, they tend to be bunched on either coast, and in the South. Similar variety applies to the proportion of profile group students currently enrolled in colleges and universities in the United States (Fonsela & Andrews, 1993).[1] Diversity based on proportional representation thus implies uneven representation across campus populations, with some institutions having few, if any, profile group students, while others would have such students representing half or more of the student body. Clearly some alternative is warranted and will likely need to be negotiated on an institution by institution basis.

4. Diversity Assumes Groups That Are Distinctive
But Not Necessarily Different

Throughout much of the literature, diversity is equated with differences (Adams, 1992) that affect the quality of the educational experience (Bowser et al., 1993). As seen in Figure 7.1, above, there is much evidence of such differences, at least with regards to the central tendencies in the profiled groups. Given the symbolic importance of terminology and language in this area of concern (Adams, 1992), these data provide support for Shang and Moore (1990) and Westbrook and Sedlacek (1991) when they argue that the widespread use of negative labels has been counterproductive.

There are two important caveats that, with few exceptions (Endo, 1990; Shang & Moore, 1990; Stage & Manning, 1992), have been glossed over in much of the literature and which I, in the above profiles, have taken some pains to underline. The first caveat is that the profiled groups are not only different from each other, and from Whites, but are also quite similar, in some areas in specific ways, in other areas in more generic   ways. Moreover, these similarities and differences are rendered more complex by what Stage and Manning (1992) have called the "heritage community" and what I have called the traditional-acculturated continuum, both referring to variation in the extent to which individual students conform with or depart from the above profiles. The second caveat concerns the importance of attending to subgroup variation, where again marked similarities and differences are in evident.

These similarities and differences at both group and subgroup levels mean that a show of respect for and even celebration of differences, while affirming and well-intentioned, nevertheless risks labeling *all* profile group students as "different" when some do not see themselves that way and would strongly resist any such identification (Grayson, 1994a). While cultural diversity policy would seek to replace negative labels with positive ones, both, when applied automatically, involve stereotyping and are to be avoided. A preferred approach would see diversity policy applied, whenever possible, to *all* students, leaving participation in any new programs or initiatives a matter of individual choice.

5. Diversity Must Be Voluntary

An extension of the preceding discussion is that diversity must be voluntary. This is so in *two* senses. In the first sense, a voluntary approach to diversity derives from the view of the university as a learning community. This is captured well in the notion of "fit" (Benjamin, 1994), the essence of which is the creation of learning environments in which students can self-select to maximize the match between what they want or need and what they get. So much of the diversity literature has been concerned with matching (Ross-Gordon et al., 1990) that the importance of self-selection appears to have been lost. Hence, diversity means more than embracing difference where it exists. It also means making difference a matter of individual expression, creating an environment of real diversity to allow for wide variation in that expression.

In the second sense, a voluntary approach to diversity derives from the university as a complex organization, with its multiple levels and divergent goals. In this context, divergent views apply among proponents of diversity policy. Some, impatient for change, insist that diversity policy must be applied coercively, from above. They cite the civil rights movement of the 1960's as an example of the use of decisive action when no other alternative was available to uphold certain central values. Certainly, in some jurisdictions, such as Ontario, governments are seriously considering introducing legislation to that effect.

Others, myself included, argue that the top-down approach significantly exaggerates the power of units at the macrosystem level, and, in turn, underestimates the power of lower-level subsystems to resist. Like a general who outruns his supply lines, macrosystem policy pronouncements are likely to be empty unless they reflect substantial consensus beforehand. Accordingly, while I am sympathetic to those who want change NOW, on a strategic basis, action that is premature in relation to the readiness of the institution in question is more likely to produce negative, unintended consequences than the desired results. Rather, while the slow process of building consensus through negotiation and consultation may take longer, it is also more likely to produce results in keeping with a "community of difference" (Tierney, 1993).

Furthermore, the voluntary approach would stress the importance of the participation of units from *all* levels of the system, since their interdependence means that all have some ability to induce change. Indeed, there is every reason to think that bottom-up efforts are likely to be as important as their top-down counterparts, especially if they occur at the same time (see below). Finally, note that the voluntary character of diversity policy is seen here as limited to acquiring institutional commitment to it. Once in place, however, voluntary involvement would become one of a variety of policy options. Others might include: attaching rewards or inducements to certain behaviors; punishing clear indications of failure to comply; and using affirmative action to promote certain kinds of change. Thus, the balance between voluntary and coercive elements would likely change, as institutions evolve in response to diversity initiatives.

6. Diversity Must Be Seen as Valued and Valuable

I spoke above of embracing diversity. While this has become something of a cliche in the literature, the point is important enough to warrant some repetition. All students, including those from profiled groups, deserve to be treated with dignity and respect. Their collective vision of the university and of what constitutes an environment in which they can learn must be valued. Their involvement in social and academic affairs, like that of all other students, must be encouraged and supported.

Therefore, to cite a second cliche, diversity should not be seen as a problem but rather as a challenge and an opportunity. It is likely to be a challenge insofar as it requires consensus building around a series of issues that are difficult, contentious and controversial. It can fruitfully be seen as an opportunity insofar as the hoped for result is a learning community that is enriched and diversified, benefiting all participants. This is not to deny the difficulties or costs in short-term disruption and conflict, but only to insist that likely benefits outweigh the presumed costs.

7. Diversity and Student Development Must Be Integrated

The rhetoric of student development has now become so widely accepted in higher education that efforts to "educate the whole student" have been incorporated in the mission statements of many universities across North America. However, as Stage and Manning (1992) note, existing theories were almost all based on research using White, middle-class men. Consequently, their application to students in profile groups will almost certainly be to the latter's disadvantage (Nettles, 1988, 1990), with "different" typically equated with "underdeveloped" or even "abnormal." Similarly, the above profiles demonstrate, that across groups, family life cycle processes vary widely, from compressed to elongated.

This is not to suggest that existing models of student development be abandoned. On the contrary, the notion that higher education should be directed toward enhancing development remains as valid as ever (Benjamin, 1990). However, the specific developmental targets suggested by available models need to be carefully reevaluated in light of the group profiles presented above. In particular, following Stage and Manning (1992) and Bronfenbrenner (1989), what seems required are developmental models that are more sensitive to context.

8. Diversity Must Be Proactive

Finally, in complex organizations, not all components are created equal. Rather, some may have more influence than others. In terms of organizational change, authors in the field agree that that initial "kick" should come from the administration, and it must be proactive (Rowe, 1993; Smith, 1989, 1990; Spann, 1988; Stage & Manning, 1992). In Spann's (1988: 7) words, "Achieving diversity requires an extraordinary effort." It is inherently complex; it is likely to arouse a wide variety of divergent opinion and will likely encounter considerable opposition as the process unfolds. Success, these authors argue, requires strong and sustained leadership from the leading lights in each institution, especially those at the peak of this inherently hierarchical organization. Further, commitment to diversity policy not only must be sustained through time but also must be consistently proactive, as the basis of establishing and maintaining the momentum for change.

Three caveats are in order. As I have argued above, while strong leadership is important, its effects are likely to be more symbolic than substantive (Stage & Hamrick, 1994). The administration can promote certain policies, but they cannot make them succeed in the daily interaction either among students or between students and faculty. Administrative concerns are, as Stage and Manning (1992) suggest, necessarily contextual. Further, administrative involvement need *not* be concerned with sweeping shifts in policy or grand gestures intended to garner attention and publicity. Rather, as suggested above in the discussion of systems theory, small, carefully selected changes can, through time, produce substantial changes in system organization. Finally, while macrosystem units may well be repositories of wisdom and innovation, they may just as easily be concentrations of reactionary and conservative thought. Thus, while the administration in some universities may well be leaders in diversity policy, in other institutions they may need to be pushed to do the right things. In this sense, units at all levels of the institution may act as agents of change; top-down initiatives are not the only way diversity policy can either be introduced or enacted. But this identifies a potential point of tension between and among macrosystem units that favor and oppose the acceptance of policies concerning cultural diversity and educational equity. Later, I will discuss the role of students, especially profile group students in helping to push reluctant administrations toward diversity policy.

DIVERSITY PROGRAMMING AT OTHER LEVELS: BUILDING ON THE PROFILES

In a multi-leveled structure, such as the university, the suprasystem level is only one of several levels at which diversity initiatives will need to be undertaken. Below, I explore the remaining three levels with an eye to considerations that will be helpful. However, no attempt will be made here to reproduce Mintz's (1993) 400-page comprehensive list of such efforts in the United States. Rather, my concern will be more generic, by linking such initiatives to the profiles developed above.

MACROSYSTEM LEVEL: ADMINISTRATIVE INITIATIVES

The macrosystem level consists of a variety of components. Below, I examine a selective list of such components, in each case proposing the types of changes diversity might entail.

Policy and Planning

Traditionally, university policies have adopted a "one-size-fits-all" approach, since university student populations have been relatively homogeneous, that is, White, middle class, single, eighteen to twenty-four years of age, largely male, full-time and residential. Demographic changes have seriously challenged the credibility of this approach. The proportion of females has risen rapidly and is now at or above 50% in many institutions and across a variety of programs. Older-than-average, part-time and married students have all become more common than ever before. Financial aid plans have made it possible for students from less affluent families to enter the university, a substantial proportion of them the first ever in their families to do so.

Diversity merely extends this trend. Indeed, as seen above, not only do profiled groups vary widely, but such variation extends to subgroup differences. It seems plain that policies aimed at serving the needs of a homogeneous student body are increasingly unreasonable.

In a similar vein, planning has traditionally involved a top-down process, with fiscal and academic matters paramount. While collaboration and consultation with students did occur, it was neither typical nor extensive, and with no assumption of future accountability. This too needs to change and, indeed, is changing. Government emphasis on institutional accountability have made institutions more willing to take a service orientation more seriously. Diversity would simply extend this trend. Given a history of inequity, students from profile groups, for example, may need to be given preferential treatment in a variety of policy areas (see below) but only with their consent, consent that may or may not be forthcoming (see Grayson, 1994a, 1994b). Similarly, diversity planning efforts, while consistent with intentionality (see above), may need to be short-term, as the formulation and implementation of policies affecting profile group students are shaped by the ongoing involvement of the students in question. In short, diversity planning may only be possible in generic terms, including the first principles discussed above; for the nuts and bolts, a more organic, trial-and-error process may be preferred. Coincidentally, this is entirely in keeping with the informal interactional styles preferred by most of the groups in question, especially the Asians, with their emphasis on group consensus.

Access and Enrollment

One of the areas in which preferential treatment would be accorded to profile group students would be access and enrollment. It is easy to imagine some of the changes this might entail, including: active recruiting of profile group students; modification of the usual grade cuts-offs for entry; expansion of assessment criteria to include consideration of life experience; and so on. However, all of these assume a body of high school graduates that are motivated to apply and who would attend if accepted. The profiles suggest that this simply may not be true with regard to Blacks, Caribbean Blacks and Hispanics. Indeed, given relatively high dropout rates, proportionately fewer students in these groups are likely to graduate from high school and thus be available for entry into university.

This has several implications for enrollment. First, it suggests that active recruitment for university begin much earlier than it normally does, that is, on high school entry rather than at high school graduation. What this suggests is a much higher degree of integration and joint effort than has hitherto been the case. While such integration is likely to benefit profile group students in particular, all students would likely get something positive out of these efforts.

Next, university recruiters must offer incentives to help motivate profile group students who would not normally consider university attendance. Quoting statistics to the effect that university graduates get better jobs than high school graduates is unlikely to be effective; for African American Blacks in particular, the veracity of such claims is debatable. Offers of financial assistance (see below) may be helpful, but likely insufficient. Rather, what the profiles suggest as critical is *parental involvement* in educational planning: recruit their parents, and profile group students may be motivated to continue and then apply. Repeatedly, the profiles make clear that parents (and other family members) play an absolutely central role in the socialization of profile group students. Without their commitment to higher education, the motivation of these students to apply to university is left in doubt.

Third, the profiles suggest that the university's message is more likely to be heard by profile group students if it comes from liaison staff who belong to their ethnic groups, thus representing persons with whom they can identify. However, given subgroup variation, this would not eliminate the need for extensive staff training in group sensitivity, including the appropriate use of language and the appeal to values central to subgroup cultures.

Finally, liaison efforts should involve a realistic portrait of what profile group students are likely to encounter when they arrive on campus. Typically already cynical and wary of White formal institutions, they need some basis for believing that the negative treatment they have received elsewhere either will not be repeated in university or, if it is, how it will be handled. This especially includes linkage between enrollment and academic and social support (see below). As seen above, for many of these students, academic failure or at least limited academic success will have been a prominent part of their academic experience to that point.

Registration and Records

In the United States, student records have long attended to matters of race. In Canada, such records have included some demographic information, but not race. In either case, record keeping has traditionally been founded, among other things, on the assumption of a homogeneously White, Christian student body. This works well for some Blacks, Caribbean Blacks, Hispanics and Asians who celebrate all the traditional Christian holidays. It is inappropriate for students who are Muslims, Hindus, Jews, Shango-Baptists, Rastafarian or Buddhists, and thus attach importance to different sets of holidays and festivals. Further, methods of celebrating even the Christian holidays have tended to favor White traditions, with its emphasis, for example, on Christmas trees, plum pudding, roast turkey and the like. Blacks, Caribbean Blacks, Hispanics and Asians who recognize Christmas may still celebrate it in ways distinctive to their respective cultures, including their own favorite foods and culturally specific rituals.

To create an integrated campus means to celebrate matters of significance to *all* students. This suggests the need to celebrate the full range of holidays and festivals and to consult students representing these groups as to how this might best be done. In addition, students who choose to be absent from class or are unable to attend an examination in recognition of such a celebration would need to be exempted from any academic penalties.

Financial Aid

Financial aid currently takes a variety of forms. National and state or provincial governments provide aid, both in the form of nonrepayable bursaries and repayable loans. Universities and a variety of outside sources offer scholarships. For diversity policy, these ways of providing access to students from low-income families is problematic in two ways (Nelson, 1994).

First, it assumes that receiving money that has, in a sense, not been earned is acceptable. Second, it assumes that such monies, since they are available in limited amounts, should be given on a priority basis to those students who show the most academic promise. The profiles show that, for some groups at least, both assumptions are false. Among Hispanics, for example, just as receiving welfare income can be a source of humiliation for men, so bursaries and scholarships might similarly be regarded. The importance of thrift among Caribbean Blacks might argue against accepting monies on loan since, it will mean emerging from university carrying a heavy burden of debt. Among Asians, especially the Indo-Chinese, it might mean losing face before the community, since it clearly suggests that the government is doing what the parents themselves cannot do.

As for tying such money to academic achievement, this too is problematic. As seen above, this would disqualify many African American, Hispanic and Indo-Chinese adolescents. It would also be inconsistent with the noncompetitive and interdependent values imbedded in Hispanic and Asians cultures.

What this suggests is the need for more creative ways of financing higher education for the families of those profile group students who cannot afford it. Several illustrative examples readily come to mind: expand the eligibility criteria to include life experience; create a pool of scholarship funds for a profile community group, who would select university candidates based on the criteria of their choice; tie bursary or loan monies to specific work guaranteed to profile group students on arrival on campus; or provide loans on an interest-free basis. Other examples might be listed but would simply reinforce the main point, that financial aid must be offered to profile group students in ways that are congruent with cultural values. Indeed, this suggests the importance of consulting with profile group students already on campus to elicit how this might best be done.

Student Services

Traditionally, student services are based on three assumptions, namely, that:

> services are provided to students who need help of one sort or another;
>
> the students in question will ask for such assistance, that is, they will see help-seeking of this sort as appropriate and acceptable; and
>
> the providers who deliver service to students are competent to do so.

The profiles suggest that all three assumptions are likely false. Of the groups profiled, all but the Jews, and especially the Hispanics and the Asians, may be quite reluctant to acknowledge the need for help, since this not only implies a personal weakness but also may cause the entire family to lose face. This is further complicated if the problem focuses on someone other than the student, as in cases of sexual harassment or professional misconduct. Here, Hispanic and Asian prohibitions against direct conflict and their tendency to "swallow the pain" may induce students from such groups to deal with the "problem" by doing nothing. Similarly, four of five groups see help-seeking in negative terms, especially when it involves dealing with formal White institutions. Finally, the profiles indicate that in the event that members of these groups do seek help, they overwhelmingly prefer to do so from a member of their own group who understands their values, speaks their language and so on. As seen above, most student services personnel are poorly equipped to provide service in this way.

This suggests five types of service underlying diversity policy. First, it suggests the need for a proactive stance. Rather than wait for students to seek service, the service should seek out students who appear to fall into one or more high-risk categories. While such efforts open the institution to charges of intrusion, acceptance of the offer of help would still be voluntary since students would be free to refuse. However, they would at least have service available to them.

Second, it suggests the need for in-service multicultural training for all service providers. Such training is now becoming available (Ivey et al., 1993; Pedersen, 1985; Sue, 1991; Sue & Sue, 1990; Sue et al., 1992), though it is still not widespread.

Third, it suggests diversification of the types of help that are available. With respect to personal counseling, for example, individual psychotherapy is the current treatment of choice for White students; however, the profiles suggest that family or group therapies might be better choices under some circumstances.

Fourth, the identity of acceptable service providers might need to be broadened. At present, only those with formal university training are recognized as qualified to provide service. Profile groups rely on a wider definition of "helper," with the use of folk healers (*curanderos*) a case in point among Hispanics. For students who prefer it, the use of such helpers, either alone or in conjunction with formally trained helpers, might prove useful in some cases, and thus deserves active consideration. Similarly, peer helpers, matched by ethnic group and trained to provide generalized support, might be helpful to students in some distress but who prefer to avoid formal sources of help. Indeed, in some universities, support centers, staffer by peers, have been created specifically with profile group students in mind.

Finally, it highlights the special importance of certain kinds or types of help, most notably, *academic support*. The profiles make clear that several groups will likely emerge from high school academically underprepared for the rigors of university performance. Academic support will thus involve four elements: supplementary assistance with such basic academic skills as reading, writing, mathematics, library use, note-taking, exam preparation and the like; the provision of service by a helper matched by ethnic group and either a staff member or perhaps a senior student "buddy" (Benjamin, 1990); an additional focus on student academic self-esteem, since lack of confidence may be as important to past failure as academic preparation; and, forward tracking to graduation or attrition (see below) as one basis for evaluating whether or not this program achieves its objectives.

Student Orientation

As depicted in Benjamin (1990), student orientation programming is organized around four objectives: to break the ice among entering students, thus promoting friendship formation; to provide information about academic work, especially lectures and note-taking; to give entering students an introduction to the campus and the rules and policies that pertain there; and, generally, to extend a warm welcome to all entering students. Further, all four concerns typically take a large group approach, with much activity accompanied by noise, hoopla and often alcohol, and with no formal recognition of diversity.

The above discussion suggests that as university policy, diversity must be on the orientation agenda. That is, students must be informed about the university's commitment to this notion, and the initiatives associated with it, including a strong stand against racism and discrimiantion on campus, wherever and from whomever it originates. As noted above, while many campuses now have such policies on their books, there is significant variation across institutions as to how they are presented and enforced.

The above profiles also suggest several changes. In making orientation welcoming for profile group students, a primary concern is to create a context that includes elements recognizable to them. This may be symbolic, as in the use of language and imagery drawn from the cultures in question, or it may be substantive, as in providing information pertinent to such students or offering culturally appropriate food and activity choices. While group activities in particular are favored by most of the profiled groups the definition of "group," as we have seen, varies across these groups, with regard to size, membership, leadership, formality and rule-related conduct. This suggests the need to provide similar variety as part of orientation programming, so that students can self-select into the contexts in which they feel most comfortable. Finally, on the assumption that such students will continue to be a minority among the larger body of White entering students, additional support might be indicated at this time. The above profiles overwhelming indicate that any support staff, whether student services staff, faculty, alumni or peers, should belong to the same group and, particularly, should speak the appropriate language.

Institutional Research

As noted above, institutional research is often far removed from diversity issues, typically confined to using registrarial data to create a rudimentary student census. The profiles suggest an expanded role of research in support of diversity objectives. At the front end, variation within and across groups as regards their position on the traditional-acculturated continuum indicates the need for a great deal of information that is not collected on a routine basis. This includes heritage beliefs; attitudes towards group membership; English language proficiency; values regarding educational equity and affirmative action; experience of racism and discrimination; expectations about coming to a mostly White college or university; and their current situation at home concerning marital status, employment, life events and the like. Further, given commitment to the principle of intentionality, such information should be gathered early, prior to arrival on campus. That information source, among others, would be used to shape diversity policy, including types of programming needs and their resource requirements.

At the back end, it is important that the university be accountable for the implementation of diversity policy. Accordingly, the institution needs to know whether and to what extent any programming initiatives have met their objectives, for example, concerning attrition rates, academic grade averages, time to graduation and especially the quality of student life (Benjamin, 1994; Benjamin & Hollings, 1995). Some of these data are available on the registrarial database. Other data would need to be obtained from students, both White and profile groups. Among the latter, this would require collaboration with profile group students, since, as we have seen, group prohibitions against direct conflict may make the evaluation of the quality of student life unusually challenging and delicate. For example, insofar as groups vary in preferred levels of formality in dealing with authority figures, the use of multiple methods of data gathering would be advised. While Asians, for example, would likely respond to "official" surveys, for recent arrivals especially, the task may be complicated by language barriers that require questionnaires translated into one or more native languages, which may have no exact equivalents in English. In contrast, the informality preferred by Hispanics might mean not only the use of Spanish, but also the use of focus groups or one-on-one interviews, as opposed to surveys. Thus, collaboration with profile group students would likely be required, both in instrument design as well as in data interpretation.

Finally, both front and back end approaches would, following Baizerman and Compton (1992), allow students, both White and profile groups, an opportunity to "tell [their] stories." It is critical that they do so, not only in relation to program evaluation but also in terms of monitoring any potential backlash of the affirmative action components of diversity policy (see below).

MESOSYSTEM LEVEL: FACULTY INITIATIVES[2]

As used here, the mesosystem level concerns faculty initiatives. Below, I examine four such policy areas.

Faculty Recruiting

The need to recruit profile group faculty as part of diversity policy stems from twin considerations. First, at most universities and colleges, the majority of faculty are White. This is clearly inconsistent with the goal of a "community of difference" (Tierney, 1993). Second, part of creating a campus environment welcoming to and comfortable for profile group students involves symbolic and substantive initiatives with which they can identify. The presence of profile group faculty, in roughly the same proportion as their student counterparts, would be important to a range of such initiatives. This is especially true given the above profiles, since these indicate that profile group students, given a choice, would prefer dealing with authority figures from their own groups.

Over the short term, say one to three years, recruiting such faculty would require extraordinary efforts (Gainen & Boice, 1993; Spann, 1988), from looking in nontraditional places to taking special care in preparing position descriptions. It also suggests taking great care to avoid exposing these faculty to the same conditions that alienate profile group students (Bernal, 1994; Davis, 1994). Rowe (1993) suggests a variety of steps toward this end, including personalized recruiting, mentoring, networking, family support programming, creation of dispute resolution mechanisms and safety programs. Over the longer term, however, say five to ten years, such efforts should become less and less problematic, as today's profile group students become part of tomorrow's professorate.

Curriculum Development

Traditional curricula in the social sciences and humanities have been confined to Western, that is, White culture. With the exception of specialized courses or programs concerned with ethnicity, much of that curricula are narrowly conceived and if any mention is made of any of the profiled groups, it is done haphazardly and very much in passing (Smith, 1990). As important, albeit implicit, has been the strong tendency to use Western cultural norms as the benchmark or standard against which all other cultures are to be compared, typically to the latter's disadvantage.

By contrast, diversity policy suggests the need for an expanded or more inclusive curricula (Moses, 1994), one that systematically includes attention to profile group perspectives, values, attitudes, history, experience and other facets of their culture, such as art, literature and the like (Border & Van Note Chism, 1992; see Bernal, 1987). To date, such changes in curricula have been largely confined to specialized programs and courses. In the future, this should be pervasive, extending to core curricula, in the process fundamentally redefining what counts as knowledge (La Belle & Ward, 1994) and how that knowledge can and should be used to promote social change in the university, the community and ultimately society at large (Nieto, 1992).

In this context, Gay (1988) proposes a series of criteria, in question form, to help educators assess the extent to which curricular change is consistent with the principles of diversity. While originally developed for application to elementary and/or high school contexts, with only minor modification, they seem equally applicable to higher education:

Does the curricular rationale reflect sensitivity to student diversity?

Does diversity permeate the core content and activities?

Are the culturally diverse content, examples, and experiences comparable to those selected from the majority culture?

Are the suggested methods for teaching content and skills, and the proposed student learning activities, responsive to the learning styles and preferences of different students?

How do the content and activities affirm the culture of diverse students?

This sort of shift may be problematic for faculty in at least three respects. First, it may be seen as inconsistent with academic freedom. That faculty may feel threatened in this area should hardly be surprising, since academic freedom has been the subject of heated debate, on the one hand the focus of criticism from feminist scholars while, on the other hand, the target of intrusive efforts by governments concerned about institutional accountability. Adding further demands based on diversity must, in some faculty at least, foster the perception of a group repeatedly confronted by unreasonable demands. Such a perception is only likely to stiffen their resistance and thus create a source of tension between faculty and the administration.

Here, Moses (1994) argues that diversity policy would not dictate curricula, but rather set up guidelines for course offerings and course content. It would then be left to faculty to voluntarily decide how to shape their own courses accordingly. Academic freedom and diversity policy need not be in conflict.

However, it does not follow that all faculty would be equally comfortable or skilled in teaching a more inclusive curricula. To encourage that shift and recognize the additional effort that it requires, two additional initiatives warrant attention. The first would involve development of training programs for faculty who wish to teach a more inclusive curricula. The second would be to reward faculty who voluntarily participate, either by a one-time monetary reward or by a lighter teaching load while the program is ongoing. The latter is conistent with La Belle and Ward (1994) who advise that selection and development of faculty be done with care, since diversity topics may be emotionally charged and since various profile group members may hold strong beliefs about who can or should teach such material.

Second, recruiting profile group faculty clearly suggests that such faculty would have some advantage over their White counterparts, in areas such as hiring, salaries, promotions and the like. On a temporary basis, until diversity targets in faculty hiring have been met, this charge is likely well-founded. Given ongoing debate regarding employment equity in hiring women faculty, similar action favoring profile group faculty must appear to some like adding insult to injury. Even so, as in all affirmative action programs, some intentional inequality cannot be avoided in the interests of a larger good. Such would be the case here, although it would likely take a benign form, with changes in faculty, for example, occurring either by addition or attrition, not by replacement. Further, as noted above, such inequality in hiring would only be over the short-term.

Finally, diversity policy might be taken to imply that only profile group faculty are qualified to teach courses specifically concerned with profile group culture, history and so on. Such need not be the case, for diversity is about empowerment, including giving people choices they did not have before. This would apply as much to faculty as it would to students. While profile group faculty, given their background, would have a unique advantage compared to their White counterparts, merit and personal preferences should be the ultimate arbiters in faculty assignments. Just as a profile group scholar would not be prevented from teaching a course in "Classical Sociological Theory" because of his or her skin color, so a White scholar specializing in "Black history," should be permitted to exercise his or her skill and talent.

Teaching Practices

Traditional teaching practices in most college and university courses have relied heavily on the formal lecture and the in-class written exam, often using the multiple choice question format. While other teaching and examination practices do apply, they have traditionally been used less widely. Accordingly, students have been forced to accommodate themselves to the system, rather than forcing the system to respond to their needs.

The above profiles have not dealt explicitly with learning styles. By implication, however, the profiles suggest that few of the groups in question would feel comfortable with this formal instructional style. Indeed, in part, this may explain why Blacks and Hispanics in particular have been notably less successful academically than their Asian, Jewish or White counterparts. Wong (1991), for example, cites research at the University of California, Berkeley, showing that the performance of Blacks in math courses is based more on a matter of teaching style than on course content.

Diversity, then, implies, *not* doing away with formal lectures. Rather, it suggests the need for two changes: introducing greater variety into current teaching practices (Border & Van Note Chism, 1992) and greater cultural sensitivity in the construction of exams (Stage & Manning, 1992).

With regard to teaching practices, this includes increased use of small group seminars, classroom discussions, field trips, slide and video presentations, group papers, student presentations, study groups and the like. Primarily, such teaching variety would be directed to choice; it would give all students numerous ways to demonstrate their talent, on the assumption that all students have a right to learning opportunities likely to be successful for them (La Belle & Ward, 1994).

With regard to testing, diversity policy assumes that while all students would be responsible for achieving the same level of content mastery, the way to help students accomplish this end is likely to vary across profile groups. Following Gay (1988), this raises concerns about traditional testing practices, and suggests assessing such methods against criteria such as: evaluation techniques that allow different ways for students to demonstrate their achievement; and that are sensitive to ethnic and cultural diversity. Furthermore, diversifying teaching practices would expose all students to different ways of learning, thus intentionally expanding their learning repertoire, with those oriented toward group approaches acquiring some ability at individual effort, and vice versa.

These sorts of shifts have direct implications for faculty development and library acquisition policy. With respect to the former, college and university teaching is one of the few professions in which incumbents are trained intensively in research skills (either in the field, the laboratory and/or the library) while being expected to acquire teaching skills by a combination of chance and talent. The result is that most professors have superior research skills, while only some possess superior teaching ability. Diversity would place additional demands on faculty teaching skills. Accordingly, diversity policy should provide a voluntary opportunity for faculty to receive supplementary training in teaching methods, with some built-in reward structure to promote participation. As to sanctions for poor performance, student evaluations are already one of a series of components (such as publishing record) used to determine faculty advancement in status and/or salary. In the short-term, while diversity policy is still new, some institutions might wish to consider additional methods, for instance, periodic peer review.

With respect to library acquisition policy, diversity policy, as we have seen, would involve an expanded curricula coupled with more flexible teaching methods. Its viability depends on more than faculty cooperation and participation. It also requires several kinds of support resources. One, the addition of personal counselors, has already been noted. Another, central to the academic task, is a library collection that reflects the diversity of students and topics likely to arise. While I know of no systematic survey in this area, my impression is that most such collections display the same Western bias noted earlier with respect to traditional curricula. It follows that a shift to diversity policy would require a corresponding shift in library acquisition policy to a more extensive collection.

It is clear that this is an ambitious objective. University libraries, like the universities in which they are located, are confronted with the constraints of recessionary economics and limited resources. Diversity policy may force them to make a hard choice: diversify the collection at the expense of keeping up with current publications, or indefinitely postpone diversity initiatives. Further, even if they choose the former, publishers, mindful of their bottomline, have historically been just as biased in favor of Western culture as faculty. It is thus far from clear whether the publications necessary for a diverse library collection are currently available. Diversity policy thus highlights the larger social contexts within which university systems operate, including their interdependence on powerful systems outside the university.

Faculty-Student Interaction
Most faculty teach because they like to interact with students, derive

pleasure in imparting their knowledge, and are genuinely concerned about the success and welfare of their students. That concern, however, is embedded in a series of assumptions about students, the thrust of which is that faculty and students share the same culture. That is, that students and faculty pretty much think the same way, are motivated by the same concerns, and interpret experience (including time, achievement, failure, grades and so on) much the same way.

The above profiles indicate such that such assumptions are more likely to be wrong than right, especially for profile group students at the traditional end of the continuum. This predicts that faculty, confronted by profile group students and with no access to the above profiles, are likely to find dealing with them confusing and very frustrating. For example, in dealing with a student complaining about a B+ grade, they may note that B+ is actually a pretty good grade, unaware that an Asian or a Jewish student might find it impossible to report such a "low" grade to their parents. In being asked to give a student an extension on a paper, they might find themselves suspicious, since the student refuses to look them in the eye, unaware that in doing so, Asian and Hispanic students are showing culturally appropriate signs of respect for an older adult.

In short, this is another instance in which diversity implies the need for transcultural training for faculty as another means of enhancing their teaching ability, not just in the classroom, but indeed in all their dealings with students. Such training would likely interact with both curricula and teaching practices issues, allowing faculty to feel comfortable and competent in dealing on a one-to-one basis with profile group students who come to them for help. Conversely, without such training, the influx of profile group students associated with diversity is likely to create another point of tension, this time between faculty and students.

MICROSYSTEM LEVEL: STUDENT INITIATIVES

As noted above, the microsystem level refers to the experience of undergraduate students. Below, I will examine *six* aspects of that experience.

Parents

As traditionally conceived, parents are thought to play a decidedly modest role in the university career of their children. While they may assist with institutional choice and with tuition, save for occasional support, parents are not traditionally seen as central to their children's college and university experience. Indeed, in keeping with a White cultural emphasis on child independence (McGoldrick, 1993), college attendance typically marks the beginning of adulthood in the family life cycle.

This view of the role of parents, while in keeping with White cultural assumptions, is more myth than reality. A review of the very scattered literature on the subject shows that parents play a critical role in student development throughout students' college careers (Benjamin, 1988a). The above profiles paint a similar picture, with parents and extended family members central to the socialization experience of profile group children; but profile group parents have a different conception of human development, especially with regard to the positive value of dependence.

For diversity policy, this highlights the positive importance of ongoing parental support and the need for the university to facilitate as much parental contact as profile group students feel they need to adjust to university life. This might involve a range of initiatives: institutions with a residence system might consider setting aside a block of rooms to provide inexpensive accommodations for visiting parents; they might strike a deal with the local telephone company to give students whose parents live some distance away a reduced rate on long distance charges; they might establish some mechanism, such as a "hotline" or "800 number," whereby parents might call to inquire about their concerns; and/or they might establish a newsletter specifically directed at parents and designed to keep them informed and encourage their sense of active involvement in their child's experience in higher education.

Malone (1992) adds an important caveat, namely, that low-income profile group parents may simply be unable to provide all the support that such students need. Under such circumstances, it will be incumbent on the university to step in, especially in the person, Malone suggests, of the academic counselor, to provide whatever support and advocacy (Stage & Manning, 1992) such students require. As regards special problems, such as sexual harassment, the academic counselor might need to share his or her advocacy function with staff specialized in the area, such as the human rights and/or the sexual harassment advisors.

Social Support

Academic achievement is not simply a matter of aptitude. Rather, it is a complex outcome that is multiply determined. As suggested above, discrepancies between teaching and learning styles may help account for the relatively poor academic performance of many Black and Hispanic students. In some cases, this may also relate to weak academic preparation in high school and social isolation amidst a sea of mostly White faces. Above, I have addressed academic support and teaching practice. Here, I address the last issue, social support.

The above profiles make clear that Blacks and Hispanics compensate for their lack of material resources by a relatively intense sociality. Social support during hard times is freely available and from a wide range of immediate and extended family members. Asians too place great emphasis on the group as opposed to individual success. In that cultural context, the shift from high school to college or university is likely to be more difficult for profile group students as compared to White students. They must not only cope with the usual difficulties associated with a major life transition

(Benjamin, 1990) but also abandon their usual support network *and* deal with culture shock *and* challenge what may be a hostile White environment.

If diversity is to mean not only increased access, but also success to graduation, then considerable social support must be part of the package. Some of this can come from parents, some from student services, but most will necessarily come from peers (Benjamin, 1990). While this will have specific implications for residence life (see below), in practical terms this will require that the university create one or more contexts where students from each profile groups will have an opportunity to meet and socialize. It also implies rethinking and augmenting existing crisis support services. While existing services are designed to cope with trauma and the "normal" crises of student life, many will be unprepared for an intensely distressed Hispanic student explaining in Spanish that they are suffering an *ataque de nervios* brought on by severe homesickness or another saying in Cantonese or Mandarin that they intend to commit suicide, having lost face for getting "only" a B+ on an exam. Such problems would not only strain available response resources, but more fundamentally challenge existing definitions of "crisis" and, in turn, would require new and innovative responses.

Residence Life

As for residence life, this is often seen by the institution as an extension of academic life, thus committed to enhancing student development (Benjamin, 1988a). Accordingly, residence life staff will have received extensive training in program development toward those aims. However, they, like their student services counterparts, will have received little or no training in diversity, nor, as noted above, are existing theories of student development of much help since "normal" is defined in terms of adolescent White males. Therefore, most will be unprepared to create meaningful programming with diversity in mind.

The above profiles suggest that such programming should be directed toward three ends. First, it should ensure that sufficient numbers of profile group students are available, either on every floor or in every building, to allow for group formation and mutual support. Placing isolated profile group students here and there is likely to be a surefire prescription for student attrition. Next, programming should be directed at making the residence environment a welcoming one for all students, including those from profiled groups. This will tax staff creativity and should necessarily involve meaningful consultation with and collaboration of profile group students. This may range from symbolic gestures, in the form of posters and artwork, to substantive additions, including cafeteria food choices, room and hall design, and activity choices. Finally, programming must be directed not just to profile group students, but to all students. Thus, White students should be exposed to transcultural information, discussions about racism and discrimination and encouraged to dispel myths and stereotypes, by regularly interacting with profile group students in a variety of informal settings, including cocurricular activities (see below).

The thrust of residence life programming in diversity is one with which residence life staff are quite familiar, namely, the development of community, where common purpose is essential in helping students, whether White or profile group, to overcome their differences.

Even so, the sort of transformation envisaged here is not likely to be quick or easy. An abundance of social psychological literature emphasizes that mutual attraction is based on the possession of culturally valued attributes (Middlebrook, 1980); however, diversity policy has often been based on "difference." Those differences can act as barriers to cordial relations and especially to friendship formation (Althen, 1994; Kitayama & Markus, 1994). In a similar vein, stereotypical ideas are notoriously resistant to evidence, however compelling or obvious. Rules and even harsh sanctions will not automatically dispense with racist or discriminatory behavior.

This predicts that as the presence of profile group students increases, the residence hall is likely to be one of the flashpoints of tension between White and profile student groups. While difficult to handle, it is important to remember that conflict per se is not destructive. Rather, it can be a source of creative energy, allowing participants to get the issues out on the table, vent their feelings, and act together to discover and work out mutually acceptable solutions (Tjosvold, 1993).

While it would be ideal if students could work out these solutions by themselves, the complexity of the issues and the intensity of associated feelings may make this impossible in some instances. Here, institutions might consider the use of a mediator. This might involve several choices, used singely or in combination, including (a) use of an outside professional (Irving & Benjamin, 1995); or (b) a faculty member or student services staff with specialized training in transcultural mediation techniques; or (c) it might involve expanding residence assistant training to include such skills.

Cocurricular Activities

University is about education in its broadest sense. This includes academic training, but extends further to encompass interpersonal relationships and social or cocurricular activities. The latter have traditionally been part of the university scene, and include various student clubs and organizations, dances, films, parties and sports.

The above profiles suggest that corresponding activities occur among the groups in question; none are foreign to them. However, the activities are often organized around different principles. For example, they are often cooperative rather than competitive and oriented towards group rather than individual achievement. In some groups, activities may also avoid the use of alcohol, or insist on a clear separation between the sexes or require the presence of adult chaperons. They may also have religious overtones and be associated with certain traditions or rituals.

For purposes of diversity policy, this suggests that, like teaching practices, cocurricular activities should become more varied or inclusive, the key principle being self-selection. Again, staff transcultural training will be important. Consider the example of the sports staff. Such training would help them prepare for profile group students, especially in the design and implementation of team-based intramural sports. Indeed, in team-based sports, the group orientation of many profile group students should assist in promoting team solidarity and spirit, and their strong orientation toward hard work and respect for authority should similarly promote superior performance.

Student Intergroup Interaction

Friendship and romantic relationships form a key feature of university life (Benjamin, 1990). Alumni routinely report that it was in college or university that friendships were formed that lasted a lifetime, or there that they met the person who would later become their spouse or partner. Such relationships are complex, their success enormously beneficial in fostering student development, while their failure and dissolution is one of the most common reasons for referral to personal counseling. Diversity policy is likely to make such processes still more complex, requiring institutions to broaden the definition of "student services" while expanding their capacity to respond to increasingly diverse student demands.

The profiles suggest that the groups in question have very different ways of behaving when dealing with family members, others from within the group or strangers from outside the group (Althen, 1994). Generally, relations between group members and strangers involve formal matters; friendship formation is frowned on, and intermarriage a source of public disgrace. Further, age-, sex- and class-related expectations differ sharply between Whites and profile groups, and religious differences only complicate matters. Finally, diversity, insofar as it may involve affirmative action, may be an added source of friction.

Thus, initially at least, diversity is likely to be a source of increased tension and conflict between White and profile group students on campus. Such conflict is likely to dissipate through time, based on sustained intergroup interaction, coupled with the integrated policy and programmatic processes described above. But, in turn, that is likely to create problems in its own right, as cross-group friendships and especially romantic relations create tension among the respective family members. Ironically, over the long term, the formation of such relationships is likely to be a key indicator of program success, as diversity policy strives to "educate all students for a pluralistic world" (Smith, 1990: 62).

Student Advocacy

Finally, I have noted above that the impetus for cultural diversity and educational equity is likely to come from several quarters, among them, governments, advocates of social justice, formal organizations, university and college administrations and students. Advocacy by students warrants further comment.

Profile group students are most likely to favor diversity policy. That is not to suggest that many White students would not favor the policy's objectives. Rather, in my experience, they are often so taken up with their own academic and social concerns that they are unlikely to place diversity high among their priorities. They may also be put off by the affirmative action components of diversity, which, on a temporary basis, might see a qualified White student passed over for an equally or differently qualified profile group student.

The student voice advocating for diversity will thus likely come from profile group students, since they clearly have a vested interest in its advancement. Advocacy generated by these students, however, is likely to be neither easy nor comfortable. As seen above, across institutions, their numbers vary widely, with corresponding variation in their capacity to influence any of the other stakeholders around this issue. Advocacy may also make them the target of attention, either positive or negative.

In one scenario, with an administration committed to diversity, profile group students are likely to be one of a variety of groups who are consulted regarding the speed, direction and consequences of diversity policy. In another scenario, with the administration resisting diversity, students may find themselves alone, pushing for change that may be widely viewed with disfavor.

In either event, it is crucial that their voices be heard, if for no other reason than to convince others that diversity is a credible, indeed necessary, choice in the views of those likely to be most directly affected by it. Saying this, however, is likely much easier than implementing it. As noted in the profiles, several groups are culturally averse to direct confrontation, especially among women. Thus, on the one hand, their vocal participation is likely to give their sentiments greater weight in the eyes of others. On the other hand, such participation is likely to create another source of tension, here between students and the administration.

DIVERSITY POLICY AND THE ECOLOGY OF UNIVERSITY SYSTEMS

The above discussion, while organized in terms of the notion of levels, was based primarily on the group profiles. In closing, it remains to re-examine this discussion in light of the university as an ecological system. Such a re-examination supports at least *six* inferences.

First, it seems plain that there is no one right way to conceptualize or implement diversity policy. The higher education system in North America is extremely heterogeneous: two-year colleges and four-year universities, public institutions and private ones, liberal arts colleges and research universities, small institutions and large multiversities, all vying for student enrollment. Such heterogeneity suggests that as ecological systems, each college and university is likely to be unique, despite generic similarities among like institutions.

This is not to imply that each system must "reinvent the wheel" regarding diversity policy. Rather, the models presented here and elsewhere indicate what diversity might eventually look like and how it might be implemented. Even so, institutional heterogeneity means that the concept-ualization and implementation of diversity policy will vary widely, to suit the unique ecological contexts in which it is applied. On similar grounds, the developmental course of this policy, once put in place,
will probably vary widely, so that any attempt to speak about diversity policy in the singular will certainly be misleading.

Second, the decision to implement diversity policy, and the speed and course of such efforts depend, in part, on the institution's readiness to do so. As shown by Kuh and Whitt (1988), institutions vary widely in terms of their "culture" or meaning systems. In this context, institutional readiness refers to both the number of system units committed to the notion as well as their power relative to other units. That is, the greater the number of units in favor of diversity policy, and the greater their power, the more the system in question will be ready to undertake this policy initiative.

This has three implications for policy implementation: diversity policy will likely go through several phases, the first of which involves getting ready; getting ready will take time, energy and resources, and should not be undertaken lightly; and diversity policy may fail for a variety of reasons, including policy initiatives undertaken when the system is not ready.

Third, diversity policy need not involve a massive commitment of resources expended all at one time. Rather, by the character of universities as systems, it can and should start small, searching for key interventions, and its advocates should commit to it over the long-term. As seen in Chapter 7, small events can be magnified through the interaction of feedback and time, to produce large effects. Thus, depending on the context, any number of small initiatives can have the desired effect, including bringing in new administrative pesonnel with fresh ideas, changing enrollment policy, making internal shifts in resource allocation and so on. Selection of these key changes will require a thorough understanding of the institution's ecology combined with intentional and creative planning.

Fourth, implementation of diversity policy will likely be associated with various points of tension and conflict. Interaction across levels is most likely to threaten to disrupt the process. That is not to suggest that conflict across units within a given level will not occur; diversity policy may temporarily promote tension across student groups based on ethnicity and pit faculty from one department against those from another. But units at the same level are likely to have related goals and shared meaning systems. That is less probable across levels, with unilateral top-down initiatives, for example, likely to be strenuously resisted by faculty. Unless their cooperation has been assured in advance, such resistance may, among other possible outcomes, seriously disrupt policy implementation. From an ecological perspective, then, diversity planners should identify key cross-level areas of tension in advance and either pre-empt such conflict as part of their readiness efforts, or put in place mechanisms apt to promote the constructive resolution of these disputes.

Fifth, the contentious character of diversity policy means that conflict associated with its implementation is likely unavoidable. That said, the unique ecology of each institution will determine whether the developmental course of diversity policy is relatively smooth and orderly, or relatively difficult and disorderly. Relations among units pursuant to diversity policy will depend on a variety of factors, including their history of interaction, their power and control over valued resources and their perception that diversity policy will or will not further their unit goals. The greater the number of units that see diversity policy as beneficial to them and the greater their power, the more likely the developmental course of diversity policy will be smooth. The more the opposite is true, the more that course will likely be disorderly. In either case, however, the complexity of university systems is such that the outcome can only be predicted in probabilistic terms. The key issue concerns system change, operationally defined as a series of attainable, short-term and medium-term objectives. Their achievement, whatever the course of change, suggests that diversity policy is succeeding.

Finally, the success or failure of diversity policy will depend in part on external constraints. University systems operate in a larger ecological field composed of federal and state or provincial legislatures, exisiting official statutes and regulations, the judiciary, alumni and parents and society at large. That larger field may be supportive of diversity policy initiatives or it may not. Above, I cited the example of library acquisition, but many additional examples could easily be given concerning aspects of diversity policy that have resource implications. The availability of those resources significantly increases the likelihood that diversity initiatives will succeed, while the absence of such resources has the opposite implication. The same holds true of public opinion. While educators may support diversity policy, it is far from clear whether such support is equally present in public opinion, especially given the levels of inequality and overt racism seen in the group profiles above. This suggests a revision to what was previously said regarding readiness, namely, that it should extend beyond the individual institution to encompass that institution's ecological field; colleges, determined to pursue diversity policy in the absence of support in the field, face an uphill battle, if not ultimate failure.

SUMMARY

Finally, cultural diversity and educational equity policies are about equality, inclusion, empowerment and, most of all, change. Fully realized, diversity policy would mean significant changes in who attends colleges and universities and what they experience on arrival. It would mean change in what students learn, how they are taught, how they are financed, how they are housed, how they are graded and, in turn, what sort of opportunities they have for their futures. Nor would these changes be confined to ethnic minority students, but would extend to all higher education personnel, with diversity emphasizing tolerance, goodwill, understanding and respect for differences in appearance, values and attitudes, perspectives, assumptions and conduct. Further still, as graduates emerge from diverse colleges and universities, they cannot but begin to change the society of which they are a part. In short, diversity policy is ultimately about changing higher education as we have known it and about changing the society in which it is rooted.

Heretofore, advocates of diversity policy have repeatedly stressed the importance of respect for difference, dedication to the cause and long-term commitment. All are vital to the acceptance and success of diversity policy. However, as I have argued above, these qualities are simply not enough. Equally crucial are three forms of knowledge: some sense of the higher-order principles needed to guide this effort; a clear-eyed view of the college or university as a complex ecological system; and, most important of all, detailed, substantive knowledge of the ethnic minority groups in question. Moreover, in using the latter, diversity advocates need to be mindful not only of the similarities and differences across the ethnic groups and between them and Whites, but also of the similarities and differences across ethnic minority subgroups.

Even with such knowledge, the sort of changes envisioned by diversity policy will come neither quickly nor easily. The aims and objectives of diversity policy are ambitious ones, and their implementation is likely to touch on a variety of delicate and emotionally charged issues. Consequently, just as it promotes solidarity among higher-order institutional units, so is it just as likely to bring division and conflict among its lower-order counterparts.

The results are likely to be mixed. In many institutions, adequate planning, resources and resolve will bring long-term success. In others, despite these attributes, diversity policy will fail, for a host of reasons, both internal and external. In still others, diversity policy will succeed in name alone, as in practice the status quo ante prevails.

Even so, I believe the exercise will have been worth it. Large scale societal changes are upon us, and their effects will only become increasingly apparent with time; they can neither be avoided nor diverted. These changes will see a North America in the twenty-first century in which plurality rules, and in which no ethnic group, including Whites, will constitute a majority. They will also see a society shaped by technological advances such that only people with higher education will have any hope of full citizenship. Diversity policy is in keeping with this future vision, and its success, and the success of related policies in others spheres, will determine whether that near-future society is one of shared hope and prosperity, or one divided into haves and have nots based on ethnicity. Whether or not one accepts this perspective, there is little question that there will be significant long-term consequences of our current, short-term choices regarding cultural diversity policy.

NOTES

1. In 1990, the proportional enrollment of profile group students in the United States varied as follows: Asians, less than 1% to 58%; Blacks, less than 1% to 31%; and Hispanics, less than 1% to 28% (Fonsela & Andrews, 1993).

2. The mesosystem includes university profesional staff as well as faculty. There is every reason to think that the comments made in this section about faculty would not apply equally to professional staff.

References

Abad, V., Ramos, J. & Boyce, E. A model for delivery of mental health services to Spanish speaking minorities. *American Journal of Orthopsychiatry*, 1974, 44, 584-595.

ABC-Clio. *The Jewish Experience in America: A Historical Bibliography*. Santa Barbara, CA: ABC-Clio, 1983.

Abella, I. *A Coat of Many Colours: Two Centuries of Jewish Life in Canada*. Toronto: Lester & Orpen Dennys, 1990.

Abella, I. & Troper, H. *None is Too Many: Canada and the Jews of Europe, 1933-1948* (3d ed.). Toronto: Lester, 1991.

Acosta, F. X., Yamamoto, J. & Evans, L. A. (Eds.). *Effective Psychotherapy for Low-Income and Minority Patients*. New York: Plenum, 1982.

Acosta-Belen, E. & Sjostrum, B. A. (Eds.). *The Hispanic Legacy in the U.S.* New York: Praeger, 1988.

Acuna, R. *Occupied America: A History of Chicanos* (3d ed.). New York: HarperCollins, 1988.

Adachi, K. with Findley, T. *The Enemy That Never Was: A History of Japanese Canadians* (Updated edition). Toronto: McClelland & Stewart, 1991.

Adams, M. Editor's Notes. In M. Adams (Ed.), *Promoting Diversity in College Classrooms: Innovative Responses for the Curriculum, Faculty, and Institution.* New Directions for Teaching & Learning, #52. San Francisco: Jossey-Bass, 1992.

Adebimpe, V. R. Overview: White norms and psychiatric diagnosis of black patients. *American Journal of Psychiatry*, 1981, 138, 279-285.

Adelman, H. *Canada and the IndoChinese Refugees*. Regina, SK: Wengl Educational Associates, 1982.

Adler, L. L. (Ed.). *Cross-Cultural Research in Human Development: Life-Span Perspective*. New York: Praeger, 1989.

Adler, L. L. (Ed.). *Women in Cross-Cultural Perspective*. New York: Praeger, 1991.

Adler, L. L. (Ed.). *International Handbook on Gender Roles*. Westport, CT: Greenwood Press, 1993.

Adler, L. L. & Gielen, U. P. (Eds.). *Cross-Cultural Topics in Psychology*. Westport, CT: Praeger, 1994.

Alba, R. D. *Italian-Americans: Into the Twilight of Ethnicity*. Englewood Cliffs, NJ:

Prentice-Hall, 1985.

Alba, R. D. *Ethnic Identity: The Transformation of White America.* New Haven, CT: Yale University Press, 1990.

Albert, R. D. Communicational and attributional differences between Hispanics and Anglo-Americans. In Y. Y. Kim (Ed.), *Interethnic Communication: Current Research.* Beverly Hills, CA: Sage, 1986.

Aldrich, H. & Waldinger, R. Ethnicity and entrepreneurship. *Annual Review of Sociology*, 1990, 16, 111-135.

Aldridge, D. P. *Black Male-Female Relationships: A Resource Book of Selected Materials.* Dubuque, IA: Kendall/Hunt, 1989.

Alers-Montalvo, M. *The Puerto Rican Migrants of New York City.* New York: AMS Press, 1985.

Alexander, K. L. & Entwisle, D. R. Achievement in the first 2 years of school: Patterns and process. *Mongraphs of the Society for Research on Child Development*, 1988, 53 (Serial 218), 1-140.

Alexander, K. L., Entwisle, D. R. & Dauber, S. L. First grade classroom behavior: Its short- and long-term consequences for school performance. *Child Development*, 1993, 64, 801-814.

Allahan, A. L. Unity and diversity in Caribbean ethnicity and culture. *Canadian Ethnic Studies*, 1993, 25 (1), 70-84.

Allen, J. P. & Turner, E. J. *We The People: An Atlas of America's Ethnic Diversity.* New York: Macmillan, 1987.

Allen, M. & Pittman, K. *Welfare and Teen Pregnancy: What Do We Know? What Do We Do?* Washington D.C.: Children's Defense Fund, 1986.

Allen, W. R. Black family research in the United States: A review, assessment and extension. *Journal of Comparative Family Studies*, 1978, 9, 166-188.

Allen, W. R. The education of Black students on White campuses: What quality the experience. In M. T. Nettles (Ed.), *Toward Black Undergraduate Student Equality in American Higher Education.* Westport, CT: Greenwood Press, 1988.

Allen, W. R. The dilemma persists: Race, class and inequality in American life. In P. Radcliffe (Ed.), *"Race", Ethnicity and Nation: International Perspectives on Social Conflict.* London: UCL Press, 1994.

Allen, W. R. & Farley, R. *The Color Line and the Quality of Life: The Problem of the Twentieth Century.* New York: Russell Sage Foundation, 1987.

Allen-Meares, P. & Burman, S. The endangerment of African American men: An appeal for social work action. *Social Work*, 1995, 40 (2), 268-274.

Almirol, E. B. *Ethnic Identity and Social Negotiation: A Study of a Filipino Community in California.* New York: AMS Press, 1985.

Altbach, P. & Lomotey, K. (Eds.). *The Racial Crisis in Higher Education.* Albany, NY: State University of New York Press, 1991.

Althen, G. Cultural differences on campus. In G. Althen (Ed.), *Learning Across Cultures.* n.p.: National Association of International Educators, 1994.

Alvirez, D. & Bean, F. D. The Mexican American family. In C. Mindel & R. Habenstein (Eds.), *Ethnic Families in America.* New York: Elsevier, 1976.

Amaro, H., Beckman, L. J. & Mays, V. M. A Comparison of Black and White women entering alcoholism treatment. *Journal of Studies on Alcohol*, 1987, 48, 220-228.

Ames, M. M. & Inglis, J. Tradition and change in British Columbia Sikh family life. In K. Ishwaran (Ed.), *The Canadian Family: A Book of Readings* (Rev. ed.).

Toronto: Holt, Rinehart & Winston, 1976.

Anderson, B. *Imagined Communities: Reflections on the Origin and Spread of Nationalism.* London: Verso, 1983.

Anderson, E. *Streetwise: Race, Class, and Change in an Urban Community.* Chicago: University of Chicago Press, 1990.

Anderson, J. M. & Lynam, M. J. The meaning of work for immigrant workers in the lower echelons of the Canadian labour force. *Canadian Ethnic Studies,* 1987, 19 (2), 67-90.

Anderson, K. J. *Vancouver's Chinatown: Racial Discourse in Canada, 1985-1990.* Kingston, ON: McGill-Queen's University Press, 1991.

Anderson, W. W. (Ed.). *Caribbean Orientations: A Bibliography of Resource Material on the Caribbean Experience in Canada.* Toronto: Organization for Caribbean Canadian Institution & William-Wallace Publishers, 1985.

Anderson, W. W. & Grant, R. W. *The New Newcomers.* Toronto: Canadian Scholars' Press, 1987.

Aponte, H. Underorganization in the poor family. In P. Guerin (Ed.), *Family Therapy: Theory and Practice.* New York: Gardner, 1976.

Aponte, H. If I don't get simple, I cry. *Family Process,* 1986, 25 (4), 531-548.

Aponte, H. *Bread and Spirit: Therapy with the New Poor: Diversity of Race, Culture, and Values.* New York: Norton, 1994.

Aranas, M. Q. *The Dynamics of Filipino Immigrants in Canada.* Edmonton, AB: Coles Printing, 1983.

Araneta, E., Jr. Filipino Americans. In A. Gaw (Ed.), *Cross-Cultural Psychiatry.* Boston: John Wright-PSG, 1982.

Arizpe, L. The rural exodus in Mexico and the Mexican migration to the United States. *International Migration Review,* 1981, 15 (6), 626-649.

Aronowitz, M. The social and emotional adjustment of immigrant children: A review of the literature. *International Migration Review,* 1984, 18, 237-257.

Aschenbrenner, J. *Lifelines: Black Families in Chicago.* Prospect Heights, IL: Waveland Press, 1975.

Astin, A. W. *Minorities in Higher Education: Recent Trends, Current Prospects and Recommendations.* San Francisco: Jossey-Bass, 1982.

Astin, A. W. Diversity and multiculturalism on the campus: How are students affected? *Change,* 1993, 25 (2), 44-49.

Atkinson, D. R., Maruyama, M. & Matsui, S. The effects of counselor race and counseling approach on Asian Americans' perceptions of counselor credibility and utility. *Journal of Counseling Psychology,* 1978, 25 (1), 76-83.

Auletta, K. *The Underclass.* New York: Vintage, 1982.

Axtell, R. E. (Ed.). *Do's and Taboos Around the World: A Guide to International Behavior.* New York: Wiley, 1985.

Aylesworth, L. S., Ossorio, P. G. & Osaki, L. T. Stress and mental health among Vietnamese in the United States. In R. Endo, Sue, S. & Wagner, N. N. (Eds.), *Asian Americans: Social and Psychological Perspectives.* Palo Alto, CA: Science & Behavior Books, 1980.

Baca Zinn, M. Chicano family research: Conceptual distortions and alternative directions. *Journal of Ethnic Studies,* 1979, 7, 59-71.

Bach, R. L., Gordon, L. W., Haines, D. W. & Howell, D. R. *The Economic Adjustment of Southeast Asian Refugees in the U.S. In United Nations Commission for Refugees, World Refugee Survey 1983.* Geneva, Switzerland: United Nations, 1984.

Badillo-Ghali S. Culture sensitivity and the Puerto Rican client. *Social Casework*, 1974, 55, 100-110.

Bagarozzi, D. A. Family therapy and the black middle class: A neglected area of study. *Journal of Marital & Family Therapy*, 1980, 6 (2), 159-166.

Baizerman, M. & Compton, D. From respondent and informant to consultant and participant: The evolution of a state agency policy evaluation. In A.-M. Madison (Ed.), *Minority Issues in Program Evaluation*. New Directions For Program Evaluation, #53. San Francisco: Jossey-Bass, 1992.

Baker, F. M. Afro-Americans. In L. Comas-Diaz & E. E. H. Griffith (Eds.), *Clinical Guidelines in Cross-Cultural Mental Health*. New York: Wiley, 1988.

Baker, H. D. R. *Chinese Family and Kinship*. New York: Columbia University Press, 1979.

Baker, M. (Ed.). *Families: Changing Trends in Canada* (2nd ed.). Toronto: McGraw-Hill Ryerson, 1990.

Ball, R. E. Family and friends: A supportive network for low-income American Black families. *Journal of Comparative Family Studies*, 1983, 14, 51-65.

Banks, J. A. *Teaching Strategies for Ethnic Studies* (5th ed.). Boston: Allyn & Bacon, 1991.

Baptiste, H. P., Baptiste, M. L. & Gollnick, D. M. (Eds.). *Multicultural Teacher Education: Preparing Educators to Provide Educational Equity (Volume 1)*. Washington D.C.: Commission on Multicultural Education, 1980.

Barr, D. J. & Strong, L. J. Embracing multiculturalism: The existing contradictions. *National Association of Student Personnel Administrators Journal*, 1989, 26 (2), 85-90.

Barrera, M. *Race and Class in the Southwest: A Theory of Racial Inequality*. Notre Dame, IN: Notre Dame University Press, 1980.

Barth, F. *Ethnic Groups and Boundaries: The Social Organization of Culture Difference*. Boston: Little, Brown, 1969.

Barth, G. *Bitter Strength: A History of the Chinese in the United States, 1850-1870*. Cambridge, MA: Harvard University Press, 1964.

Bass, B. A., Wyatt, G. E. & Powell, G. J. *The Afro-American Family: Assessment, Treatment, and Research Issues*. New York: Grune & Stratton, 1982.

Baum, C., Hyman, P. & Michael, S. *The Jewish Woman in America*. New York: Dial Press, 1975.

Baureiss, G. & Driedger, L. Winnipeg's Chinatown: Demographic, ecological and organizational change, 1900-80. *Urban Historical Review*, 1982, 10 (3), 11-24.

Bean, F. D. Components of income and expected family size among Mexican Americans. *Social Science Quarterly*, 1973, 54, 103-116.

Bean, F. D. & Tienda, M. *The Hispanic Population of the United States*. New York: Russell Sage Foundation, 1987.

Bean, F. D., King, A. G. & Passel, J. S. The number of illegal immigrants of Mexican origin in the United States: Sex ratio-based estimates for 1980. *Demography*, 1983, 20 (1), 99-109.

Bean, F. D., Swicegood, C. G. & King, A. G. Role incompatibility and the relationship between fertility and labor supply among Hispanic women. In G. Borjas & M. Tienda (Eds.), *Hispanics in the U.S. Economy*. Orlando, FL: Academic, 1985.

Beaudry, J. S. Synthesizing research in multiculural teacher education: Findings and issues for evaluation of cultural diversity. In A.-M. Madison (Ed.), *Minority Issues in Program Evaluation*. New Directions for Program Evaluation, #53. San

Francisco: Jossey-Bass, 1992.

Beckett, J. O. Working wives: A racial comparison. *Social Work*, 1976, 21, 463-471.

Bender, P. S. & Ruiz, R. A. Race and class in differential determinants of underachievment and underaspiration among Mexican Americans. *Journal of Educational Research*, 1974, 68, 51-56.

Benjamin, M. General systems theory, family systems theories, and family therapy: Towards an integrated recursive model of family process. In A. Bross (Ed.), *Family Therapy: A Recursive Model of Strategic Practice*. New York: Guilford, 1983.

Benjamin, M. Student development and family systems: Critical review and implications for theory and practice. *Student Development Monograph Series* (Volume 2). (ERIC ED 346792). Guelph, Ontario: University of Guelph, Student-Environment Study Group, 1988a.

Benjamin, M. Residence life systems and student development: A critical review and reformulation. *Student Development Monograph Series* (Volume 3). (ERIC ED346793). Guelph, Ontario: University of Guelph, Student-Environment Study Group, 1988b.

Benjamin, M. Freshman daily experience: Implications for policy, research and theory. *Student Development Monograph Series* (Volume 4). (ERIC ED 346794). Guelph, Ontario: University of Guelph, Student-Environment Study Group, 1990.

Benjamin, M. The quality of student life: Toward a coherent conceptualization. *Social Indicators Research*, 1994, 31, 205-264.

Benjamin, M. & Hollings, A. Toward a theory of student satisfaction: An exploratory study of the "quality of student life." *Journal of College Student Devlopment*, 1995, 36 (6), 574-586.

Benkin, R. L. Ethnicity and organization: Jewish communities in Eastern Europe and the United States. *Sociological Quarterly*, 1978, 19, 614-625.

Bensimon, E. M. (Ed.). *Multicultural Teaching and Learning: Strategies for Change in Higher Education*. University Park, PA: National Center on Postsecondary Teaching, Learning, & Assessment, 1994.

Berdichewsky, B. *Los Latinamericanos en la Columbia Britanica*. Vancouver: LARC, 1984.

Berdichewsky, B. *Ethnicity and Multiculturalism in Canada* (booklet). Vancouver: Future Publications, 1988.

Bernal, M. *Black Athena: The Afroasiatic Roots of Classical Civilization*. New Brunswick, NJ: Rutgers University Press, 1987.

Bernal, M. E. Integration of ethnic minorities into academic psychology: How it has been and what it could be. In E. J. Trickett, R. J. Watts & D. Birman (Eds.), *Human Diversity: Perspectives on People in Context*. San Francisco: Jossey-Bass, 1994.

Berry, F. B. & Blassingame, J. W. *Long Memory: The Black Experience in America*. New York: Oxford University Press, 1982.

Betzig, L. Causes of conjugal dissolution: A cross-cultural study. *Current Anthropology*, 1989, 30 (5), 654-676.

Billingsley, A. *Black Families in America*. New York: Simon & Schuster, 1988.

Billingsley, A. *Climbing Jacob's Ladder: The Enduring Legacy of African-American Families*. New York: Simon & Schuster, 1992.

Birman, D. Acculturation and human diversity in a multicultural society. In E. J. Trickett, R. J. Watts & D. Birman (Eds.), *Human Diversity: Perspectives on People in Context*. San Francisco: Jossey-Bass, 1994.

Birnbaum, P. *A Book of Jewish Concepts* (Rev. ed.). New York: Hebrew Publishing, 1975.

Birnbaum, R. *How Colleges Work: The Cybernetics of Academic Organization and Leadership.* San Francisco: Jossey-Bass, 1988.

Blalock, B. Race versus class: Distinguishing reality from artifacts. *National Journal of Sociology,* 1990, 3 (2), 127-143.

Blau, Z. S. The strategy of the Jewish mother. In M. Sklare (Ed.), *The Jews in American Society.* New York: Behrman House, 1974.

Blea, I. I. *Bessemer: A Sociological Perspective of a Chicano Bario.* New York: AMS Press, 1985.

Block, F., Coward, R., Ehrenreich, B. & Piven, F. F. (Eds.). *The Mean Season: The Attack on the Welfare State.* New York: Pantheon, 1987.

Bobo, L. & Kluegel, J. R. Opposition to race-targeting: Self-interest, stratification ideology, or racial attitudes? *American Sociological Review,* 1993, 58, 443-464.

Bonacich, E. A theory of middleman minorities. *American Sociological Review,* 1973, 38, 583-594.

Bonacich, E. Inequality in America: The failure of the American system for people of color. In G. E. Thomas (Ed.), *U.S. Race Relations in the 1980s and 1990s: Challenges and Alternatives.* New York: Hemisphere, 1990.

Bonacich, E. & Modell, J. *The Economic Basis of Ethnic Solidarity: Small Business in the Japanese-American Community.* Berkeley, CA: University of California Press, 1980.

Bonilla, F. A. & Campos, R. Imperialist initiatives and the Puerto Rican workers: From Foraker to Reagan. *Contemporary Marxism,* 1982, 5, 1-18.

Borden, V. H. & Banta, T. W. (Eds.). *Using Performance Indicators to Guide Strategic Decision Making.* New Directions for Institutional Research, #82. San Francisco: Jossey-Bass, 1994.

Border, L. L. B. & Van Note Chism, N. (Eds.). *Teaching for Diversity.* New Directions for Teaching & Learning, #49. San Francisco: Jossey-Bass, 1992.

Boswell, T. D. & Curtis, J. R. *The Cuban-American Experience.* Totowa, NJ: Rowman & Allanheld, 1984.

Boswell, T. E. A split labor market analysis of discrimination against Chinese immigrants, 1850-1882. *American Sociological Review,* 1986, 51, 352-371.

Bouvier, L. F. *Peaceful Invasions: Immigration and Changing America.* Lanham, MD: University Press of America, 1991.

Bowser, B. P., Auletta, G. S. & Jones, T. *Confronting Diversity Issues on Campus.* Thousand Oaks, CA: Sage, 1993.

Boyd, M. The status of immigrant women in Canada. *Canadian Review of Sociology & Anthropology,* 1975, 12, 406-416.

Boyd, M. Immigrant women. In S. S. Halli, F. Trovato & L. Driedger (Eds.), *Ethnic Demography: Canadian Immigrant, Racial and Cultural Variations.* Ottawa: Carleton University Press, 1990.

Boyd-Franklin, N. *Black Families in Therapy: A Multisystem Approach.* New York: Guilford, 1989.

Boyd-Franklin, N. Race, class, and poverty. In F. Walsh (Ed.), *Normal Family Processes* (2nd ed). New York: Guilford, 1993.

Braddock, J. H., II & McPartland, J. M. How minorities continue to be excluded from equal employment opportunities: Research on labor market and institutional barriers. *Journal of Social Issues,* 1987, 43 (1), 5-39.

Bradshaw, B. & Bean, F. D. Some aspects of fertility of Mexican Americans. In C. S. Westoff & R. Parke, Jr. (Eds.), *Demographic and Social Aspects of Population Growth.* Washington, D.C.: U.S. Government Printing Office, 1972.

Bramble, L. *Black Fugitive Slaves in Early Canada.* St. Catherines, ON: Vanwell Pubishers, 1987.

Braverman, L. Jewish mothers. *Journal of Feminist Family Therapy*, 1990, 2 (2), 9-14.

Breton, R., Isajiw, W. W., Kalbach, W. E. & Reitz, J. G. *Ethnic Identity and Equality: Varieties of Experience in a Canadian City.* Toronto: University of Toronto Press, 1990.

Breunster, K. L. Race differences in sexual activity among adolescent women: The role of neighbourhood characteristics. *American Sociological Review*, 1994, 59 (3), 408-424.

Breyfogle, D. & Dworaczek, M. *Blacks in Ontario: A Selected Bibliography, 1965-1976.* Toronto: Ontario Ministry of Labour, 1977.

Brice, J. West Indian families. In M. McGoldrick, J. K. Pearce & J. Giordano (Eds.), *Ethnicity and Family Therapy.* New York: Guilford, 1982.

Briody, E. K. *Household Labor Patterns among Mexican Americans in South Texas: Buscando Trabajo Seguro.* New York: AMS Press, 1985.

Bronfenbrenner, U. Ecological Systems Theory. In R. Vast (Ed.), *Annals of Child Development* (Volume 6). Greenwich, CT: JAI Press, 1989.

Brooks-Gunn, J. & Chase-Lansdale, L. Correlates of adolescent pregnancy and parenthood. In C. G. Fisher & R.M. Lerner (Eds.), *Applied Developmental Psychology.* Cambridge, MA: McGraw-Hill, 1993.

Brown, C. Increasing minority access to college: Seven efforts for success. *National Association of Student Personnel Administrators Journal*, 1991, 28 (3), 224-230.

Brown, L. & Root, M. P. P. (Eds.). *Diversity and Complexity in Feminist Therapy.* New York: Haworth Press, 1990.

Bruce, J. D. & Rodman, H. Black-White marriages in the United States: A review of the empirical literature. In I. R. Stuart & L. Edwin (Eds.), *Interracial Marriage: Expectations and Realities.* New York: Grossman, 1973.

Brym, R. J., Shaffir, W. & Weinfeld, M. (Eds.). *The Jews in Canada.* Toronto: Oxford University Press, 1993.

Buchignani, N. & Indra, D. M. with Srivastana, R. *Continuing Journey: A Social History of South Asians in Canada.* Toronto: McClleland & Stewart, 1985.

Buenker, J. D. & Ratner, L. A. (Eds.). *Multiculturalism in the United States: A Comparative Guide to Acculturation and Ethnicity.* Westport, CT: Greenwood Press, 1992.

Buenker, J. D. & Ratner, L. A. Bibliographical essay. In J. D. Buenker & L. A. Ratner (Eds.), *Multiculturalism in the United States: A Comparative Guide to Acculturation and Ethnicity.* Westport, CT: Greenwood Press, 1992.

Bulka, R. P. *Jewish Marriage: A Halakhic Ethic.* New York: KTAV Publishing, 1986.

Buriel, R. Cognitive styles among three generations of Mexican children. *Journal of Cross-Cultural Psychology*, 1975, 6, 417-429.

Burton, L. M. *Early and On-Time Grandmotherhood in Multigenerational Black Families.* Unpublished doctoral dissertation, Department of Sociology, University of Southern California, 1985.

Burton, L. M. Teenage childbearing as an alternative life-course strategy in multigeneration Black families. *Human Nature*, 1990, 1, 123-143.

Cabezas, A. & Kawaguchi, G.   Empirical evidence for continuing Asian American income inequality: The human capital model and labor market segmentation. In G. Y. Okihiro, S. Hune, A. A. Hansen & J. M. Liu (Eds.), *Reflections on Shattered Windows: Promises and Prospects for Asian American Studies.* Pullman, WA: Washington State University Press, 1988.

Canino, G. & Canino, I. A.   Culturally syntonic family therapy for migrant Puerto Ricans. *Hospital & Community Psychiatry*, 1982, 33, 299-303.

Cardoza, J.   Colleges alerted: Pay attention to minorities or risk future survival. *ETS Development*, 1986, 32 (3), 8-10.

Carter, B. & McGoldrick, M. (Eds.).   *The Changing Family Life Cycle: A Framework for Family Therapy* (2nd ed.). New York: Gardner, 1988.

Carter, V. & Carter, L.   *The Black Canadians: Their History and Constitution.* Edmonton, AB: Reidmore Books, 1989.

Castex, G. M.   Providing services to Hispanic/Latino populations: Profiles in diversity. *Social Work*, 1994, 39 (3), 288-96.

Cazenave, N. A.   Middle income Black families: An analysis of the provider's role. *Family Coordinator*, 1979, 28 (4), 583-593.

Centre of Criminology.   *Workshop on Collecting Race and Ethnicity Statistics in the Criminal Justice System.* Toronto: Centre of Criminology, University of Toronto, 1991.

Cerhan, J. U.   The Hmong in the United States: An overview for mental health professionals. *Journal of Counseling & Development*, 1990, 69 (1), 88-92.

Chadney, J. G.   *The Sihks of Vancouver.* New York: AMS Press, 1984.

Chan, A.   *Gold Mountain.* Vancouver, BC: New Star Books, 1983.

Chan, K. B. & Helly, D. (Eds.).   Coping with racism: The Chinese experience in Canada. *Canadian Ethnic Studies*, Special Issue, 1987, 19 (3).

Chao, C. M.   The inner heart: Therapy with Southeast Asian families. In L. A. Vargas & J. D. Koss-Chioino (Eds.), *Working with Culture: Psychotherapeutic Interventions with Ethnic Minority Children and Adolescents.* San Francisco: Jossey-Bass, 1992.

Chapman, A. B.   *Entitled to Good Loving: Black Men and Women and the Battle for Power and Love.* New York: Henry Holt, 1995.

Chase-Lansdale, L. & Brooks-Gunn, J.   Children having children: Effects on the family system. *Pediatric Annals*, 1991, 20, 467-481.

Chavez, L. R. (Ed.).   Immigrants in U.S. cities. *Urban Anthropology*, Special Issue, 1990, 19 (1-2).

Cheatham, H. E. (Ed.).   *Cultural Pluralism on Campus.* Alexandria, VA: American College Personnel Association, 1991.

Cheek, D.   *Assertive Blacks, Puzzled Whites.* San Louis Obispo, CA: Impact, 1976

Chen, A. B.   Kinship and internal migration: Filipinos in Thunder Bay. In D. R. Webster (Ed.), *The Southeast Asian Environment.* Ottawa: University of Ottawa Press, 1983.

Chen, A. B.   Studies on Filipinos in Canada: State of the art. *Canadian Ethnic Studies*, 1990, 12 (1), 83-95.

Cheng, D., Leong, F. T. L. & Geist, R.   Cultural differences in psychological distress between Asian and Caucasian American college students. *Journal of Multicultural Counseling & Development*, 1993, 21, 182-190.

Cheng, E.   *The Elder Chinese.* San Diego, CA: Center on Aging, San Diego State

University, 1978.

Cheng, M., Tsuji, G., Yau, M. & Ziegler, S. *The Every Secondary Student Survey, Fall, 1987.* Toronto: Toronto Board of Education, Research Services, Report No. 191, 1989.

Chin, J. & Cheung, Y. W. Ethnic resources and business enterprise: A study of Chinese businesses in Toronto. *Human Organization*, 1985, 44, 142-154.

Chin J. L. & Associates. *Transference and Empathy in Asian American Psychotherapy: Cultural Values and Treatment Needs.* Westport, CT: Praeger, 1993.

Chiswick, B. Labor supply and investment in child quality: A study of Jewish and non-Jewish women. *Contemporary Jewry*, 1988, 9, 35-61.

Chiswick, B. The postwar economy of American Jews. *Studies in Contemporary Jewry*, 1992, 5, 85-117.

Christiansen, J. M., Thornley-Brown, A. & Robinson, J. A. *West Indians in Toronto: Implications for Helping Professionals.* Toronto: Family Service Association of Metropolitan Toronto, 1982.

Clabrese, R. L. The public school: A source of alienation for minority parents. *Journal of Negro Education*, 1990, 59 (2), 148-154.

Clairmont, D. H. & Magill, D. W. *Africville: The Life and Death of a Canadian Black Community* (Rev. ed.). Toronto: Candian Scholars' Press, 1987.

Cleary, P. D. & Demone, H., Jr. Health and social service needs in a Northeastern metropolitan area: Ethnic group differences. *Journal of Sociology & Social Welfare*, 1988, 15 (4), 63-76.

Cohen, J. A. Chinese mediation on the eve of modernization. *California Law Review*, 1966, 54, 1201-1266.

Cohen, L. Controlarse and the problems of life among Latino immigrants. In W. A. Vega & M. R. Miranda (Eds.), *Stress and Hispanic Mental Health: Relating Research to Service Delivery.* Rockville, MD: National Institue of Mental Health, 1985.

Cohen, R. Women of color in white households: Coping strategies of live-in domestic workers. *Qualitative Sociology*, 1991, 14 (2), 197-215.

Cole, E., Espin, O. M. & Rothblum, E. (Eds.). *Refugee Women and their Mental Health: Shattered Societies, Shattered Lives.* New York: Haworth Press, 1992.

Coleman, J. S. Social capital in the creation of human capital. *American Journal of Sociology*, 1988, 94, 595-620.

Coleman, J. S. *Equality and Achievement in Education.* Boulder, CO: Westview Press, 1990.

Collins, S. M. The marginalization of the Black middle class. *Social Problems*, 1989, 36, 317-331.

Collins, S. M. Blacks on the bubble: The vulnerability of Black executives in White corporations. *Sociological Quarterly*, 1993, 34, 429-447.

Colman, C. International family therapy: A view from Kyoto, Japan. *Family Process*, 1986, 25, 651-664.

Colon, F. The family life cycle of the multiproblem poor family. In E. A. Carter & M. McGoldrick (Eds.), *The Family Life Cycle: A Framework for Family Therapy.* New York: Gardner, 1980.

Comas-Diaz, L. Culturally relevant issues and treatment implications for Hispanics. In D. R. Koslow & E. P. Salett (Eds.), *Cross Cultures in Mental Health.* Washington, D.C.: SIETAR International, 1989.

Comas-Diaz, L. & Greene, B. (Eds.). *Women of Color and Mental Health.* New York: Guilford, in press.

Commission on Minority Participation in Education & American Life. *One-Third of a Nation.* Washington, D.C.: American Council on Education, 1988.

Con, H., Con, R. J., Johnson, G., Wichberg, E. & Willmott, W. E. *From China to Canada: A History of the Chinese Community in Canada.* Toronto: McClleland & Stewart, 1982.

Coner-Edwards, A. F. & Spurlock, J. (Eds.). *Black Families in Crisis: The Middle Class.* New York: Brunner/Mazel, 1988.

Connolly, P. R. The perception of personal space among Black and White Americans. *Central States Speech Journal,* 1975, 26, 21-28.

Connor, J. W. Acculturation and family continuities in three generations of Japanese-Americans. *Journal of Marriage & the Family,* 1974a, 36, 159-165.

Connor, J. W. Acculturation and changing need patterns in Japanese-American and Caucasian-American students. *Journal of Social Psychology,* 1974b, 93, 293-294.

Connor, J. W. *Tradition and Change in Three Generations of Japanese Americans.* Chicago: Nelson Hall, 1977.

Conquergood, D., Thao, P. & Thao, X. *I Am a Shaman: A H'Mong Life Story with Ethnographic Commentary.* Minneapolis, MN: Southeast Asian Refugee Studies Project, Center for Urban & Regional Affairs, University of Minnesota, 1989.

Cordasco, F. *The Immigrant Women in North America: An Annotated Bibliography of Selected References.* Metuchen, NJ: Scarecrow Press, 1985.

Cox, F. D. *Human Intimacy: Marriage, the Family and Its Meaning* (6th ed.). Minneapolis, MN: West Publishing, 1993.

Cox, J. L. (Ed.). *Transcultural Psychiatry.* London: Croom Helm, 1986.

Cretser, G. A. (Ed.). *Intermarriage in the United States.* New York: Haworth Press, 1982.

Crissman, L. W. The segmentary structure of urban overseas Chinese communities. *Man,* 1967, 2, 185-204.

Cromwell, R. & Ruiz, R. The myth of macho dominance in decision making with Mexican-American and Chicano families. *Hispanic Journal of Behavioral Science,* 1979, 1, 355-373.

Cross, H. with G. Kenney, J. Mell & W. Zimmerman. *Employer Hiring Practices: Differential Treatment of Hispanic and Anglo Job Seekers.* Report 90-4. Washington D.C.: Urban Institute Press, 1990.

Cross, M. (Ed.). *Ethnic Minorities and Industrial Change in Europe and North America.* New York: Cambridge University Press, 1992.

Crosson, P. Four year college and university environments for minority degree achievement. *Review of Higher Education,* 1988, 11 (4), 365-382.

Cushman, P. Why the self is empty: Towards a historically situated psychology. *American Psychologist,* 1990, 45 (5), 599-611.

Dalton, J. (Ed.). *Racism on Campus: Confronting Racial Bias Through Peer Interventions.* New Directions for Student Services, # 56. San Francisco: Jossey-Bass, 1991.

Daly, A., Jennings, J., Becizett, J. U. & Leashord, B. R. Effective coping strategies of African Americans. *Social Work,* 1995, 40 (2), 240-248.

Dana, R. H. *Multicultural Assessment Perspectives for Professional Psychology.* Boston: Allyn & Bacon, 1993.

Daniel, J. H. Cultural and ethnic issues: The Black family. In E. H. Newberger & R. Bourne (Eds.), *Unhappy Families: Clinical and Research Perspectives on Family Violence.* Littleton, MA: PSG Publishing, 1985.

Danziger, M. H. *Returning to Tradition: The Contemporary Revival of Orthodox Judaism.* New Haven, CT: Yale University Press, 1989.

Danziger, S. & Radin, N. Absent does not equal uninvolved: Predictors of fathering in teen mother families. *Journal of Marriage & the Family,* 1990, 52 (3), 636-642.

Dasgupta, S. *On the Trail of Uncertain Dreams: India Immigrant Experience in America.* New York: AMS Press, 1989.

Davenport, D. S. & Yurich, J. M. Multicultural gender issues. *Journal of Counseling & Development,* 1991, 70 (1), 64-71.

Davidman, L. *Tradition in a Rootless World: Women Turn to Orthodox Judaism.* Berkeley, CA: University of California Press, 1991.

Davis, G. & Watson, G. *Blacks in Corporate America.* Garden City, NY: Doubleday, 1983.

Davis, J. D. (Ed.). *Coloring the Halls of Ivy: Leadership and Diversity in the Academy.* Boston: Anker Publishing, 1994.

Davis, J. E. Reconsidering the use of race as an explanatory variable in program evaluation. In A.-M. Madison (Ed.), *Minority Issues in Program Evaluation.* New Directions for Program Evaluation, # 53. San Francisco: Jossey-Bass, 1992.

Davis, L. G. *The Black Family in the United States: A Revised, Updated, Selectively Annotated Bibliography.* New York: Greenwood Press, 1986.

Dawidowitz, L. S. *The War Against the Jews, 1933-1945.* New York: Holt, Rinehart and Winston, 1975.

Dawson, R. *The Chinese Chameleon: An Analysis of European Conceptions of Chinese Civilization.* London: Oxford University Press, 1967.

Delacancera, V., Guamaccia, P. J. & Carillo, E. Psychosocial distress among Latinos: A critical analysis of ataque de nervios. *Humanity & Society,* 1986, 10, 431-447.

De la Garza, R. O., Bean, F. D., Bonjean, C. M., Romo, R. & Alvarez, R. (Eds.). *The Mexican-American Experience: An Interdisciplinary Anthology.* Austin, TX: University of Texas Press, 1985.

Del Castillo, R. G. *La Familia: Chicano Families in the Urban Southwest, 1848 to the Present.* Notre Dame, IN: University of Notre Dame Press, 1984.

Delgado, M. Natural support systems in the Puerto Rican community. In E. H. Newberger & R. Bourne (Eds.), *Unhappy Families: Clinical and Research Perspectives on Family Violence.* Littleton, MA: PSG Publishing, 1985.

Delgado, M. Groups in Puerto Rican spiritism: Implications for clinicians. In C. Jacobs & D. D. Bowles (Eds.), *Ethnicity and Race: Critical Concepts in Social Work.* Silver Springs, MD: National Association of Social Work, 1988.

Delgado-Gaitan, C. Socializing young children in Mexican-American families: An intergenerational perspective. In P. M. Greenfield & R. R. Cocking (Eds.), *Cross-Cultural Roots of Minority Child Development.* Hillsdale, NJ: Lawrence Erlbaum, 1994.

De Mente, B. *The Japanese Influence on America: The Impact, Challenges and Opportunity.* Lincolnwood, IL: Passport Books, 1989.

De Ridder, L. M. Teenage pregnancy: Etiology and educational interactions. *Educational Psychology Review,* 1993, 5 (1), 87-107.

DeSilva, A. *Earnings of Immigrants: A Comparartive Analysis.* Ottawa: Economic Council of Canada, 1992.

Deutscher, I., Pestello, F. P. & Pestello, F. G. *Sentiments and Acts.* New York: Aldine de Gruyter, 1993.

DeVaney, S. & Hughey, A. W. Multiculturalism in higher education: Moving from awareness to action. *New Directions in Educational Reform*, 1992, 1 (1), 27-34.

Devereux, G. *From Anxiety to Method in the Behavioral Sciences*. The Hague, Netherlands: Mouton, 1967.

Devore, W. & Schlesinger, E. G. *Ethnic-Sensitive Social Work Practice* (2nd ed.). New York: Macmillan, 1987.

De Vos, G. A. Afterword. In D. K. Reynolds, *The Quiet Therapies: Japanese Pathways to Personal Growth*. Honolulu: University of Hawaii Press, 1980.

Diaz-Guerrero, R. *Psychology of the Mexican: Culture and Personality*. Austin, TX: University of Texas Press, 1975.

Diaz-Guerrero, R. Contemporary psychology in Mexico. *Annual Review of Psychology*, 1984, 35, 83-112.

Dickson, L. The future of marriage and family in Black America. *Journal of Black Studies*, 1993, 23 (4), 472-491.

Dillard, J. L. *Black English: Its History and Usage in the United States*. New York: Knopf, 1973.

Dilworth-Anderson, P. & McAdoo, H. P. The study of ethnic minority families: Implications for practitioners and policy makers. *Family Relations*, 1988, 37 (3), 265-267.

Dilworth-Anderson, P., Burton, L. M. & Johnson, L. B. Reframing theories for understanding race, ethnicity, and families. In P. G. Boss, W. J. Doherty, R. LaRossa, W. R. Schumm & S. K. Steinmetz (Eds.), *Sourcebook of Family Theories and Methods: A Contextual Approach*. New York: Plenum, 1993.

Dinerman, I. R. Patterns of adaptation among households of U.S. bound migrants from Michoaccan, Mexico. *International Migration Review*, 1978, 12 (4), 485-501.

Dion, K. K. & Dion, K. L. Individualistic and collectivistic perspectives on gender and the cultural context of love and intimacy. *Journal of Social Issues*, 1993, 49 (3), 53-69.

Doi, L. T. *The Anatomy of Self: The Individual versus Society*. (Trans. M. A. Harbison). Tokyo: Kodansha International, 1985.

Doi, M. L., Lin, C. & Vohra-Sahu, I. *Pacific/Asian American Research: An Annotated Bibliography*. Chicago: Pacific/Asian American Mental Health Research Center, 1981.

Donohue, W. A. Ethnicity and mediation. In W. B. Gudykunst, L. P. Stewart & S. Ting-Toomey (Eds.), *Communication, Culture, and Organizational Processes*. Beverly Hills, CA: Sage, 1985.

Doo, L. Dispute settlement in Chinese-American communities. *American Journal of Comparative Law*, 1973, 21, 627-663.

Dorais, L. J. Les associations Vietnamiennes a Montreal. *Canadian Ethnic Studies*, 1992, 14 (1), 79-95.

Dorais, L. J., Pilon-Le, L. & Nguyen, H. *Exile in a Cold Land: A Vietnamese Community in Canada*. New Haven, CT: Yale Southeast Asian Studies, 1987.

Dornbusch, S., Carlsmith, J. M., Bushwall, S., Ritter, P., Leiderman, H., Hastorf, A. & Gross, R. Single parents, extended households, and the control of adolescents. *Child Development*, 1985, 56, 326-341.

Downing, K. E., MacAdams, B. & Nichols, D. P. *Reaching a Multicultural Student Community: A Handbook for Academic Librarians*. Westport, CT: Greenwood Press, 1993.

D'Oyley, V. (Ed.). *Black Presence in Multi-Ethnic Canada*. Abridged. Vancouver, BC: University of British Columbia, Centre for the Study of Curriculum & Instruction, Faculty of Education, 1977/1982.

Drachman, D. (Ed.). *Social Services to Refugee Populations.* Washington, D.C.: National Institute of Mental Health, 1990.

Drachman, D. Immigration statutes and their influence on service provision, access and use. *Social Work,* 1995, 40 (2), 188-197.

Dressler, W. W. Extended family relationships, social support, and mental health in a southern Black community. *Journal of Health & Social Behavior,* 1985, 26, 39-48.

Driedger, L. *Ethnic Canada: Identities and Inequalities.* Toronto: Copp Clark Pitman, 1987.

D'Souza, D. *Illiberal Education: The Politics of Race and Sex on Campus.* New York: Free Press, 1991.

Duncan, G., Hill, M. & Rogers, W. The changing fortunes of young and old. *American Demographics,* 1986, 8 (8), 26-33.

Dunning, R. W. Changes in marriage and the family among the northern Ojibwa. In K. Ishwaran (Ed.), *The Canadian Family: A Book of Readings.* Toronto: Holt, Rinehart & Winston, 1971.

Duran, R. P. *Hispanics' Education and Background: Predictors of College Achievement.* New York: College Entrance Examination Board, 1983.

Duryea, M. L. *Culture and Conflict: A Literature Review and Bibliography.* Victoria, BC: UVic Institute for Dispute Resolution, 1992.

Duryea, M. L. & Gundison, J. B. *Conflict and Culture: Research in Five Communities in Vancouver, British Columbia.* Victoria, BC: UVic Institute for Dispute Resolution, 1993.

Edelman, M. W. The Black family in America. In L. Tepperman & S. Wilson (Eds.), *Next of Kin.* Englewood Cliffs, NJ: Prentice-Hall, 1993.

Ehrenberg, R. G. & Murphy, S. H. What price diversity? The death of need-based financial aid at selective private colleges and universities. *Change,* 1993, 25 (4), 64-73.

Ehrenreich, B. *Fear of Falling: The Inner Life of the Middle Class.* New York: Pantheon, 1989.

Ellenson, D. *Rabbi Esriel Hildesheimer and the Creation of a Modern Jewish Orthodoxy.* Tuscaloosa, AB: University of Alabama Press, 1990.

Elliston, I. Counselling West Indian immigrants: Issues and answers. In R. J. Samuda & A. Wolfgang (Eds.), *Intercultural Counselling and Assessment: Global Perspectives.* Toronto: Hogrefe Publishing, 1985.

Endo, J. J. Assessing the educational performance of minority students: The case of Asian and Pacific Americans. In M. T. Nettles (Ed.), *The Effect of Assessment on Minority Student Populations.* New Directions for Institutional Research, # 65. San Francisco: Jossey-Bass, 1990.

Entwisle, D. R. & Alexander, K. L. Entry into school: The beginning school transition and educational stratification in the United States. *Annual Review of Sociology,* 1993, 19, 401-423.

Epstein, H. *Children of the Holocaust.* New York: Putnam, 1979.

Erickson, F. Talking down: Some cultural sources of miscommunication in interracial interviews. In A. Wolfgang (Ed.), *Nonverbal Communication: Applications and Cultural Implications.* New York: Academic, 1979.

Espin, O. Psychotherapy with Hispanic women. In P. Peddersen (Ed.), *Handbook of Cross-Cultural Counseling and Therapy.* Westport, CT: Greenwood Press, 1985.

Evans, E. N. *The Provincials.* New York: Atheneum, 1973.

Evans, L. A., Acosta, F. X., Yamamoto, J. & Hurwicz, H. L. Patient requests:

Correlates and therapeutic implications for Hispanic, Black, and Caucasian patients. *Journal of Clinical Psychology*, 1986, 42, 213-221.

Fabrega, H., Mezzich, J. & Ulrich, R. F. Black-white differences in psychopathology in an urban psychiatric population. *Comprehensive Psychiatry*, 1988, 29, 285-297.

Falicov, C. J. Mexican families. In M. McGoldrick, J. K. Pearce & J. Giordano (Eds.), *Ethnicity and Family Therapy*. New York: Guilford, 1982.

Falicov, C. J. *Latino Families in Therapy*. New York: Guilford, in press.

Falicov, C. J. & Karrer, B. M. Cultural variations in the family life cycle: The Mexican-American family. In E. A. Carter & M. McGoldrick (Eds.), *The Family Life Cycle: A Framework for Family Therapy*. New York: Gardner, 1980.

Farley, F. *Blacks and Whites: Narrowing the Gap?* Cambridge, MA: Harvard University Press, 1984.

Farley, J. E. Disproportionate Black and Hispanic unemployment in U.S. metropolitan areas. *American Journal of Economic Sociology*, 1987, 46, 129-150.

Farley, R. Blacks, Hispanics and White ethnic groups: Are Blacks uniquely disadvantaged? *American Economic Review*, 1990, 80, 237-241.

Favazza, A. R. & Faheem, A. D. *Themes in Cultural Psychiatry: An Annotated Bibliography 1975-1980*. Columbia, MO: University of Missouri Press, 1982.

Favazza, A. R. & Oman, M. *Anthropological and Cross-Cultural Themes in Mental Health: An Annotated Bibliography 1925-1974*. Columbia, MO: University of Missouri Press, 1977.

Feagin, J. R. The continuing significance of racism: Discrimination against Black students in White Colleges. *Journal of Black Studies*, 1992, 22, 546-578.

Fernandez-Kelly, M. P. & Garcia, A. Power surrendered, power restored: The politics of home and work among Hispanic women in Southern California and Southern Florida. In L. A. Tilly & P. Gurin (Eds.), *Women, Change, and Policies*. New York: Russell Sage Foundation, in press.

Fernando, S. Depression in ethnic minorities. In J. L. Cox (Ed.), *Transcultural Psychiatry*. London: Croom Helm, 1986.

Fetgin, N. Factors contributing to the academic excellence of American Jewish and Asian students. *Sociology of Education*, 1995, 68 (1), 18-30.

Findley, S. E. & Williams, L. *Women who go and women who stay: Reflections of family migration processes in a changing world*. Geneva, Switzerland: World Employment Programme, Working Paper #176, 1991.

Fine, M., Schwebel, A. I. & James-Myers, L. Family stability in black families: Values underlying three different perspectives. *Journal of Comparative Family Studies*, 1987, 18 (1), 1-23.

Fischer, M. M. J. Ethnicity and the post-modern arts of memory. In J. Clifford & G. E. Marcus (Eds.), *Writing Culture: The Poetics and Politics of Ethnography*. Berkeley, CA: University of California Press, 1986.

Fisher, S. *From Margin to Mainstream: The Social Progress of Black Americans* (2nd ed.). Lanham, MD: Rowman & Littlefield, 1992.

Fitzpatrick, J. *Puerto Rican Americans: The Meaning of Migration to the Mainland*. Englewood Cliffs, NJ: Prentice-Hall, 1971.

Fitzpatrick, J. & Gurak, D. *Hispanic Intermarriage in New York City*. New York: Fordham University Hispanic Research Center, 1979.

Flanagan, T. & Foster, J. (Eds.). The Metis: Past and present. *Canadian Ethnic Studies*, Special Issue, 1985, 17 (2).

Fleming, J. *Blacks in College: A Comparative Study of Students' Success in Black and White Institutions*. San Francisco: Jossey-Bass, 1984.

Flowers, R. B. *Minorities and Criminality.* Westport, CT: Greenwood Press, 1988.

Foggo, C. *Pourin' Down Rain.* Calgary, AB: Detselig Enterprises, 1990.

Fong, S. L. M. Assimilation and changing roles of Chinese Americans. *Journal of Social Issues,* 1973, 29, 115-127.

Fong, T. P. *The First Suburban Chinatown: The Remaking of Monterey Park, California.* Philadelphia, PA: Temple University Press, 1993.

Fonsela, J. W. & Andrews, A. C. *The Atlas of American Higher Education.* New York: New York University Press, 1993.

Foster, D. W. *Sourcebook of Hispanic Culture in the United States.* Chicago: American Library Association, 1982.

Fowler, F. J. *1975 Community Survey: A Study of the Jewish Population of Greater Boston.* Boston, MA: Combined Jewish Philanthropies of Greater Boston, 1977.

Franklin, D. L. Race, class, and adolescent pregnancy: An ecological analysis. *American Journal of Orthopsychiatry,* 1988a, 58 (3), 339-354.

Franklin, D. L. The impact of early childbearing on developmental outcomes: The case of black adolescent parenting. *Family Relations,* 1988b, 37 (3), 268-274.

Franklin, A. J. Therapy with African-American men. *Families in Society,* 1992, 73 (6), 350-355.

Freeman, R. B. & Holzer, H. J. (Eds.). *The Black Youth Employment Crisis.* Chicago: University of Chicago Press, 1986.

Fugita, S. F. & O'Brien, D. J. *Japanese American Ethnicity: The Persistance of Community.* Seattle, WA: University of Washington Press, 1991.

Fulani, L. (Ed.). *The Politics of Race and Gender in Therapy.* New York: Haworth, 1988.

Fulmer, R. H. Lower-income and professional families: A comparison of structure and life cycle process. In B. Carter & M. McGoldrick (Eds.), *The Changing Family Life Cycle: A Framework for Family Therapy* (2nd ed.). New York: Gardner, 1988.

Furstenberg, F. Teen mothers 17 years later: They've recovered but their children are maladjusted. *Professional Newsletter of Family Therapy Practitioners,* 1986, 46, 11.

Furstenberg, F., Brooks-Gunn, J. & Chase-Lansdale, L. Teenaged pregnancy and childbearing. *American Psychologist,* 1989, 44, 315-318.

Gaff, J. Beyond politics: The educational issues inherent in multicultural education. *Change,* 1992, 24 (1), 31-35.

Gainen, J. & Boice, R. (Eds.). *Building a Diverse Faculty.* New Directions for Teaching & Learning, #53. San Francisco: Jossey-Bass, 1993.

Ganesan, S., Fine, S. & Lin, T. Y. Psychiatric symptoms in refugee families from South-East Asia: Therapeutic challenges. *American Journal of Psychotherapy,* 1989, 43, 218-228.

Gann, L. H. *The Hispanics in the United States: A History.* Boulder, CO: Westview Press, 1986.

Gans, H. J. Deconstructing the underclass. *Journal of the American Planning Association,* 1990, 56, 271-277.

Garbarino, J. *Children in Danger: Coping with the Consequences of Community Violence.* San Francisco: Jossey-Bass, 1992.

Garcia, E. E. "Hispanic" children: Homicide, equality, and related policy issues. *Educational Psychology Review,* 1992, 4 (1), 69-93.

Garcia, R. L. *Teaching in a Pluralistic Society: Concepts, Models, Strategies.* New York: Harper & Row, 1982.

Garcia-Preto, N.   Puerto Rican families. In M. McGoldrick, J. K. Pearce & J. Giordano (Eds.), *Ethnicity and Family Therapy.* New York: Guilford, 1982.

Gareau, J.   *The Nine Nations of North America.* Boston: Houghton Mifflin, 1981.

Garfinkel, B. & Northrup, G. (Eds.).   *Adolescent Suicide.* New York: Haworth, 1990.

Gary, L. E. (Ed.).   *Black Men.* Beverly Hills, CA: Sage, 1981.

Gary, L. E.   Attitudes of Black adults towards community mental health centers. *Hospital & Community Psychiatry,* 1987, 38, 1100-1105.

Gaw, A.   Chinese Americans. In A. Gaw (Ed.), *Cross-Cultural Psychiatry.* Boston: John Wright-PSG, 1982.

Gay, G.   Designing relevant curricula for diverse learners. *Education & Urban Society,* 1988, 20 (4), 327-340.

Gelfand, D. E.   *Aging: The Ethnic Factor.* Boston: Little, Brown 1982.

Gelfand, D. E. & Barresi, C. M. (Eds.).   *Ethnic Dimensions of Aging.* New York: Springer, 1987.

Gelfand, D. E. & Bialik-Gilad, R.   Immigration reform and social work. *Social Work,* 1989, 34 (1), 23-27.

Gelfand, D. E. & Yee, B. W. K.   Trends and forces: Influence of immigration, migration, and acculturation on the fabric of aging in America. In E. P. Stanford & F. M. Torres-Gil (Eds.), *Diversity: New Approaches to Ethnic Minority Aging.* Amityville, NY: Baywood Publishing, 1992.

Gendrot, S. & Turner, J.   Ethnicity and class: Politics on Manhattan's Lower East Side. *Ethnic Groups,* 1983, 5, 79-108.

Gibbs, J. T.   The interpersonal orientation in mental health consultation: Toward a model of ethnic variations in counseling. *Journal of Community Psychology,* 1980, 8, 195-207.

Gibbs, J. T.   Black adolescents and youth: An endangered species. *American Journal of Orthopsychiatry,* 1984, 54 (1), 6-21.

Gibbs, J. T.   Black adolescents and youth: An update on an endangered species. In R. Jones (Ed.), *Black Adolescents.* Berkeley, CA: Cobb & Henry, 1989a.

Gibbs, J. T.   Black American adolescents. In J. T. Gibbs, L. Huang & Associates (Eds.), *Children of Color: Psychological Intervention with Minority Youth.* San Francisco: Jossey-Bass, 1989b.

Gibson, A., with Lewis, C.   *A Light in the Dark Tunnel: Ten Years of Westindian Concern and Caribbean House.* London: Centre for Caribbean Studies, 1985.

Gibson, M. & Ogbu, J. (Eds.).   *Minority Status and Schooling: A Comparative Study of Immigrant and Involuntary Minorities.* New York: Garland, 1991.

Giddings, P.   *When and Where I Enter: The Impact of Black Women on Race and Sex in America.* New York: Bantam, 1984.

Gilbert, D. & Kahl, J. A.   *The American Class Structure: A New Synthesis.* Chicago: Dorsey, 1987.

Glasgow, D.   *The Black Underclass.* New York: Vintage, 1981.

Glazer, N. (Ed.).   *Clamor at the Gates.* San Francisco: Institute for Contemporary Studies, 1985.

Glenn, E. N.   *Issei, Nisei, War Bride: Three Generations of Japanese-American Women in Domestic Service.* Philadelphia, PA: Temple University Press, 1986.

Godfrey, B. J.   *Neighbourhoods in Transition: The Making of San Francisco's Ethnic and Nonconformist Communities.* Berkeley, CA: University of California Press, 1988.

Goldscheider, C. R.   *Jewish Community and Change: Emerging Patterns in America.*

Bloomington, IN: Indiana University Press, 1985.

Goldscheider, C. R. & Kobrin, F. E. Ethnic continuity and the process of self-employment. *Ethnicity*, 1980, 7, 256-278.

Goldscheider, C. R. & Zuckerman, A. *The Transformation of the Jews.* Chicago: University of Chicago Press, 1984.

Goldsmith, P. D. *When I Rise Cryin' Holy: Afro-American Denominationalism on the Georgia Coast.* New York: AMS Press, 1989.

Goldstein, J. & Segall, A. Ethnic intermarriage and ethnic identity. *Canadian Ethnic Studies*, 1985, 17 (3), 60-71.

Goldstein, S. & Kosmin, B. Religious and ethnic self-identification in the United States 1989-90: A case study of the Jewish population. *Ethnic Groups*, 1992, 9, 219-245.

Goldwurm, H. *History of the Jewish People: The Second Temple Era.* New York: Mesorah, 1982.

Gollnick, D. M., Osayande, K. I. M. & Levy, J. (Eds.). *Multicultural Teacher Education: Case Studies of Thirteen Programs* (Volume 2). Washington, D.C.: Commission on Multicultural Education, 1981.

Gonzalez, A. The sex roles of the traditional Mexican family: A comparison of Chicano and Anglo students' attitudes. *Journal of Cross-Cultural Psychology*, 1982, 13, 330-339.

Goossen, J. The migration of French West Indian women to Metropolitan France. *Anthropological Quarterly*, 1976, 49 (1), 45-52.

Gordon, A. I. *Intermarriage.* Boston: Beacon Press, 1964.

Gordon, M. M. *Assimilation in American Life.* New York: Oxford University Press, 1964.

Grayson, J. P. *The Social Construction of 'Visible Minority' for Students of Chinese Origin.* Toronto: Institute for Social Research, York University, 1994a.

Grayson, J. P. *Racialization and Black Student Identity at York University.* Toronto: Institute for Social Research, York University, 1994b.

Grayson, J. P. *Race on Campus: Outcomes of the First Year Experience at York University.* Toronto: Institute for Social Research, York University, 1994c.

Green, M. F. *Minorities on Campus: A Handbook for Enhancing Diversity.* Washington, D.C.: American Council on Education, 1988.

Greenblum, J. Medical and health orientations of American Jews: A case of diminishing distinctiveness. *Social Science & Medicine*, 1974, 8, 127-134.

Greenfield, P. M. & Cocking, R. R. (Eds.). *Cross-Cultural Roots of Minority Child Development.* Hillsdale, NJ: Lawrence Erlbaum, 1994.

Gregorovich, A. *Canadian Ethnic Groups Bibliography: A Selected Bibliography of Ethnocultural Groups in Canada and the Province of Ontario.* Toronto: Ontario Department of the Provincial Secretary & Citizenship, 1972.

Grier, W. & Cobbs, P. *Black Rage.* New York: Basic, 1968.

Griffin, J. Emotional support providers and psychological distress among Anglo- and Mexican-Americans. *Community Mental Health Journal*, 1984, 20, 182-201.

Griffith, J. E. & Villavicencio, S. Relationship among acculturation, sociodemographic characteristics, and social support in Mexican American adults. *Hispanic Journal of Behavioral Sciences*, 1985, 7, 75-92.

Gross, M. *Learning Readiness in Two Jewish Groups: A Study of Cultural Deprivation.* New York: Center for Urban Education, 1967.

Gross, S. R. & Mauro, R. *Death and Discrimination: Racial Disparities in Capital*

Sentencing. Boston: Northeastern University Press, 1989.

Guamaccia, P. J. Nervios and ataque de nervios in the Latin community: Socio-somatic expressions of distress. *Sante, Culture, Health*, 1989, 6 (1), 25-37.

Guttentag, M. & Secord, P. F. *Too Many Women? The Sex Ratio Question.* Beverly Hills, CA: Sage, 1983.

Hacker, A. *Two Nations: Black and White, Separate, Hostile, Unequal.* New York: Scribners, 1992.

Haglund, E. Japan: Cultural considerations. *International Journal of Intercultural Relations*, 1984, 8, 61-76.

Hale-Benson, J. E. *Black Children: Their Roots, Culture, and Learning Styles.* Baltimore, MD: Johns Hopkins University Press, 1982.

Hall, E. T. *The Silent Language.* New York: Fawcett, 1959.

Hall, E. T. *The Hidden Dimension.* Garden City, NY: Anchor, 1969.

Hall, E. T. *Beyond Culture.* Garden City, New York: Anchor Books, 1976.

Halli, S. S. Minority group status and fertility of Chinese and Japanese in Canada. *Canadian Ethnic Studies*, 1987a, 19 (2), 44-66.

Halli, S. S. *How Minority Status Affects Fertility.* Westport, CT: Greenwood Press, 1987b.

Halli, S., Trovato, F. & Driedger, L. (Eds.). *Ethnic Demography: Canadian Immigrant, Racial and Cultural Variations.* Ottawa: Carleton University Press 1990a.

Halli, S., Trovato, F. & Driedger, L. The social demography of ethnic groups. In S. Halli, F. Trovato & L. Driedger (Eds.), *Ethnic Demography: Canadian Immigrant, Racial and Cultural Variations.* Ottawa: Carleton University Press 1990b.

Hampton, R. L. *Black Family Violence: Current Research & Theory.* Lexington, MA: DC Heath, 1991.

Hansen, J. C. & Falicov, C. E. (Eds.). *Cultural Perspectives in Family Therapy.* Rockville, MD: Aspen Systems Corporation, 1983.

Hardy, K. V. The theoretical myth of sameness: A critical issue in family therapy and treatment. In G. Saba, B. Karrer & K. V. Hardy (Eds.), *Minorities and Family Therapy.* New York: Haworth, 1990.

Harris, F. & Wilkins, R. *Quiet Riots: Race and Poverty in the United States.* New York: Pantheon, 1988.

Harris, M. G. *Cholas: Latino Girls and Gangs.* New York: AMS Press, 1986.

Harris, P. R. & Moran, R. T. *Managing Cultural Differences: High-Performance Strategies for a New World of Business* (3d ed.). Houston, TX: Gulf Publishing, 1991.

Harrison, A., Serafica, F. & McAdoo, H. Ethic families of color. In R. D. Parke (Ed.), *Review of Child Development Research* (Volume 7): The Family. Chicago: University of Chicago Press, 1984.

Harrison, B. Non parlo ne inglese, ne francese: "I can't speak English or French." *Canadian Social Trends*, 1993, 31, 26-28.

Harrison, B. & Bluestone, B. *The Great U-Turn.* New York: Basic, 1988.

Harrison, D. F., Woderaska, J. S. & Thyer, B. A. (Eds.). *Cultural Diversity and Social Work Practice.* Springfield, IL: Thomas, 1992.

Hartzman, C. A. *Not Yet Canadians: The Latin American Immigrant in Nova Scotia.* Halifax, NS: International Education Centre, St. Mary's University, 1991.

Hawkes, G. & Taylor, M. Power structure in Mexican and Mexican American farm labor families. *Journal of Marriage & the Family*, 1975, 31, 807-811.

Hawkins, D. F. (Ed.). *Homicide Among Black Americans*. New York: University Press of America, 1986.

Hawkins, D. F. Explaining the Black homicide rate. *Journal of Interpersonal Violence*, 1990, 5, 151-163.

Hawkins, D. F. Crime and ethnicity. In B. Forst (Ed.), *The Socioeconomics of Crime and Justice*. New York: Sharpe, 1993.

Hawkins, D. F. Ethnicity: The forgotten dimension of American social control. In G. S. Bridges & M. A. Myers (Eds.), *Inequality, Crime, and Social Control*. Boulder, CO: Westview Press, 1994.

Hawkins, F. *Canada and Immigration: Public Policy and Public Concern* (2nd ed.). Kingston: McGill-Queen's University Press, 1988.

Hawkins, F. *Critical Years in Immigration: Canada and Australia Compared* (2nd ed.). Kingston: McGill-Queen's University Press, 1991.

Hayes-Bautista, D. E. Young Latinos, older Anglos, and public policy: Lessons from California. In E. P. Stanford & F. M. Torres-Gil (Eds.), *Diversity: New Approaches to Ethnic Minority Aging*. Amityville, NY: Baywood Publishing, 1992.

Head, W. *The Black Presence in the Canadian Mosaic: A Study of Perception and the Practice of Discrimination Against Blacks in Metropolitan Toronto*. Toronto: Human Rights Commission, 1975.

Health and Welfare Canada. *Canada Task Force in Mental Health Issues Affecting Immigrants and Refugees: Review of the Literature on Migrant Mental Health*. Ottawa: Health & Welfare Canada, 1988.

Heer, D. M. The trend of interfaith marriages in Canada: 1922-1957. In K. Ishwaran (Ed.), *The Canadian Family: A Book of Readings*. Toronto: Holt, Rinehart & Winston, 1971.

Heer, D. M. The prevalence of Black-White marriage in the United States, 1960 and 1970. *Journal of Marriage & the Family*, 1974, 36, 246-258.

Heer, D. M. The trend of interfaith marriages in Canada: 1922-1972 In K. Ishwaran (Ed.), *The Canadian Family: A Book of Readings* (Rev. ed.). Toronto: Holt, Rinehart & Winston, 1976.

Hegar, R. L. & Grief, G. L. Parental abduction of children from interracial and cross-cultural marriages. *Journal of Comparative Family Studies*, 1994, 25 (1), 135-142.

Heilman, S. & Cohen, S. M. *Cosmopolitan Parochials: Modern Orthodox Jews in America*. Chicago: University of Chicago Press, 1989.

Helmreich, W. B. *The World of the Yeshiva: An Intimate Portrait*. New Haven, CT: Yale University Press, 1986.

Helms, J. E. Toward a theoretical explanation of the effects of race on counseling: A Black and White Model. *Counseling Psychologist*, 1984, 12 (4), 153-164.

Helms, J. E. (Ed.). *Black and White Racial Identity: Theory, Research and Practice*. New York: Greenwood Press, 1990.

Henricks, G. L. *The Dominican Diaspora: From the Dominican Republic to New York City*. New York: Columbia University, Teachers College Press, 1974.

Henry, F. *Forgotten Canadians: The Blacks of Nova Scotia*. Toronto: Longman Canada, 1973.

Henry, F. & Ginzberg, E. *Who Gets the Work: A Test of Racial Discrimination in Employment*. Toronto: Urban Alliance on Race Relations & Social Planning Council of Metropolitan Toronto, 1986.

Herberg, E. N. *Ethnic Groups in Canada: Adaptations and Transitions*. Toronto: Nelson, 1989.

Herz, F. M. & Rosen, E. J. Jewish families. In M. McGoldrick, J. K. Pearce & J. Giordano (Eds.), *Ethnicity and Family Therapy.* New York: Guilford, 1982.

Hill, P. J. Multiculturalism: The crucial philosophy and organizational issues. *Change,* 1991, 23 (4), 38-47.

Hill, R. *The Strengths of Black Families.* New York: Emerson-Hall, 1972.

Hill, R. *Informal Adoption Among Black Families.* Washington, D.C.: National Urban League, 1977.

Hilliard, A. Alternatives to IQ testing: An approach to the identification of gifted minority children. In J. E. Hale-Benson (Ed.), *Black Children: Their Roots, Culture, and Learning Styles.* Baltimore, MD; John Hopkins University Press, 1986.

Hines, P. M. The family life cycle of poor black families. In B. Carter & M. McGoldrick (Eds.), *The Changing Family Life Cycle: A Framework for Family Therapy* (2nd ed.). New York: Gardner, 1988.

Hines, P., Garcia-Preto, N., McGoldrick, M., Almeida, R. & Weltman, S. Intergenerational relationships across cultures. *Families in Society,* 1992, 73 (6).

Hines, P. M. African American mothers. *Journal of Feminist Family Therapy,* 1990, 2 (2), 23-32.

Hines, P. M. & Boyd-Franklin, N. Black families. In M. McGoldrick, J. K. Pearce & J. Giordano (Eds.), *Ethnicity and Family Therapy.* New York: Guilford, 1982.

Hirata, L. C. *Free, Indentured, Enslaved: Chinese Prostitutes in Nineteenth Century America.* Boston: Houghton-Mifflin, 1979.

Hirschman, C. & Wong, M. G. Trends in socioeconomic achievement among immigrant and native-born Asian-Americans. *Sociological Quarterly,* 1981, 22, 495-513.

Hirschman, C. & Wong, M. G. The extraordinary educational attainment of Asian Americans: A search for historical evidence and explanation. *Social Forces,* 1986, 65, 1-27.

Ho, C. G. T. The internationalization of kinship and the feminization of Caribbean migration: The case of Afro-Trinidadian immigrants in Los Angeles. *Human Organization,* 1993, 52 (1), 32-40.

Ho, D. Y. F. On the concept of face. *American Journal of Sociology,* 1976, 81, 867-884.

Ho, D. Y. F. Cognitive socialization in Confucian heritage cultures. In P. M. Greenfield & R. R. Cocking (Eds.), *Cross-Cultural Roots of Minority Child Development.* Hillsdale, NJ: Lawrence Erlbaum, 1994.

Ho, H. K. *Family Therapy with Ethnic Minorities.* Newbury Park, CA: Sage, 1987.

Ho, M. K. Differential application of treatment modalities with Asian American youth. In L. A. Vargas & J. D. Koss-Chioino (Eds.), *Working with Culture: Psychotherapeutic Interventions with Ethnic Minority Children and Adolescents.* San Francisco: Jossey-Bass, 1992a.

Ho, M. K. *Minority Children and Adolescents in Therapy.* Newbury Park, CA: Sage, 1992b.

Hofstede, G. *Cultural Consequences: International Differences in Work-Related Values.* Beverly Hills, CA: Sage, 1984.

Hogan, D. P. *Transitions and Social Change: The Early Lives of American Men.* New York: Academic, 1981.

Hogan, D. P. The demography of life-span transitions: Temporal and gender comparisons. In A. Rossi (Ed.), *Gender and the Life Course.* New York: Aldine, 1985.

Holder, M. *History of the Jewish People: From Yavneh to Pumbedisa.* New York:

Mesorah, 1986.

Hong, G. K. Application of cultural and environmental issues in family therapy with immigrant Chinese Americans. *Journal of Strategic & Systemic Therapies*, 1989, 8, 14-21.

Hooks, B. Representing whiteness in the black imagination. In L. Grossberg (Ed.), *Cultural Studies*. New York: Routledge, 1992.

Hopper, K., Susser, E. & Conover, S. Economics of makeshift: Deindustrialization and homelessness in New York City. *Urban Anthropology*, 1985, 13 (2), 183-236.

Hornby, J. *Black Islanders: Prince Edward Islands Historical Black Community*. Charlettetown, PEI: Institute of Island Studies, 1991.

Horowitz, R. *Honor and the American Dream: Culture and Identity in a Chicano Community*. New Brunswick, NJ: Rutgers University Press, 1983.

Howze, B. Black suicides: Final act of alienation. *Human Behavior*, 1979, 8 (2), 59-60.

Hsia, J. *Asian Americans in Higher Education and at Work*. Hillsdale, NJ: Lawrence Erlbaum, 1988.

Hsu, F. *Iemoto: The Heart of Japan*. Cambridge, MA: Schenkman, 1975.

Huang, K. & Uba, L. Premarital sexual behavior among Chinese college students in the United States. *Archives of Sexual Behavior*, 1992, 21, 227-240.

Hunter, A. G. & Ensinger, M. The diversity and fluidity of children's living arrangements: Family transitions in an urban, Afro-American community. *Journal of Marriage & the Family*, 1992, 54 (2), 418-426.

Hurh, W. M. & Kim, K. C. *Korean Immigrants in America: A Structural Analysis of Ethnic Confinement and Adhesive Adaptation*. Washington, D.C.: Association of University Presses, 1984.

Irish, D. P., Lundquist, K. F. & Nelsen, V. J. (Eds.). *Ethnic Variations in Dying, Death and Grief: Diversity in Universality*. Washington, D.C.: Taylor & Francis, 1993.

Irving, H. H. & Benjamin, M. *Family Mediation: Contemporary Issues*. Thousand Oaks, CA: Sage, 1995.

Irving, H. H. & Benjamin, M. *Family Mediation in Canada and Israel: A Comparative Analysis*. Jerusalem: The Hebrew University of Jerusalem, Occasional Paper #11, 1992.

Ishwaran, K. (Ed.). *The Canadian Family: A Book of Readings*. Toronto: Holt, Rinehart & Winston, 1971.

Ishwaran, K. (Ed.). *The Canadian Family: A Book of Readings* (Rev. ed.). Toronto: Holt, Rinehart & Winston, 1976.

Ishwaran, K. (Ed.). *Childhood and Adolescence in Canada*. Toronto: McGraw-Hill Ryerson, 1979.

Ishwaran, K. (Ed.). *The Canadian Family*. Toronto: Gage, 1983.

Ivey, A. E. Cultural intentionality: The core of effective helping. *Counselor Education & Supervision*, 1987, 26, 168-172.

Ivey, A. E., Ivey, M. B. & Simek-Morgan, L. *Counseling and Psychotherapy: A Multicultural Perspective* (3d ed.). Boston: Allyn & Bacon, 1993.

Jacobs, A. G. Social integration of Salvadoran refugees. *Social Work*, 1994, 39 (3), 307-312.

Jacobs, J. *Revolving Doors: Sex Segregation and Women's Careers*. Stanford, CA: Stanford University Press, 1989.

Jasso, G. & Rosenzweig, M. *The New Chosen People: Immigrants in the United States.* New York: Russell Sage Foundation, 1990.

Jaynes, G. D. & Williams, R. M., Jr. *A Common Destiny: Blacks and American Society.* Washington, D.C.: National Academy Press, 1989.

Jencks, C. *Rethinking Social Policy: Race, Poverty, and the Underclass.* New York: Harper Perennial, 1992.

Jencks, C. & Peterson, P. E. (Eds.). *The Urban Underclass.* Washington, D.C.: Brookings Institute, 1991.

Jenkins, S. & Diamond, B. Ethnicity and foster care: Census data as predictors of placement variables. *American Journal of Orthopsychiatry*, 1985, 55 (2), 267-276.

Jiobu, R. M. Ethnic hegemony and the Japanese in California. *American Sociological Review*, 1988, 53, 353-367.

Johnson, F. A., Marsella, A. J. & Johnson, C. L. Social and psychological aspects of verbal behavior in Japanese Americans. *American Journal of Psychiatry*, 1974, 131, 580-583.

Johnson, G. E. Chinese family and community in Canada: Tradition and change. In J. L. Elliot (Ed.), *Two Nations, Many Cultures: Ethnic Groups in Canada.* Toronto: Prentice-Hall, 1979.

Johnson, L. & Smith, S. *Dealing with Diversity Through Multicultural Fiction: Library-Classroom Partnerships.* Chicago: American Library Association, 1993.

Jones, A. C., Terrell, M. C. & Duggar, M. The role of student affairs in fostering cultural diversity in higher education. *National Association of Student Personnel Administrators Journal*, 1991, 28 (2), 121-127.

Jones, E. L. Courtesy bias in South-East Asian surveys. *International Social Science Journal*, 1963, 15, 70-76.

Jones, J. *Labor of Love, Labor of Sorrow: Black Women, Work, and the Family From Slavery to the Present.* New York: Basic, 1985.

Jones, J. M. Our similarities are different: Toward a psychology of affirmative diversity. In E. J. Trickett, R. J. Watts & D. Birman (Eds.), *Human Diversity: Perspectives on People in Context.* San Francisco: Jossey-Bass, 1994.

Jones, R. L. (Ed.). *Black Psychology.* New York: Harper-Collins, 1972.

Jones, W. T. Perspectives on ethnicity. In L. V. Moore (Ed.), *Evolving Theoretical Perspectives on Students.* New Directions for Student Services, #51. San Francisco: Jossey-Bass, 1990.

Jones, E. F. & Associates. *Teenage Pregnancy in Industrialized Countries: A Study.* New Haven: Yale University Press, 1986.

Joy, A. *Ethnicity in Canada: Social Accomodation and Cultural Persistence among the Sihks and the Portuguese.* New York: AMS Press, 1989.

Kaczmarek, P., Backlund, B. & Biemer, P. The dynamics of ending a romantic relationship: An empirical account of grief in college students. *Journal of College Student Development*, 1990, 31 (4), 319-324.

Kadushin, C. *The American Intellectual Elite.* Boston: Little, Brown, 1974.

Kaganoff, N. M. Judaica Americana. *American Jewish History*, 1990-91, 80 (2), 230-267.

Kahn, A. *Listen While I Tell You: A Story of the Jews of St. John's, Newfoundland.* St. John's, NF: ISER Publishing, 1987.

Kalbach, W. E. Propensities for intermarriage in Canada, as reflected in the ethnic origins of husbands and their wives: 1961-1971. In K. Ishwaran (Ed.), *Marriage and Divorce in Canada.* Toronto: Methuen, 1983.

Kallen, E. Family lifestyles and Jewish culture. In K. Ishwaran (Ed.), *The Canadian Family* (Rev. ed.). Toronto: Holt, Rinehart & Winston, 1976.

Kallen, E. *Ethnicity and Human Rights in Canada* (2nd ed.). Toronto: Oxford University Press, 1995.

Kamen, R. M. *Growing Up Hasidic: Education and Socialization in the Bobover Hasidic Community.* New York: AMS Press, 1985.

Kasarda, J. D. Urban industrial transition and the underclass. *Annals of the American Academy of Political & Social Sciences,* 1989, 501, 26-47.

Kasinitz, P. *Caribbean New York: Black Immigrants and the Politics of Race.* Ithaca, NY: Cornell University Press, 1992.

Katz, J. H. *White Awareness: Handbook for Anti-Racism Training.* Norman, OK: University of Oklahoma Press, 1978.

Katz, M. *The Undeserving Poor: From the War on Poverty to the War on Welfare.* New York: Pantheon, 1989.

Katz, M. (Ed.). *The "Underclass" Debate and the Transformation of Urban America.* New York: Social Science Research Council, in press.

Katz, M. B. *In the Shadow of the Poorhouse: A Social History of Welfare in America.* New York: Basic, 1986.

Kaufman, D. R. *Rachel's Daughter: Newly Orthodox Jewish Women.* New Brunswick, NJ: Rutgers University Press, 1991.

Keefe, S. E. Real and ideal extended familism among Mexican-Americans and Anglo-Americans: On the meaning of 'close' family ties. *Human Organization,* 1984, 43, 65-70.

Keefe, S. E. & Padilla, A. M. *Chicano Ethnicity.* Albuquerque, NM: University of New Mexico Press, 1987.

Keefe, S. E., Padilla, A. M. & Carlos, L. M. *Emotional Support Systems in Two Cultures: A Comparison of Mexican Americans and Anglo Americans.* Los Angeles: University of California, 1978.

Keefe, S. E., Padilla, A. M. & Carlos, L. M. The Mexican-American extended family as an emotional support system. *Human Organization,* 1979, 38, 144-152.

Keller, G. D., Deneen, J. R. & Magallan, R. J. (Eds.). *Assessment and Access: Hispanics in Higher Education.* Albany, NY: State University of New York Press, 1991.

Kendis, K. O. *A Matter of Comfort: Ethnic Maintenance and Ethnic Style Among Third Generation Japanese.* New York: AMS Press, 1989.

Kenkel, W. Black-white differences in age at marriage: Expectations of low-income high school girls. *Journal of Negro Education,* 1981, 50, 425-438.

Kiefer, C. W. Notes on anthropology and the minority elderly. *The Gerontologist,* 1971, 1, 94-98.

Kiefer, C. W. *Changing Cultures, Changing Lives: An Ethnographic Study of Three Generations of Japanese Americans.* San Francisco: Jossey-Bass, 1974.

Kikumura, A. *Through Harsh Winters: The Life of Japanese Immigrant Women.* Novato, CA: Chandler & Sharp, 1981.

Kim, B. L. C. *The Asian Americans: Changing Patterns, Changing Needs.* Montclair NJ: Association of Korean Christian Scholars in North America, 1978.

Kim, E.-Y. Career choice among second-generation Korean-Americans: Reflections of a cultural model of success. *Anthropology & Education,* 1993, 24 (3), 224-248.

Kim, H.-C. *A Legal History of Asian America, 1790-1990.* Westport, CT: Greenwood Press, 1994.

Kim, I. *The New Urban Immigrants: The Korean Community in New York*. Princeton, NJ: Princeton University Press, 1981.

Kim, I. The Koreans: Small business in an urban frontier. In N. Foner (Ed.), *New Immigrants in New York*. New York: Columbia University Press, 1987.

Kim, U. & Choi, S.-H. Individualism, collectivism, and child development: A Korean perspective. In P. M. Greenfield & R. R. Cocking (Eds.), *Cross-Cultural Roots of Minority Child Development*. Hillsdale, NJ: Lawrence Erlbaum, 1994.

Kim, U., Triandis, H. C., Kagitcibasi, G., Choi, S.-C. & Yoon, G. (Eds.). *Individualism and Collectivism: Theory, Method and Applications*. Cross-Cultural Research and Methodology Series (Volume 18). Thousand Oaks, CA: Sage, 1994.

Kirmayer, L. J. Culture, affect and somatization. *Transcultural Psychiatric Research Review*, 1984, 21, 159-188.

Kirschenman, J. & Neckerman, K. M. "We'd love to hire them, but": The meaning of race for employers. In C. Jencks & P. E. Peterson (Eds.), *The Urban Underclass*. Washinton, D.C.: Brookings Institute, 1991.

Kitano, H. H. L. *Japanese Americans: The Evolution of a Sub-Culture* (2nd ed.). Englewood Cliffs, NJ: Prentice-Hall, 1976.

Kitano, H. H. L. & Daniels, R. *Asian Americans: Emerging Minorities*. Englewood Cliffs, NJ: Prentice-Hall, 1990.

Kitano, H. H. L. & Yeung, W.-T. Chinese interracial marriage. *Marriage & Family Review*, 1982, 5, 35-48.

Kitano, H. H. L., Yeung, W.-T., Chai, L. & Hatanaka, H. Asian American interracial marriage. *Journal of Marriage & the Family*, 1984, 46, 179-190.

Kitayama, S. & Markus, H. R. (Eds.). *Emotion and Culture: Empirical Studies of Mutual Influence*. Washington, D.C.: American Psychological Association, 1994.

Knoll, T. *Becoming American: Asian Sojourners, Immigrants, and Refugees in Western United States*. Portland, OR: Coast to Coast Books, 1982.

Knox, D. H. Spirituality: A tool in the assessment and treatment of Black alcoholics and their families. *Alcoholism Treatment Quarterly*, 1985, 2 (3/4), 31-44.

Kochman, T. Orality and literacy as factors of 'Black' and 'White' communication behavior. *Linguistics*, 1974, 136, 91-117.

Kochman, T. *Black and White Styles in Conflict*. Chicago: University of Chicago Press, 1981.

Kochman, T. Black verbal dueling strategies in interethnic communication. In Y. Y. Kim (Ed.), *Interethnic Communication: Current Research*. Beverly Hills, CA: Sage, 1986.

Kolody, B., Vega, W., Meinhardt, K. & Bensussen, G. The correspondence of health complaints and expressive symptoms among Mexican Americans and Anglos. *Journal of Nervous & Mental Disease*, 1986, 174, 221-228.

Koltun, E. *The Jewish Woman*. New York: Schocken, 1976.

Kong, S. L. Counselling Chinese immigrants: Issues and answers. In R. J. Samuda & A. Wolfgang (Eds.), *Intercultural Counselling and Assessment: Global Perspectives*. Toronto: Hogrefe Publishing, 1985.

Koss-Chioino, J. D. & Vargas, L. A. Through the cultural looking glass: A model for understanding culturally responsive psychotherapies. In L. A. Vargas & J. D. Koss-Chioino (Eds.), *Working with Culture: Psychotherapeutic Interventions with Ethnic Minority Children and Adolescents*. San Francisco: Jossey-Bass, 1992.

Kozol, J. *Savage Inequalities*. New York: Crown, 1991.

Kralt, J. *Ethnic Origins of Canadians*. Ottawa: Census Canada, Profile Studies,

Demographic Characteristics, Bulletin 5, Catalogue 99-790, 1977.

Kramer, M. & Weiner, S. S. *Dialogues for Diversity: Community and Ethnicity on Campus.* Pheonix, AZ: Oryx Press, 1994.

Kuh, G. D. & Whitt, E. J. *The Invisible Tapestry: Culture in American Colleges and Universities.* ASHE-ERIC Higher Education Report No. 1. Washington, D.C.: Association for the Study of Higher Education, 1988.

Kumabe, K., Nishida, C. K. & Hepworth, D. H. *Bridging Ethnocultural Diversity in Social Work and Health.* Honolulu: University of Hawaii, School of Social Work, 1985.

Kung, S. W. *Chinese in American Life: Some Aspects of their History, Status, Problems, and Contributions.* Seattle, WA: University of Washington Press, 1962.

Kunjufu, J. *Countering the Conspiracy to Destroy Black Boys* (Volume 1). Chicago: African-American Images, 1985.

Kuo, C.-L. *Social and Political Change in New York's Chinatown: The Role of Voluntary Associations.* New York: Praeger, 1977.

Kwong, P. *ChinaTown, New York: Labor and Politics, 1930-1950.* New York: Monthly Review, 1979.

Kwong, P. *The New Chinatown.* New York: Hill & Wang, 1987.

La Belle, T. J. *Nonformal Education in Latin America and the Caribbean.* New York: Praeger, 1986.

La Belle, T. J. & Ward, C. R. *Multiculturalism and Education: Diversity and Its Impact on Schools and Society.* Albany, NY: State University of New York Press, 1994.

Laguerre, M. S. The impact of migration on the Haitian family and household organization. In A. Marks & R. A. Romer (Eds.), *Family and Kinship in Middle America and the Caribbean.* Curacao, Netherland Antilles: University of Netherland Antilles, 1978.

Laguerre, M. S. *American Odyssey: Haitians in New York City.* Ithaca, NY: Cornell University Press, 1984.

Lai, D. C. *Chinatowns: Towns Within Cities in Canada.* Vancouver, BC: University of British Columbia Press, 1988.

Lai, M. C. & Yue, K. M. K. The Chinese. In N. Waxler-Morrison & Associates (Eds.), *Cross-Cultural Caring.* Vancouver, BC: University of British Columbia Press, 1990.

Lai, V. The new Chinese immigrants in Toronmto. In J. L. Elliott (Ed.), *Minority Canadians* (Volume 2). Scarborough: Prentice-Hall, 1973.

Lam, L. Searching for a safe haven: The migration and settlement of Hong Kong Chinese immigrants in Toronto, Canada. In R. Skeldon (Ed.), *Reluctant Exiles: Hong Kong Communities Overseas.* New York: Sharpe, & Hong Kong: University of Hong Kong Press, 1993.

Lamb, M. E. (Ed.). *The Father's Role: Cross-Cultural Perspectives.* Hillsdale, NJ: Lawrence Erlbaum, 1987.

Lancaster, J. & Hamburg, B. (Eds.). *Schoolage Pregnancy and Parenthood: Biosocial Dimensions.* New York: Aldine, 1986.

Landau-Stanton, J. Adolescents, families, and cultural transition: A treatment model. In M. P. Mirkin & S. L. Koman (Eds.), *Handbook of Adolescents and Family Therapy.* New York: Gardner, 1985.

Landry, B. *The Black Middle Class.* Berkeley, CA: University of California Press, 1987.

Lane, R. *The Roots of Violence in Black Philadelphia.* Cambridge, MA: Harvard University Press, 1985.

Lang, M. Barriers to Blacks' educational achievement in higher education: A statisical and conceptual review. *Journal of Black Studies*, 1992, 22, 510-522.

Langan, P. Racism on trial: New evidence to explain the racial composition of prisons in the United States. *Journal of Criminal Law & Criminology*, 1985, 76, 666-683.

Lareau, A. Social class differences in family school relationships: The importance of cultural capital. *Sociology of Education*, 1987, 60, 73-85.

Larson, L. E. & Munro, B. Religious intermarriage in Canada in the 1980s. *Journal of Comparative Family Studies*, 1990, 21 (2), 239-250.

Lassiter, J. F. A minority experience of private practice. In E. A. Margenau (Ed.), *The Encyclopedic Handbook of Private Practice.* New York: Gardner, 1990.

Lau, A. Family therapy across cultures. In J. L. Cox (Ed.), *Transcultural Psychiatry.* London: Croom Helm, 1986.

Lee, C. C. & Richardson, B. L. (Eds.). *Multicultural Issues in Counseling: New Approaches to Diversity.* Alexandria, VA: American Association for Counseling and Development, 1991.

Lee, E. Assessment and treatment of Chinese-American families. *Journal of Psychotherapy & the Family*, 1989, 6, 99-122.

Lee, R. H. *The Chinese in the United States of America.* New York: Oxford University Press, 1960.

Leggon, C. Career, marriage and motherhood: "Copping out" or coping. In C. E. Obudho (Ed.), *Black Marriage and Family Therapy.* Westport, CT: Greenwood Press, 1983.

Lemoine, J. Shamanism in the context of H'Mong resettlement. In G. L. Hendricks, B. T. Downing & A. S. Deinard (Eds.), *The H'Mong in Transition.* New York: Center for Migration Studies, 1986.

LeResche, D. Comparison of the American mediation process with a Korean-American harmony restoration process. *Mediation Quarterly*, 1992, 9 (4), 323-339.

Leung, P. & Sakata, R. Asian Americans and rehabilitation: Some important variables. *Journal of Applied Rehabilitation Counseling*, 1988, 9 (4), 16-20.

Levine, A. & Cureton, J. The quiet revolution: Eleven facts about multiculturalism and the curriculum. *Change*, 1992, 24 (1), 25-29.

Levine, G. & Rhodes, C. *The Japanese American Community: A Three Generation Study.* New York: Praeger, 1981.

Levine, G. N. & Montero, D. M. Socioeconomic mobility among three generations of Japanese Americans. *Journal of Social Issues*, 1973, 29, 33-48.

Lewis, J. & Looney, J. *The Long Struggle: Well-Functioning Working-Class Black Families.* New York: Brunner/Mazel, 1983.

Li, P. The economic cost of racism to Chinese-Canadians. *Canadian Ethnic Studies*, 1987, 19 (3), 102-113.

Li, P. S. The stratification of ethnic immigrants: The case of Toronto. *Canadian Review of Sociology & Anthropology*, 1978, 15, 31-40.

Li, P. S. *Ethnic Inequality in a Class Society.* Toronto: Wall & Thompson, 1988a.

Li, P. S. *The Chinese in Canada.* Toronto: Oxford University Press, 1988b.

Li, P. S. Race and ethnicity. In P. S. Li (Ed.), *Race and Ethnic Relations in Canada.* Toronto: Oxford University Press, 1990a.

Li, P. S. The emergence of a new middle class among the Chinese in Canada. *Asian Culture*, 1990b, 14, 187-94.

Li, P. S. Ethnic enterprise in transition: Chinese business in Richmond, B.C., 1980-1990. *Canadian Ethnic Studies*, 1992, 14 (1), 120-138.

Lichter, D. T. Racial differences in underemployment in American cities. *American Journal of Sociology*, 1988, 93 (4), 771-792.

Light, I. *Ethnic Enterprise in America.* Berkeley, CA: University of California Press, 1972.

Light, I. From vice districts to tourist attraction: The moral career of American Chinatowns, 1840-1940. *Pacific Historical Review*, 1974, 43, 367-394.

Light, I. Disadvantaged minorities in self-employment. *International Journal of Comparative Sociology*, 1979, 20, 31-45.

Light, I. & Bonacich, E. *Immigrant Entrepreneurs: Koreans in Los Angeles.* Berkeley, CA: University of California Press, 1988.

Lin, K. M., Inui, T. S., Kleinman, A. M. & Womack, W. M. Sociocultural determinants of the help-seeking behavior of patients with mental illness. *Journal of Nervous & Mental Disease*, 1982, 170, 78-85.

Lin, T. Y. Ethnicity and patterns of help-seeking. *Culture, Medicine & Psychiatry*, 1978, 2, 3-13.

Lindblad-Goldberg, M. & Dukes, J. Social support in Black, low-income, single-parent families: Normative and dysfunctional patterns. *American Journal of Orthopsychiatry*, 1985, 55 (1), 42-58.

Lindblad-Goldberg, M., Dukes, J. & Lasley, J. Stress in Black, low-income, single-parent families: Normative and dysfunctional patterns. *American Journal of Orthopsychiatry*, 1988, 58 (1), 104-129.

Little, K. Women in African towns south of the Sahara. In T. Bromsen & B. Bromsen (Eds.), *Women and World Development.* Washington, D.C.: Overseas Development Council, 1976.

Llanes, J. *Cuban-Americans: Masters of Survival.* Cambridge, MA: Abt Publishing, 1982.

Locher, U. *Rural-urban migration and the alleged demise of the extended family: The Haitian case in comparative perspective.* Montreal: McGill University Centre for Developing-Area Studies Working Paper Series #20, 1977.

Logan, R. Immigration during the 1980s. *Canadian Social Trends*, 1991, 20, 10-13.

Logan, S. M. L., Freeman, E. M. & McDay, R. G. (Eds.). *Social Work Practice with Black Families.* New York: Longmans, 1990.

Loo, C. *Chinatown: Most Time, Hard Time.* New York: Praeger, 1991.

Loo, C. & Rolison, G. Alienation of ethnic minority students at a predominantly white university. *Journal of Higher Education*, 1986, 57 (1), 59-77.

Looney, J. Assessing minorities for graduate admissions. In M. T. Nettles (Ed.), The *Effect of Assessment on Minority Student Populations.* New Directions for Institutional Research, #65. San Francisco: Jossey-Bass, 1990.

Lopez, S. Mexican-American usage of mental health facilities: Underutilization reconsidered. In A. Baron, Jr. (Ed.), *Explorations in Chicano Psychology.* New York: Praeger, 1981.

Luthar, S. S. & Quinlan, D. M. Parental images in two cultures: A study in India and America. *Journal of Cross-Cultural Psychology*, 1993, 24 (2), 186-202.

Lyman, S. M. *Chinese Americans.* New York: Random House, 1974.

Ma, C. *Chinese Pioneers.* Vancouver, BC: Versatile Press, 1979.

Maas, E. H. *The Jews of Houston: An Ethnographic Study.* New York: AMS Press, 1989.

MacLeod, J. *Ain't No Making It: Lowered Aspiration in a Low Income Neighborhood.* Boulder, CO: Westview Press, 1987.

Madhubuti, H. *Black Men: Obsolete, Single, Dangerous?* Chicago: Third World Press, 1990.

Madison, A.-M. Editor's Notes. In A.-M. Madison (Ed.), *Minority Issues in Program Evaluation.* New Directions For Program Evaluation, #53. San Francisco: Jossey-Bass, 1992.

Majors, R. G. & Gordon, J. U. (Eds.). *The American Black Male: His Present Status and His Future.* Chicago: Nelson-Hall, 1994.

Makabe, T. *Ethnic group identity: Canadian born Japanese in Metropolitan Toronto.* Unpublished doctoral dissertation, Department of Sociology, University of Toronto, 1976.

Makabe, T. Ethnic identity and social mobility: The case of the second generation of Japanese in Metropolitan Toronto. *Canadian Ethnic Studies*, 1978, 10 (1), 106-123.

Makabe, T. Ethnic identity scale and social mobility: The case of the Nisei in Toronto. *Canadian Review of Sociology & Anthropology*, 1979, 16 (2), 136-146.

Makabe, T. The theory of the split market: A comparison of the Japanese experience in Brazil and Canada. *Social Forces*, 1981, 59, 786-809.

Maldonado, D., Jr. The Chinese aged. *Social Work*, 1975, 20, 213-216.

Maldanado, L. A. Latino ethnicity: Increasing diversity. *Latino Studies Journal*, 1991, 2, 49-57.

Malik, I. H. *Pakistanis in Michigan: A Study of Third Culture and Acculturation.* New York: AMS Press, 1989.

Malone, R. M. Counseling the disadvantaged Black urban college student: A study of family support expectations. *National Association of Student Personnel Administrators Journal*, 1992, 29 (4), 268-273.

Malong, C. (Ed.). *The Evil Eye.* New York: Columbia University Press, 1976.

Malson, M. R. Black families and childrearing support networks. In H. Z. Lopata & J. H. Peck (Eds.), *Research in the Interweave of Social Roles: Jobs and Families* (Volume 3). Greenwich, CT: JAI Press, 1983.

Manning, K. Multicultural theories for multicultural practice. *National Association of Student Personnel Administrators Journal*, 1994, 31 (3), 176-185.

Manning, K. & Coleman-Boatwright, P. Student affairs initiatives toward a multicultural campus. *Journal of College Student Development*, 1991, 32, 367-374.

Marin, G. & Triandis, H. C. Allocentrism as an important characteristic of the behavior of Latin Americans and Hispanics. In R. Diaz-Guerrero (Ed.), *Cross-Cultural and National Studies in Social Psychology.* 23rd Proceedings of the International Congress of Psychology of the International Union of Psychological Science, Acapulco, Mexico, September 2-7, 1984. Volume 2. Amsterdam: North-Holland, 1985.

Marks, C. The urban underclass. *Annual Review of Sociology*, 1991, 17, 445-466.

Marmot, M. G. & Syme, S. L. Acculturation and coronary heart disease in Japanese-Americans. *American Journal of Epidemiology*, 1976, 104, 225-247.

Marsella, A., Devos, G. & Hsu, F. *Culture and Self: Asian and Western Perspectives.* New York: Tavistock, 1985.

Marsiglia, F. F. *The Ethnic Warriors: Ethnic Identity and School Achievement as Perceived by a Group of Selected Mainland Puerto Rican Students.* Unpublished doctoral dissertation, School of Social Work, Case Western Reserve University, Cleveland, Ohio, 1991.

Martin, E. & Martin, J. M. *The Black Extended Family*. Chicago: University of Chicago Press, 1978.

Martinez, C. Hispanics: Psychiatric issues. In C. B. Wilkinson (Ed.), *Ethnic Psychiatry*. New York: Plenum Medical Books, 1986.

Martinez, J. R., Jr. (Ed.). *Chicano Psychology*. San Diego, CA: Academic, 1977.

Martinez, J. R., Jr. & Mendoza, R. H. *Chicano Psychology* (2nd ed.). San Diego, CA: Academic, 1984.

Massey, D. S. Hispanic residential segregation: A comparison of Mexicans, Cubans, and Puerto Ricans. *Sociological & Social Research*, 1981, 65, 311-322.

Massey, D. S. American apartheid: Segregation and the making of the underclass. *American Journal of Sociology*, 1990, 96 (2), 329-357.

Massey, D. S. & Denton, N. A. *American Apartheid: Segregation and the Making of the Underclass*. Cambridge, MA: Harvard University Press, 1993.

Massey, D. S. & Eggers, M. The ecology of inequality: Minorities and the concentration of poverty. *American Journal of Sociology*, 1990, 95 (5), 1153-1188.

Massey, D. S., Gross, A. B. & Shibuya, K. Migration, segregation, and the geographic constitution of poverty. *American Sociological Review*, 1994, 59 (3), 425-445.

Massey, D. S. & Schnabel, K. M. Recent trends in Hispanic immigration to the United States. *International Migration Review*, 1983, 17 (2), 212-244.

Mata, F. Latin American immigration to Canada: Some reflections on the immigration statistics. *Canadian Journal of Latin American & Caribbean Studies*, 1985, 10, 27-42.

Matsuoka, J. K. Differential acculturation among Vietnamese refugees. *Social Work*, 1990, 35 (4), 341-345.

Mayers, R. S., Kail, B. & Watts, T. (Eds.). *Hispanic Substance Abuse*. Springfield, IL: Thomas, 1993.

Maykovich, M. K. Japanese and Mennonite childhood socialization. In K. Ishwaran (Ed.), *Childhood and Adolescence in Canada*. Toronto: McGraw-Hill Ryerson, 1979.

Maykovich, M. K. Acculturation versus familism in three generations of Japanese-Canadians. In K. Ishwaran (Ed.), *Canadian Families: Ethnic Variations*. Toronto: McGraw-Hill Ryerson, 1980.

Mayo, C. & LaFrance, P. *Moving Bodies: Nonverbal Communication in Social Relationships*. Monterey, CA: Brooks/Cole, 1978.

McAdoo, H. P. Factors related to stability in upwardly mobile black families. *Journal of Marriage & the Family*, 1978, 40 (4), 761-776.

McAdoo, H. P. Black kinship. *Psychology Today*, 1979, 12, 155-169.

McAdoo, H. P. (ed.) *Black Families*. Beverly Hills: Sage, 1981a.

McAdoo, H. P. Patterns of upward mobility in Black families. In H. P. McAdoo (Ed.), *Black Families*. Beverly Hills, CA: Sage, 1981b.

McAdoo, H. P. (Ed.). *Black Families* (2nd ed.). Newbury Park, CA: Sage, 1988.

McAdoo, H. P. (Ed.). *Family Ethnicity*. Newbury Park, CA: Sage, 1993.

McAdoo, H. P. & McAdoo, J. *Black Children*. Newbury Park, CA: Sage, 1985.

McClain, C. J. *In Search of Equality: The Chinese Struggle Against Discrimination in Nineteenth-Century America*. Berkeley, CA: University of California Press, 1994.

McCready, W. C. (Ed.). *Culture, Ethnicity and Identity: Current Issues in Research*. New York: Academic Press, 1983.

McDaniel, S. The changing Canadian family. In S. Burt, L. Code & L. Dorney (Eds.), *Changing Patterns: Women in Canada.* Toronto: McClelland & Stewart, 1988.

McDowell, C. L. Standardized tests and program evaluation: Inappropriate measures in critical times. In A.-M. Madison (Ed.), *Minority Issues in Program Evaluation.* New Directions for Program Evaluation, #53. San Francisco: Jossey-Bass, 1992.

McEwen, M., Roper, L., Bryant, D. & Langa, M. Incorporating the development of African-American students into psychosocial theories of student development. *Journal of College Student Development*, 1990, 31 (5), 429-436.

McEwen, M. K. & Roper, L. D. Incorporating multiculturalism into student affairs preparation programs: Suggestions from the literature. *Journal of College Student Development*, 1994, 35, 46-53.

McGill, D. Language, cultural psychology, and family therapy: Japanese examples from an international perspective. *Contemporary Family Therapy*, 1987, 9, 282-293.

McGoldrick, M. Ethnicity and family therapy: An overview. In M. McGoldrick, J. K. Pearce & J. Giordano (Eds.), *Ethnicity and Family Therapy.* New York: Guilford, 1982a.

McGoldrick, M. Normal families: An ethnic perspective. In F. Walsh (Ed.), *Normal Family Processes.* New York: Guilford, 1982b.

McGoldrick, M. Ethnicity and the family life cycle. In B. Carter & M. McGoldrick (Eds.), *The Changing Family Life Cycle: A Framework for Family Therapy* (2nd ed.). New York: Gardner, 1988.

McGoldrick, M. Ethnicity, cultural diversity, and normality. In F. Walsh (Ed.), *Normal Family Processes* (2nd ed.). New York: Guilford, 1993.

McGoldrick, M. & Preto, N.G. Ethnic intermarriage: Implications for therapy. *Family Process*, 1984, 23 (3), 347-362.

McGoldrick, M., Garcia-Preto, N., Hines, P. M. & Lee, E. Ethnicity and women. In M. McGoldrick, C. M. Anderson & F. Walsh (Eds.), *Women in Families: A Framework for Family Therapy.* New York: Norton, 1989.

McInnis, K. M., Petracchi, H. E. & Morgenbesser, M. *The Hmong in America: Providing Ethnic-Sensitive Health, Educations, and Human Services.* Dubuque, IA: Kendall/Hunt, 1990.

McLeod, K. A. (Ed.). *Intercultural Education and Community Development.* Toronto: University of Toronto, Guidance Centre, Faculty of Education, 1980.

McMahon, A. & Allen-Meares, P. Is social work racist? A content analysis of recent literature. *Social Work*, 1992, 37 (6), 533-539.

McManus, W., Gould, W. & Welch, F. Earnings of Hispanic men: The role of English language proficiency. *Journal of Labor Economics*, 1983, 1, 101-130.

Medjuck, S. *Jews of Atlantic Canada.* St. John's, NF: Breakwater Books, 1986.

Meierding, N. R. The impact of cultural and religious diversity in the divorce mediation process. *Mediation Quarterly*, 1992, 9 (4), 297-305.

Menaghan, E. G. Work experiences and family interaction processes: The long reach of the job? *Annual Review of Sociology*, 1991, 17, 419-444.

Michel, R. Economic growth and income inequality since the 1982 recession. *Journal of Policy Analysis & Management*, 1991, 10, 181-203.

Middlebrook, P. N. *Social Psychology and Modern Life* (2nd ed.). New York: Knopf, 1980.

Miller, L. S. *An American Imperative: Accelerating Minority Educational Achievement.* New Haven, CT: Yale University Press, 1994.

Miller, S. *The Unwelcome Immigrant: The American Image of the Chinese, 1785-1882.* Berkeley, CA: University of California Press, 1969.

Min, P. G. *Ethnic Business Enterprise: Korean Small Business in Atlanta.* New York: CMS, 1988.

Mincy, R. & Ricketts, E. Growth of the underclass 1970-1980. *Journal of Human Resources*, 1990, 25, 137-145.

Mindel, C. H. Extended families among urban Mexican Americans, Anglos and Blacks. *Hispanic Journal of Behavioral Sciences*, 1980, 2, 1-34.

Mindel, C. H., Habenstein, R. W. & Wright, R., Jr. (Eds.). *Ethnic Families in America* (3rd ed.). New York: Elsevier, 1988.

Ministry of Industry, Science and Technology. *The Current Demographic Analysis: Report on the Demographic Situation in Canada, 1988.* Ottawa: Ministry of Supply & Services, 1990.

Mintz, S. D. (Ed.). *Sources: Diversity Initiatives in Higher Education.* Washington, D.C.: Office of Minorities in Higher Education, American Council on Education, 1993.

Minuchin, S. *Families and Family Therapy.* Cambridge, MA: Harvard University Press, 1974.

Minuchin, S. & Montalvo, B. Techniques for working with disorganized low socioeconomic families. *American Journal of Orthopsychiatry*, 1967, 37 (5), 880-887.

Minuchin, S., Montalvo, B., Guerney, B., Rosman, B. & Schumer, F. *Families of the Slums.* New York: Basic, 1967.

Miralles, M. A. *A Matter of Life and Death: Health-Seeking Behavior of Guatemalan Refugees in South Florida.* New York: AMS Press, 1989.

Mirande, A. *The Chicano Experience: An Alternative Perspective.* Notre Dame, IN: Notre Dame University Press, 1985.

Mizio, E. Impact of external systems on the Puerto Rican family. *Social Casework*, 1974, 55, 76-83.

Mizio, E. *Puerto Rican Task Report: Project on Ethnicity.* New York: Family Service Association, 1979.

Modell, J. *The Economics and Politics of Racial Accomodation: The Japanese of Los Angeles, 1900-1942.* Urbana, IL: University of Ilinois Press, 1977.

Mokuan, N. Social worker's perceptions of counseling effectiveness for Asian American clients. *Social Work*, 1987, 32, 331-335.

Montalvo, B. & Gutierrez, M. A perspective for the use of the cultural dimension in family therapy. In J. C. Hansen & C. E. Falicov (Eds.), *Cultural Perspectives in Family Therapy.* Rockville, MD: Aspen Systems Corporation, 1983.

Montero, D. The Japanese Americans: Changing patterns of assimilation over three generations. *American Sociological Review*, 1981, 46, 829-839.

Moodley, K. A. (Ed.). *Beyond Multicultural Education: International Perspective.* Calgary, AT: Detselig Enterprises, 1992.

Moore, J. & Glick, R. (Eds.). *Drugs in Hispanic Communities.* New Brunswick, NJ: Rutgers University Press, 1991.

Moore, J. W. & Pachon, H. *Hispanics in the United States.* Englewood Cliffs, NJ: Prentice-Hall, 1985.

Mora, M. & Del Castillo, R. (Eds.). *Mexican Women in the United States.* Los Angeles: UCLA Chicano Studies Research Center, 1980.

Morales, A. T. Therapy with Latino gang members. In L. A. Vargas & J. D. Koss-Chioino (Eds.), *Working with Culture: Psychotherapeutic Interventions with Ethnic Minority Children and Adolescents*. San Francisco; Jossey-Bass, 1992.

Morales, R. F. *Makibaka: The Filipino American Struggle*. Darby, Montana: Mountain View Press, 1974.

Moreau, J. Changing faces: Visible minorities in Toronto. *Canadian Social Trends*, 1991, 23, 26-28.

Morishima, J. K. & Associates. *Handbook of Asian American/Pacific Islander Mental Health* (Volume 1). Washington, D.C.: U.S. Government Printing Office, 1979.

Morris, L. *Dangerous Classes: The Underclass and Social Citizenship*. London: Routledge, 1994.

Morris, S. V. (Ed.). *Multicultural and Intercultural Education: Building Canada*. Calgary, AT: Detselig Enterprises, 1989.

Morsbach, H. Aspects of Japanese marriage. In M. Corbin (Ed.), *The Couple*. London: Penguin, 1978.

Morton, J. W. *In the Sea of Sterile Mountains: The Chinese in British Columbia*. Vancouver, BC: Douglas, 1973.

Moses, Y. T. *Black Women in Academe: Issues and Strategies*. Washington, D.C.: American Association of Colleges, 1989.

Moses, Y. T. The challenge of diversity: Anthropological perspectives on university culture. *Education & Urban Society*, 1990, 22 (4), 402-412.

Moses, Y. T. *The Recruitment and Retention of Minority Faculty and Students*. Women at the Helm: Pathfinding Presidents at American Colleges and Universities. New York: University Press Association, 1991.

Moses, Y. T. Quality, excellence, and diversity. In D. G. Smith (Ed.), *Studying Diversity in Higher Education*. New Directions for Institutional Research, #81. San Francisco: Jossey-Bass, 1994.

Mow, S. L. & Nettles, M. T. Minority student access to, and persistence and performance in, college: A review of trends and research literature. In J. C. Smart (Ed.), *Higher Education: Handbook of Theory and Research* (Volume 6). New York: Agathon, 1990.

Muecke, M. A. In search of healers: Southeast Asian refugees in the American health care system. *Western Journal of Medicine*, 1983, 139, 835-840.

Muir, K. L. S. *The Strongest Part of the Family: A Study of Lao Refugee Women in Columbus, Ohio*. New York: AMS Press, 1985.

Muller, C. Parent involvement an academic achievement: An analyses of family resources available to the child. In B. Schneider & J. S. Coleman (Eds.), *Parents, Their Children and Schools*. Boulder, CO: Westview, 1993.

Munro-Blum, H., Boyle, M. H., Offord, D. R. & Kates, N. Immigrant children: Psychiatric disorder, school performance and service utilization. *American Journal of Orthopsychiatry*, 1989, 59, 510-519.

Murase, K., Egawa, J. & Tashima, N. Alternative mental health services models in Asian/Pacific communities. In T. C. Owan (Ed.), *Southeast Asian Mental Health Treatment Prevention Services Training and Research*. Washington, D.C.: National Institute of Mental Health, 1985.

Murguia, E. *Assimilation, Colonialism, and the Mexican American People*. New York: University Press America, 1989.

Murguia, E. & Cazares, R. Intermarriage among Mexican-Americans. *Marriage & Family Review*, 1982, 5, 91-100.

Murillo, N. The Mexican-American family. In C. Hernandez, M. J. Haug & N. N.

Wagner (Eds.), *Chicano: Social and Psychological Perspective*. St. Louis, MO: Mosby, 1970.

Murillo, N. The Mexican-American family. In R. A. Martinez, Jr. (Ed.), *Hispanic Culture and Health Care: Fact, Fiction, Folklore*. St. Louis, MO: Mosby, 1976.

Murillo-Rhode, I. Family life among mainland Puerto Ricans in New York City slums. *Perspectives in Psychiatric Care*, 1976, 14, 174-179.

Mutran, E. Intergenerational family support among Blacks and Whites: Response to culture or to socioeconomic differences. *Journal of Gerontology*, 1985, 40, 382-389.

Muzny, C. C. *The Vietnamese in Oklahoma City: A Study of Ethnic Change*. New York: AMS Press, 1989.

Nagasawa, R. & Espinosa, D. J. Educational achievement and the adaptive strategy of Asian American college students: Facts, theory, and hypotheses. *Journal of College Student Development*, 1992, 33, 137-142.

National Center for Educational Statistics. *Youth Indicators 1993: Trends in the Well-Being of American Youth*. Washington, D.C.: U.S. Department of Education, Office of Educational Research & Improvement, NCES 93-242, 1993.

National Commission on Testing & Public Policy. *From Gatekeeper to Gateway: Transforming Testing in America*. Boston: National Commission on Testing & Public Policy, 1990.

National Council of Welfare. *The Working Poor: People and Programs*. Ottawa: NCW, 1981.

National Council of Welfare. *Women and Poverty Revisited*. Ottawa: NCW, 1990.

National Council of Welfare. *Poverty Profile, 1980-1990*. Ottawa: NCW, 1992.

Nee, V. & Nee, B. D. *Longtime Californ': A Documentary Study of an American Chinatown*. New York: Random House, 1972.

Nee, V. & Wong, H. Y. Asian American socioeconomic achievment. *Sociological Perspectives*, 1985, 28, 281-306.

Neisser, U. (Ed.). *The School Achievement of Minority Children: New Perspectives*. Hillsdale, NJ: Lawrence Erlbaum, 1986.

Nelson, C. & Tienda, M. The structuring of Hispanic ethnicity: Historical and contemporary perspectives. *Ethnic Racial Studies*, 1985, 8, 49-74.

Nelson, W. L. Receptivity to institutional assistance: An important variable for African-American and Mexican-American student achievement. *Journal of College Student Development*, 1994, 35 (5), 378-383.

Nett, E. M. *Canadian Families: Past & Present* (2nd ed.). Toronto: Butterworths, 1993.

Nettler, G. *Killing One Another*. Volume 2, Criminal Careers Series. Cincinnati, OH: Anderson, 1982.

Nettles, M. (Ed.). *Toward Black Undergraduate Student Equality in American Higher Education*. Westport, CT: Greenwood Press, 1988.

Nettles, M. T. (Ed.). *The Effect of Assessment on Minority Student Populations*. New Directions for Institutional Research, #65. San Francisco: Jossey-Bass, 1990.

Nettles, M. T., Theony, A. R. & Gosman, E.J. Comparing and predicting the college performance of black and white students. *Higher Education Abstracts*, 1984, 20 (1), 3.

Newhill, C. E. The role of culture in the development of paranoid symptomatology. *American Journal of Orthopsychiatry*, 1990, 60 (2), 176-185.

Newman, K. S. *Falling From Grace: The Experience of Downward Mobility in the*

American Middle Class. New York: Free Press, 1988.

Nguyen, N. A. & Williams, H. L.   Transition from East to West: Vietnamese adolescents and their parents. *Journal of the American Academy of Child & Adolescent Psychiatry*, 1989, 28 (4), 505-515.

Nicholson, N.   The transition cycle: Causes, outcomes, processes, and forms. In S. Fisher & C. L. Cooper (Eds.), *On the Move: The Psychology of Change and Transition*. New York: Wiley, 1990.

Nieto, S.   *Affirming Diversity: The Sociopolitical Context of Multicultural Education*. New York: Longman, 1992.

Nobles, W.   *African Psychology: Toward a Reclamation, Reascension, and Revitalization*. Oakland, CA: Black Family Institute, 1986.

Nora, A.   Two-year colleges and minority students' educational aspirations: Help or hindrance? In J. C. Smart (Ed.), *Higher Education: Handbook of Theory and Research* (Volume 9). New York: Agathon, 1993.

Notman, M. T. & Zilbach, J. J.   Family aspects of nonuse of contraceptives in adolescence. In H. Hirsch (Ed.), *The Family*. Basel, Switzerland: Karger, 1975.

O'Brien, D. J. & Fugita, S. S.   Middleman minority concept: Its explanatory value in the case of the Japanese in California agriculture. *Pacific Sociological Review*, 1982, 25, 185-204.

O'Brien, D. J. & Fugita, S. S.   Generational differences in Japanese Americans' perceptions and feelings about social relationships between themselves and Caucasian Americans. In W. C. McReady (Ed.), *Culture, Ethnicity, and Identity: Current Issues in Research*. New York: Academic, 1983.

O'Brien, E. M.   *Latinos in Higher Education*. Washington, D.C.: American Council on Education, Research Brief Reports, Volume 4 (4), Division of Policy Analysis & Research, 1993.

Odell, M. & Mock, J. J. (Eds.).   *A Crucial Agenda: Making College and University Work Better for Minority Students*. Boulder, CO: Western Interstate Commission for Higher Education, 1989.

Ogbu, J.   Origins of human competence: A cultural ecology perspective. *Child Development*, 1981, 52, 413-429.

Ogbu, J.   The consequence of the American caste system. In U. Neisser (Ed.), *The School Achievement of Minority Children: New Perspectives*. Hillsdale, NJ: Lawrence Erlbaum, 1986.

Okana, Y.   *Japanese Americans and Mental Health*. Los Angeles: Coalition for Mental Health, 1977.

Olivas, M. A. (Ed.).   *Latino College Students*. New York: Teachers College Press, 1986.

Olivas, M. A.   The attack on affirmative action: Lives in parallel universes. *Change*, 1993, 25 (2), 16-20.

Olzak, S.   *The Dynamics of Ethnic Competition and Conflict*. Stanford, CA: Stanford University Press, 1992.

Omolade, B.   *It's a Family Affair: The Real Lives of Single Black Mothers*. Latham, New York: Kitchen Table: Women of Color Press, 1986.

Ong, P.   An ethnic trade: The Chinese laundries in early California. *Journal of Ethnic Studies*, 1981, 8, 95-113.

Ooms, T. (Ed.).   *Teenage Pregnancy in a Family Context*. Philadelphia: Temple University Press, 1981.

Orlans, H. Affirmative action in higher education. *Annals of the American Academy of Political & Social Science*, 1992, 523, 144-158.

Osterweis, M., Solomon, F. & Green, M. (Eds.). *Bereavement: Reactions, Consequences, and Care.* Washington, D.C.: National Academy Press, 1978.

Pachai, B. *Blacks.* Tantallon, NS: Four East Publications, 1987.

Painter, D. H. Black women and the family. In J. R. Chapman & M. Gates (Eds.), *Women into Wives: The Legal and Economic Impact of Marriage.* Beverly Hills, CA: Sage, 1977.

Pallas, A., Natriello, G. & McDill, E. The changing nature of the disadvantaged population: Current dimensions and future trends. *Educational Researcher*, 1989, 18, 16-22.

Papajohn, J. & Spiegel, J. *Transactions in Families.* San Francisco: Jossey-Bass, 1975.

Paris, E. *Jews: An Account of Their Experience in Canada.* Toronto: Macmillan, 1980.

Parker, W. M. *Consciousness-Raising: A Primer for Multicultural Counseling.* Springfield, IL: Thomas, 1988.

Patton, M. Q. Editor's notes. In M. Q. Patton (Ed.), *Culture and Evaluation.* New Directions for Program Evaluation, #25. San Francisco: Jossey-Bass, 1985.

Pavkov, T. W., Lewis, D. A. & Lyons, J. S. Psychiatric diagnosis and racial bias: An empirical investigation. *Professional Psychology*, 1990, 20, 364-368.

Pedersen, P. The intercultural context of counseling and therapy. In A. J. Marsella & G. M. White (Eds.), *Cultural Conceptions of Mental Health and Therapy.* Dordrecht, Holland: Reidel, 1984.

Pedersen, P. *Handbook of Cross-Cultural Counseling and Therapy.* Westport, CT: Greenwood Press, 1985.

Pedersen, P. *A Handbook for Developing Multicultural Awareness.* Alexandria, VA: American Association for Counseling and Development, 1988.

Pedersen, P. Multiculturalism as a generic approach to counseling. *Journal of Counseling & Development*, 1991, 70 (1), 6-12.

Pedersen, P. B. & Ivey, A. *Culture-Centered Counseling and Interviewing Skills: A Practical Guide.* Westport, CT: Praeger, 1994.

Pedraza, S. Women and migration: The social consequences of gender. *Annual Review of Sociology*, 1991, 17, 303-325.

Pedraza-Bailey, S. *Political and Economic Migrants in America: Cubans and Mexicans.* Austin, TX: University of Texas Press, 1985.

Peel Board of Education. *Race/Ethnicity Survey.* Halton, ON: Peel Board of Education, 1989.

Perez, L. Immigrant economic adjustment and family organization: The Cuban success story reexamined. *International Migration Review*, 1986, 20, 4-20.

Perlman, J. Beyond New York: The occupations of Russian Jewish immigrants in Providence, R.I., and other small Jewish communities, 1900-1915. *American Jewish History*, 1983, 72, 369-394.

Perlman, J. *Ethnic Differences: Schooling and Social Structure among the Irish, Italians, Jews, and Blacks in an American City, 1880-1935.* New York: Cambridge University Press, 1988.

Persell, C. H., Catsambis, S. & Cookson, P. W., Jr. Differential asset conversion: Class and gendered pathways to selective colleges. *Sociology of Education*, 1992, 65, 208-225.

Peters, J. Cultural variations: Past & Present. In M. Baker (Ed.), *Families: Changing*

Trends in Canada (2nd ed.). Toronto: McGraw-Hill Ryerson, 1990.

Petersen, W. Chinese Americans amd Japanese Americans. In T. Sowell (Ed.), *Essays and Data on American Ethnic Groups.* Washington, D.C.: Urban Institute, 1978.

Petersilia, J. *Racial Disparities in the Criminal Justice System.* Santa Monica, CA: Rand, 1983.

Phinney, J. S. & Rotheram, M. J. (Eds.). *Children's Ethnic Socialization: Pluralism and Development.* Newbury Park, CA: Sage, 1987.

Pinderhughes, E. Afro-American families and the victim system. In M. McGoldrick, J. K. Pearce & J. Giordano (Eds.), *Ethnicity and Family Therapy.* New York: Guilford, 1982.

Piotrkowski, C. S. & Hughes, D. Dual-earner families in context: Managing family systems and work systems. In F. Walsh (Ed.), *Normal Family Processes* (2nd ed.). New York: Guilford, 1993.

Pittman, K. & Adams, G. *Teenage Pregnancy: An Advocate's Guide to the Numbers.* Washington, D.C.: Adolescent Pregnancy Prevention Clearinghouse, 1988.

Plath, D. W. Contours of consociation: Lessons from a Japanese narrative. In P. B. Baltes & O. G. Brim, Jr. (Eds.), *Life-Span Development & Behavior* (Volume 3). New York: Academic, 1980.

Ponce, D. E. The Filipinos of Hawaii. In W. S. Tseng, J. F. McDermott & T. W. Maretzki (Eds.), *Adjustment in Intercultural Marriage.* Honolulu: University Press of Hawaii, 1974.

Porter, J. R. & Washington, R. E. Black identity and self-esteem: A review of studies of black self-concept: 1968-1978. *Annual Review of Sociology*, 1979, 5, 53-74.

Porter, J. R. & Washington, R. E. Developments in research on black identity and self-esteem: 1979-88. *Review of International Psychology & Sociology*, 1989, 2, 341-353.

Porter, J. R. & Washington, R. E. Minority identity and self-esteem. *Annual Review of Sociology*, 1993, 19, 139-161.

Portes, A. The social origins of the Cuban enclave economy of Miami. *Sociological Perspectives*, 1987, 30, 340-372.

Portes, A. & Bach, R. L. *Latin Journey: Cuban and Mexican Immigrants in the United States.* Berkeley, CA: University of California Press, 1985.

Portes, A., Castells, M. & Benton, L. (Eds.). *The Informal Economy: Studies in Advanced and Less Developed Nations.* Baltimore, MD: Johns Hopkins University Press, 1989.

Portes, A. & Rumbaut, R. *Immigrant America: A Portrait.* Berkeley, CA: University of California Press, 1990.

Portes, A. & Truelove, C. Making sense of diversity: Recent research on Hispanic minorities in the United States. *Annual Review of Sociology*, 1987, 13, 359-385.

Postsecondary Education Opportunity. No progress for Blacks and Hispanics on equity in 1992. *Postsecondary Education Opportunity*, 1993a, February, 1-5.

Postsecondary Education Opportunity. Blacks still only half as likely as Whites to attain baccalaureate degree. *Postsecondary Education Opportunity*, 1993b, November, 1-6.

Postsecondary Education Opportunity. Parental educational attainment drives educational attainment by their children. *Postsecondary Education Opportunity*, 1993c, May, 1-5.

Powell, G. J. Self-concept among Afro-American students in racially isolated minority schools: Some regional differences. *Journal of the American Academy of Child Psychiatry*, 1985, 24, 142-149.

Pratt, M., Smith, B. & Bulkin, E. (Eds.). *Yours in Struggle.* New York: Long Haul Press, 1984.

Preto, N. G. Hispanic mothers. *Journal of Feminist Family Therapy*, 1990, 2 (2), 15-21.

Price, C. *The Great White Walls are Built: Restrictive Immigration to North America and Australia, 1836-1888.* Canberra, Australia: Australian University Press, 1974.

Price, J. A. Canadian Indian families. In K. Ishwaran (Ed.), *The Canadian Family.* Toronto: Gage, 1983.

Quality Education for Minorities Project. *Education That Works.* Cambridge, MA: MIT, 1990.

Quevedo-Garcia, E. L. Facilitating the development of Hispanic college students. In D. J. Wright (Ed.), *Responding to the Needs of Today's Minority Students.* New Directions for Student Services, #38. San Francisco: Jossey-Bass, 1987.

Radcliffe, P. (Ed.). *"Race," Ethnicity and Nation: International Perspectives on Social Conflict.* London: UCL Press, 1994.

Radetsky, D. S., Handelsman, M. M. & Browne, A. Individual and family environment patterns among Jews and non-Jews. *Psychological Reports*, 1984 55, 787-793.

Ralston, H. Ethnicity, class and gender among South Asian women in Metropolitan Halifax: An exploratory study. *Canadian Ethnic Studies*, 1988, 20 (3), 63-83.

Ram, B. Intermarriage among ethnic groups. In S. S. Halli, F. Travato & L. Driedger (Eds.), *Ethnic Demography: Canadian Immigrant, Racial and Cultural Variations.* Ottawa: Carleton University Press, 1990.

Ramcharan, S. The economic adaptation of West Indians in Toronto Canada. *Canadian Review of Sociology & Anthropology*, 1976, 13, 295-304.

Ramirez, M. *Psychology of the Americas: Mestizo Perspectives on Personality and Mental Health.* Elmsford, NY: Pergamon, 1983.

Ramirez, M. Combining modernism and traditionalism: Coping effectively with economic and acculturation stress. In R. Diaz-Guerrero (Ed.), *Cross-Cultural and National Studies in Social Psychology.* 23rd Proceedings of the International Congress of Psychology of the International Union of Psychological Science, Acapulco, Mexico, September 2-7, 1984. Volume 2. Amsterdam: North-Holland, 1985.

Ramirez, M. & Castenaeda, A. *Cultural Democracy, Bicognitive Development and Education.* New York: Academic, 1974.

Raymond J., Rhoads, D. & Raymond, R. The relative impact of family and social involvement on Chicano mental health. *American Journal of Community Psychology*, 1980, 5, 557-569.

Reddy, M. T. *Crossing the Color Line: Race, Parenting, and Culture.* New Brunswick, NJ: Rutgers University Press, 1994.

Reich, A. H. *The Cultural Construction of Ethnicity: Chicanos in the University.* New York: AMS Press, 1989.

Reichert, J. & Massey, D. S. History and trends in U.S. bound migration from a Mexican town. *International Migration Review*, 1980, 14 (4), 475-491.

Reid, P. & Comas-Diaz, L. Gender and ethnicity: Perspectives on dual status. *Sex Roles*, 1990, 22, 397-407.

Reimer, C. W. A comparative analysis of the wages of Hispanics, Blacks, and non-Hispanic Whites. In G. Borjas & M. Tienda (Eds.), *Hispanics in the U.S.*

Economy. Orlando, FL: Academic, 1985.

Reischauer, E. O. *The Japanese.* Cambridge, MA: Harvard University Press, 1981.

Return to the Source. *Selected Articles on Judaism and Teshuva.* New York: Feldheim, 1984.

Reynolds, D. K. *The Quiet Therapies: Japanese Pathways to Personal Growth.* Honolulu: University of Hawaii Press, 1980.

Richard, M. *Ethnic Group and Marital Choices: Ethnic History and Marital Assimilation in Canada, 1871-1971.* Vancouver, BC: University of British Columbia Press, 1991.

Richardson, R. C. & Skinner, E. F. *Achieving Quality and Diversity: Universities in a Multicultural Society.* New York: ACE/Macmillan, 1991.

Riche, M. F. We're all minorities now. *American Demographics,* 1991, 13, 26-34.

Rischin, M. *The Promised City.* Cambridge, MA: Harvard University Press, 1962.

Rischin, M. (Ed.). *The Jews of North America.* Detroit, MI: Wayne State University Press, 1987.

Robinson, I., Anctil, P. & Butovsky, M. (Eds.). *An Everyday Miracle: Yiddish Culture in Montreal.* Montreal: Vehicule Press, 1990.

Robinson, J. B. Clinical treatment of Black families: Issues and strategies. *Social Work,* 1989, 34 (4), 323-329.

Rodriguez, C. E. *Puerto Ricans: Born in the USA.* Boston, MA: Unwin Hyman, 1992.

Rodriguez, C. E. & Melendez, E. Puerto Rican poverty and labor markets: An introduction. *Hispanic Journal of Behavioral Science,* 1992, 14, 4-15.

Roland, A. *In Search of Self in India and Japan: Toward a Cross-Cultural Psychology.* Princeton, NJ: Princeton University Press, 1988.

Romero, M. Twice protected? Assessing the impact of affirmative action on Mexican-American women. In W. A. Van Horne & T. V. Tonnensen (Eds.), *Ethnicity and Women.* Madison, WI: University of Wisconsin, 1986.

Romero, M. Chicanas modernize domestic service. *Qualitative Sociology,* 1988, 11 (4), 319-334.

Root, M. P. P. *Racially Mixed People in America.* Newbury Park, CA: Sage, 1992.

Rose, P. I. *Strangers in Their Midst: A Sociological Study of the Small-Town Jew and his Neighbours.* Unpublished doctoral dissertation, Department of Sociology, Cornell University, Ithaca, NY, 1959.

Rosenberg, S. E. *The Search for Jewish Identity in America.* New York: Anchor, 1965.

Rosentraub, M. & Taebel, D. Jewish enterprise in transition: From collective self-help to orthodox capitalism. In S. Cummings (Ed.) *Self-Help in Urban America.* Port Washington, NY: Kennikat Press, 1980.

Ross, D. P. & Shillington, R. *The Canadian Fact Book on Poverty 1989.* Ottawa: Canadian Council on Social Development, 1989.

Ross-Gordon, J. M., Martin, L. G. & Brisco, D. B. Editor's Notes. In J. M. Ross-Gordon, L. G. Martin & D. B. Brisco (Eds.), *Serving Culturally Diverse Populations.* New Directions for Adult and Continuing Education, #48. San Francisco: Jossey-Bass, 1990.

Rossi, P. H. *Down and Out in America: The Origins of Homelessness.* Chicago: University of Chicago Press, 1989.

Rowe, M. P. Fostering diversity: Some major hurdles remain. *Change,* 1993, 25 (2), 35-39.

Royse, D. & Turner, G. Strengths of Black families: A Black community's perspective. *Social Work*, 1980, 25 (5), 407-409.

Ruggles, S. The origin of African-American family studies. *American Sociological Review*, 1994, 59 (1), 136-151.

Ruiz, P. & Langrod, J. Psychiatrists and spiritual healers: Partners in community mental health. In J. Westermeyer (Ed.), *Anthropology and Mental Health: Setting a New Course*. The Hague, Netherlands: Mouton, 1976.

Rutledge, E. Marital interaction goals of Black women: Strengths and effects. In L. Rose (Ed.), *The Black Woman*. Beverly Hills, CA: Sage, 1980.

Ryerse, C. *Thursday's Child: Child Poverty in Canada: A Review of the Effects of Poverty on Children*. Ottawa: National Youth in Care Network, 1990.

Saba, G., Karrer, B. M & Hardy, K. *Minorities and Family Therapy*. New York: Haworth, 1990.

Sabogal, F., Marin, G., Otero-Sabogal, R., VanOss Martin, B. & Perez-Sable, E. J. Hispanic familism and acculturation: What changes and what doesn't? *Hispanic Journal of Behavioral Science*, 1987, 9, 397-402.

Safa, H. I. Female employment and the social reproduction of the Puerto Rican working class. *International Migration Review*, 1984, 18 (4), 1168-1187.

Safa, H. I. Migration and identity: A comparison of Puerto Rican and Cuban migrants to the U.S. In E. Acosta-Belen & B. Sjostrum (Eds.), *The Hispanic Experience in the U.S.* New York: Praeger, 1988.

Sagaria, M. A. & Johnsrud, L. K. Recruiting, advancing, and retaining minorities in student affairs: Moving from rhetoric to results. *National Association of Student Personnel Administrators Journal*, 1991, 28 (2), 105-120.

Salgado de Snyder, V. N. & Padilla, A. M. Transmission of sociocultural functioning between parents and children in interethnic families. In R. Diaz-Guerrero (Ed.), *Cross-Cultural and National Studies in Social Psychology*. 23rd Proceedings of the International Congress of Psychology of the International Union of Psychological Science, Acapulco, Mexico, September 2-7, 1984. Volume 2. Amsterdam: North-Holland, 1985.

Salter, C. *San Francisco's Chinatown: How Chinese a Town?* San Francisco: R & E Research Associates, 1978.

Samora, J. Conceptions of health and disease among Spanish-Americans. In R. A. Martinez (Ed.), *Hispanic Culture and Health Care*. St. Louis, MO: Mosby, 1978.

Sampson, E. E. The debate on individualism: Indigenuous psychologies of the individual and their role in personal and social functioning. *American Psychologist*, 1988, 43, 15-22.

Sampson, R. J. Urban Black violence: The effects of male joblessness and family disruption. *American Journal of Sociology*, 1987, 93, 348-382.

Sanchez-Korrol, V. *From Colonia to Community*. Westport, CT: Greenwood Press, 1983.

Sanday, P. R., Boardman, A. & Davis, O. The cultural context of American education. In P. R. Sanday (Ed.), *Anthropology and the Public Interest*. New York: Academic, 1977.

Sanders, W. B. *Gangbangs and Drive-bys: Grounded Culture and Juvenile Gang Violence*. New York: Aldine de Gruyter, 1994.

Sanjek, R. & S. Colen (Eds.). *At Work in Homes: Domestic Workers in World Perspective*. Washington D.C.: American Anthropological Society, 1990.

Sanua, V. D. The contemporary Jewish family: A review of the social science literature. In G. Babis (Ed.), *Serving the Jewish Family*. New York: KTAV, 1978.

Sanua, V. D. Familial and sociocultural antecedents of psychopathology. In H. C. Triandis & J. G. Draguns (Eds.), *Handbook of Cross-Cultural Psychology* (Volume 6): Psychopathology. Boston, MA: Allyn & Bacon, 1980.

Sanua, V. D. The family and sociocultural factors of psychopathology. In L. L'Abate (Ed.), *The Handbook of Family Psychology and Therapy* (Volume 2). Homewood, IL: Dorsey, 1985.

Sassen, S. Economic restructuring and the American city. *Annual Review of Sociology*, 1990, 16, 465-490.

Saunders, M. *Multicultural Teaching: A Guide for the Classroom.* London: McGraw-Hill, 1982.

Scanzoni, J. *The Black Family in Modern Society.* Boston: Allyn & Bacon, 1971.

Schlesinger, B. *The Jewish Family: A Survey and Annotated Bibliography.* Toronto: University of Toronto Press, 1971.

Schlesinger, B. *Jewish Family Issues: A Resource Guide.* New York: Garland, 1987.

Schneider, B., Hieshima, J. A., Lee, S. & Plank, S. East-Asian academic success in the United States: Family, school, and community explanations. In P. M. Greenfield & R. R. Cocking (Eds.), *Cross-Cultural Roots of Minority Child Development.* Hillsdale, NJ: Lawrence Erlbaum, 1994.

Schneider, S. W. *Jewish and Female: Choices and Changes in Our Lives.* New York: Simon & Schuster, 1984.

Schoem, D. (Ed.). *Inside Separate Worlds: Life Stories of Young Blacks, Jews, and Latinos.* Ann Arbor, MI: University of Michigan Press, 1991.

Schoonmaker, A. N. *Negotiate to Win: Gaining the Psychological Edge.* Englewood Cliffs, NJ: Prentice-Hall, 1989.

Schwartzman, J. Normality from a cross-cultural perspective. In F. Walsh (Ed.), *Normal Family Processes.* New York: Guilford, 1982.

Sena-Rivera, J. Extended kinship in the United States: Competing models and the case of la familia chicana. *Journal of Marriage & the Family*, 1979, 41, 121-129.

Sev'er, A. *Women and Divorce in Canada: A Sociological Analysis.* Toronto: Canadian Scholars Press, 1992.

Sev'er, A., Isajiw, W. W. & Driedger, L. Anomie as powerlessness: Sorting ethnic group prestige, class, and gender. *Canadian Ethnic Studies*, 1993, 25 (2), 84-99.

Sewell, D. *Knowing People: A Mexican-American Community's Concept of a Person.* New York: AMS Press, 1989.

Shadd, A. L. Dual labour markets in "core" and "periphery" regions of Canada: The position of black males in Ontario and Nova Scotia. *Canadian Ethnic Studies*, 1987, 19 (2), 91-116.

Shamai, S. Ethnicity and educational achievement in Canada, 1941-1981. *Canadian Ethnic Studies*, 1992, 14 (1), 43-57.

Shang, P. & Moore, L. V. Applying cultural theory: The environmental variable. In L. V. Moore (Ed.), *Evolving Theoretical Perspectives on Students.* New Directions for Student Services, #51. San Francisco: Jossey-Bass, 1990.

Shibutani, T. & Kwan, K. M. *Ethnic Stratification.* New York: Macmillan, 1965.

Shih-Shan, H. T. *The Chinese Experience in America.* Indianapolis, IN: University of Indianapolis Press, 1986.

Shimkin, D., Shimkin, E. & Frate, D. (Eds.). *The Extended Family in Black Society.* Chicago: University of Chicago Press, 1978.

Shlay, A. B. & Rossi, P. H. Social science research and contemporary studies of homelessness. *Annual Review of Sociology*, 1992, 18, 129-160.

Shon, S. P. & Ja, D. Y. Asian families. In M. McGoldrick, J. K. Pearce & J.

Giordano (Eds.), *Ethnicity and Family Therapy.* New York: Guilford, 1982.

Shuval, J. T. Migration and stress. In L. Goldberger & S. Breznitz (Eds.), *Handbook of Stress: Theoretical and Clinical Aspects* (2nd ed.). New York: Free Press, 1993.

Sidel, R. *Women and Child Care in China.* New York: Penguin, 1982.

Siegel, R. J. & Cole, E. (Eds.). *Jewish Women in Therapy: Seen But Not Heard.* New York: Haworth, 1991.

Siggelkow, R. A. Racism in higher education: A permanent condition? *National Association of Student Personnel Administrators Journal,* 1991, 28 (2), 98-104.

Sikkema, M. & Niyekana, A. *Design for Cross-Cultural Learning.* Yarmouth, ME: Intercultural Press, 1987.

Silberman, C. E. *A Certain People: American Jews and Their Lives Today.* New York: Summit, 1985.

Silverman, M. *Strategies for Social Mobility: Family, Kinship and Ethnicity within Jewish Families in Pittsburgh.* New York: AMS Press, 1989.

Simmons, A. B. & Turner, J. E. The socialization of sex-roles and fertility ideals: A study of two generations in Toronto. In G. Kurian (Ed.), *Parent-Child Interaction in Transition.* Contributions in Family Studies, No. 10. Westport, CT: Greenwood Press, 1986.

Sims, S. J. *Diversifying Historically Black Colleges and Universities: A New Higher Education Paradigm.* Westport, CT: Greenwood Press, 1994.

Skansie, J. E. *Death is for All: Death and Death-Related Beliefs of Rural Spanish-Americans.* New York: AMS Press, 1985.

Sklare, M. *American Jews.* New York: Random House, 1972.

Sklare, M. (Ed.). *The Jews in American Society.* New York: Behrman House, 1974.

Skolnick, A. *Embattled Paradise: The American Family in an Age of Uncertainty.* New York: Basic, 1991.

Sleeter, C. & Grant, C. An analysis of multicultural education in the United States. *Harvard Educational Review,* 1988, 57, 421-444.

Sluzki, C. E. The latin lover revisited. In M. McGoldrick, J. K. Pearce & J. Giordano (Eds.), *Ethnicity and Family Therapy.* New York: Guilford, 1982.

Smedley, B. D., Myles, H. F. & Harrell, S. P. Minority status stresses and the college adjustment of ethnic minority freshmen. *Journal of Higher Education,* 1993, 64 (4), 434-452.

Smith, D. G. *The Challenge of Diversity: A Question of Involvement or Alienation.* Washington, D.C.: American Association of Higher Education, 1989.

Smith, D. G. Challenge of diversity: Implications for institutional research. In M. T. Nettles (Ed.), *The Effect of Assessment on Minority Student Populations.* New Directions for Institutional Research, #65. San Francisco: Jossey-Bass, 1990.

Smith, D. G., Wolf, L. E. & Levitan, T. (Eds.). *Studying Diversity in Higher Education.* New Directions for Institutional Research, #81. San Francisco: Jossey-Bass, 1994a.

Smith, D. G., Wolf, L. E. & Levitan, T. Introduction to studying diversity: Lessons from the field. In D. G. Smith, L. E. Wolf & T. Levitan (Eds.), *Studying Diversity in Higher Education.* New Directions for Institutional Research, #81. San Francisco: Jossey-Bass, 1994b.

Smith, D. J. (Ed.). *Understanding the Underclass.* London: Policy Studies Institute, 1992.

Smith, S. L. *Commission of Inquiry on Canadian University Education.* Ottawa: Association of Universities and Colleges of Canada, 1991.

Snipp, C. M.   Sociological perspectives on American Indians. *Annual Review of Sociology*, 1992, 18, 351-371.

Snyder, C. R.   *Alcohol and the Jews: A Cultural Study of Drinking and Sobriety.* Glencoe, IL: Free Press, 1958.

Sodowsky, G. R. & Plake, B. S.   A study of acculturation differences among international people and suggestions for sensitivity to within-group differences. *Journal of Counseling & Development*, 1992, 71, 53-59.

Sollars, W.   *The Invention of Ethnicity.* New York: Oxford University Press, 1989.

Solomon, P.   Racial factors in mental health service utilization. *Psychosocial Rehabilitation Journal*, 1988, 11, 3-12.

South, S.   Racial and ethnic differences in the desire to marry. *Journal of Marriage & the Family*, 1993, 55 (2), 357-370.

Sowell, T.   *Ethnic America.* New York: Basic, 1981.

Spanier, G. B. & Thompson, L.   *Parenting: The Aftermath of Separation and Divorce.* Beverly Hills, CA: Sage, 1984.

Spann, J.   *Achieving Faculty Diversity: A Sourcebook of Ideas and Success Stories.* Madison, WI: University of Wisconsin System, 1988.

Spurlock, J.   Development of self-concept in Afro-American children. *Hospital & Community Psychiatry*, 1986, 37 (1), 66-70.

Srole, L., Langer, T. S., Michael, S. T., Opler, M. K. & Rennie, T. A. C.   *Mental Health in the Metropolis: The Midtown Manhattan Study.* New York: McGraw-Hill, 1962.

Stack, C.   *All Our Kin: Strategies for Survival in a Black Community.* New York: Harper & Row, 1974.

Stage, F. K. & Hamrick, F. A.   Diversity issues: Fostering campuswide development of multiculturalism. *Journal of College Student Development*, 1994, 35 (5), 331-336.

Stage, F. K. & Manning, K.   *Enhancing the Multicultural Campus Environment: A Cultural Brokering Approach.* New Directions for Student Services, #60. San Francisco: Jossey-Bass, 1992.

Staggers, B.   Health care of Black adolescents. In R. Jones (Ed.), *Black Adolescents.* Berkeley, CA: Cobb & Henry, 1989.

Stanton-Salazar, R. D. & Dornbusch, S. M.   Social capital and the reproduction of inequality: Information networks among Mexican-origin high school students. *Sociology of Education*, 1995, 68 (2), 116-135.

Staples, R.   The myth of the Black matriarchy. *The Black Scholar*, 1981, 12 (6), 26-34.

Staples, R.   Changes in Black family structure: The conflict between family ideology and structural conditions. *Journal of Marriage & the Family*, 1985, 47 (4), 1005-1013.

Staples, R.   The Black American family. In C. H. Mindel, R. W. Haberstein & R. Wright, Jr. (Eds.), *Ethnic Families in America: Patterns and Variations.* New York: Elsevier, 1988.

Staples, R.   *The Black Family: Essays and Studies* (4th ed.). Belmont, CA: Wadsworth, 1991.

Staples, R. & Johnson, L. B.   *Black Families at the Crossroads.* San Francisco: Jossey-Bass, 1993.

State Higher Education Executive Officers.   *A Difference of Degrees: State Initiative to Improve Minority Student Achievement.* Research Report. Denver, CO: State Higher Education Executive Officers, 1987.

Statistics Canada. *Homicide in Canada, 1987.* Ottawa: Statistics Canada, Catalogue 85-209, 1988.

Statistics Canada. *Homicide in Canada, 1988.* Ottawa: Statistics Canada, Catalogue 85-209, 1989.

Statistics Canada. The inner city transition. *Canadian Social Trends,* 1990a, 16, 27-30.

Statistics Canada. *Homicide. Canadian Social Trends,* 1990b, 17, 14-17.

Statistics Canada. *Report on the Demographic Situation in Canada 1991: Current Demographic Analysis.* Ottawa: Statistics Canada, Catalogue 91-209E Annual, 1991.

Steenbarger, B. N. Emerging contextualist themes in counseling and development. *Journal of Counseling & Development,* 1991, 70 (2), 288-296.

Stein, H. F. Values and family therapy. In J. Schwartzman (Ed.), *Families and Other Systems: The Macrosystemic Context of Family Therapy.* New York: Guilford, 1985.

Steinberg, S. *The Ethnic Myth: Race, Ethnicity and Class in America.* New York: Atheneum, 1981.

Steiner, S. *Fusang: The Chinese Who Built America.* New York: Harper & Row, 1979.

Stern, E. M. (Ed.). *Psychotherapy and the Poverty Patient.* New York: Haworth, 1991.

Stern, S. & Cicala, J. A. *Creative Ethnicity: Symbols and Strategies of Contemporary Ethnic Life.* Logan, UT: University of Utah Press, 1991.

Stevens, E. Machismo and marianismo. *Transaction-Society,* 1973, 10 (6), 57-63.

Steward, R. J., Germain, S. & Johnson, J. D. Alienation and interactional style: A study of successful Anglo, Asian and Hispanic university students. *Journal of College Student Development,* 1992, 33(3), 149-156.

Stewart, D. & Vaux, A. Social support resources, behaviors, and perceptions among Black and White college students. *Journal of Multicultural Counseling & Development,* 1986, 14, 65-72.

Stewart, R. J., Jackson, M. R. & Jackson J. K. Alienation and interactional style in a predominantly white environment: A study of successful Black students. *Journal of College Student Development,* 1990, 31 (6), 509-515.

Stikes, C. S. *Black Students in Higher Education.* Carbondale, IL: Southern Illinois University Press, 1984.

Stockdill, S. H., Duhon-Sells, R. M., Olson, R. A. & Patton, M. Q. Voices in the design and evaluation of a multicultural education program: A developmental approach. In A.-M. Madison (Ed.), *Minority Issues in Program Evaluation.* New Directions For Program Evaluation, #53. San Francisco: Jossey-Bass, 1992.

Stricker, G. & Associates (Eds.). *Toward Diversification in Psychology Education and Training.* Washington, D.C.: American Psychological Association, 1990.

Student-Environment Study Group. *Educational Equity and Cultural Diversity: A Discussion Paper.* Guelph, Ontario: Student-Environment Study Group, 1992.

Sue, D. W. *Counseling the Culturally Different: Theory and Practice.* New York: Wiley, 1981.

Sue, D. W. A diversity perspective on contextualism. *Journal of Counseling & Development,* 1991, 70 (2), 300-301.

Sue, D. W., Arrendondo, P. & McDavis, R. J. Multicultural counseling competencies and standards: A call to the profession. *Journal of Counseling & Development,* 1992, 70 (4), 477-486.

Sue, D. W. & Sue, D. Asian Americans. In N. Vacc, J. Wittmer & S. DeVaney (Eds.), *Experiencing and Counseling Multicultural and Diverse Populations.* Muncie, IN: Accelerated Development, 1988.

Sue, D. W. & Sue, D. *Counseling the Culturally Different: Theory and Practice* (2nd ed.). New York: Wiley, 1990.

Sue, S. & Morishima, J. K. *The Mental Health of Asian Americans: Contemporary Issues in Identifying and Treating Mental Problems.* San Francisco: Jossey-Bass, 1982.

Sue, S. & Zane, N. The role of culture and cultural techniques in psychotherapy: A critique and reformulation. *American Psychologist,* 1987, 42 (1), 37-45.

Suen, H. K. Alienation and attitudes of Black college students at a predominantly white campus. *Journal of College Student Personnel,* 1993, 24 (2), 117-121.

Suginasiui, S. H. J. The literature of Canadians of South Asian origin: An overview. *Canadian Ethnic Studies,* 1985, 17 (1), 1-21.

Sullivan, J. J. *Invasion of the Salarymen: The Japanese Business Presence in America.* Westport, CT: Praeger, 1992.

Sullivan, M. L. *Getting Paid: Youth Crime and Work in the Inner City.* Ithaca, NY: Cornell University Press, 1989.

Sunahara, A. *The Politics of Racism: The Uprooting of Japanese Canadians During the Second World War.* Toronto: Lorimer, 1981.

Sung, B. L. *Mountain of Gold.* New York: Macmillan, 1967.

Sung, B. L. *Chinese America: History and Perspectives.* San Francisco: Chinese Historical Society of America, 1987.

Suzuki, B. H. The Asian American family. In M. Fantini & R. Cardenas (Eds.), *Parenting in a Multicultural Society.* New York: Longmans, 1980.

Suzuki, B. Curriculum transformation for multicultural education. *Education & Urban Society,* 1984, 16 (3), 294-322.

Syrtash, J. T. *Religion and Culture in Canadian Family Law.* Toronto: Butterworths, 1992.

Szalay, L. B. & Diaz-Guerrero, R. Similarities and differences between subjective cultures: A comparison of Latin, Hispanic, and Anglo Americans. In R. Diaz-Guerrero (Ed.), *Cross-Cultural and National Studies in Social Psychology.* 23rd Proceedings of the International Congress of Psychology of the International Union of Psychological Science, Acapulco, Mexico, September 2-7, 1984. Volume 2. Amsterdam: North-Holland, 1985.

Taieb-Carlen, S. Monocultural education in a pluralist environment: Ashkenazi curricula in Toronto Jewish educational institutions. *Canadian Ethnic Studies,* 1992, 14 (3), 75-86.

Takaki, R. *Strangers from a Different Shore: A History of Asian Americans.* Boston: Little, Brown, 1989.

Takaki, R. *A Different Mirror: A History of Multicultural America.* Boston: Little, Brown, 1993.

Takamishi, R. Continuities and discontinuities in the cognitive socialization of Asian-originated children: The case of Japanese Americans. In P. M. Greenfield & R. R. Cocking (Eds.), *Cross-Cultural Roots of Minority Child Development.* Hillsdale, NJ: Lawrence Erlbaum, 1994.

Takash, P. C. & Zavella, P. (Eds.). Social construction of gender in U.S. Latino communities. *Urban Anthropology,* Special Issue, 1993, 23 (3-4).

Takata, T. *Nikkei Legacy: The Story of Japanese Canadians from Settlement to Today.* Toronto: NC Press, 1983.

Tamura, T. & Lau, A. Connectedness versus separateness: Applicability of family therapy to Japanese families. *Family Process*, 1992, 31 (4), 319-340.

Tan, J.-Y. & Roy, P. E. *The Chinese in Canada.* Ottawa: Canadian Historical Association, 1985.

Tang, J. Whites, Blacks, and Asians in science and engineering: A reconsideration of their economic prospects. *Research in Social Stratification & Mobility*, 1993a, 12, 249-291.

Tang, J. The career attainment of Caucasian and Asian engineers. *Sociological Quarterly*, 1993b, 34, 467-496.

Tavuchis, N. Ethnicity and the family. In G. N. Ramu (Ed.), *Marriage and the Family in Canada Today.* Toronto: Prentice-Hall, 1989.

Taylor, A. & Sanchez, E. A. Out of the White box: Adapting mediation to the needs of Hispanic and other minorities within American society. *Family & Conciliation Courts Review*, 1991, 29 (2), 114-127.

Taylor, R. Receipt of support from family among Black Americans: Demographic and familial differences. *Journal of Marriage & the Family*, 1986, 48, 67-77.

Tchen, J. K. W. (Ed.). *The Chinese Laundryman: A Study of Social Isolation, Paul C. P. Siu.* New York: New York University Press, 1988.

Teachman, J. Early marriage, premarital fertility and marital dissolution. *Journal of Family Issues*, 1982, 4, 105-116.

Terrel, S. J. *This Other Kind of Doctor: Traditional Medical Systems in Black Neighborhoods in Austin, Texas.* New York: AMS Press, 1989.

Terrell, M. C. (Ed.). *Diversity, Disunity, and Campus Community.* Washington, D.C.: National Association of Student Personnel Administrators, 1992.

Thelin, J. R. The curriculum crusades and the conservative backlash. *Change*, 1992, 24 (1), 17-23.

Thomas, A. & Sillen, S. *Racism and Psychiatry.* Secaucus, NJ: Citadel, 1974.

Thomas, G. E. (Ed.). *Black Students in Higher Education: Conditions and Experiences.* Westport, CT: Greenwood Press, 1981.

Thomas, L. *The Medusa and the Snail: More Notes of a Biology Watcher.* New York: Viking, 1979.

Thompson, R. H. *Toronto's Chinatown: The Changing Social Organization of an Ethnic Community.* New York: AMS Press, 1989.

Thomson, C. A. *Blacks in Deep Snow: Black Pioneers in Canada.* Toronto: Dent, 1979.

Tienda, M. Market characteristics and Hispanic earnings: A comparison of natives and immigrants. *Social Problems*, 1983, 31 (1), 59-72.

Tienda, M. Race, ethnicity and the portrait of inequality: Approaching the 1990s. In G. E. Thomas (Ed.), *U.S. Race Relations in the 1980s and 1990s: Challenges and Alternatives.* New York: Hemisphere, 1990.

Tierney, W. G. An anthropological analysis of student participation in college. *Journal of Higher Education*, 1992, 63, 603-618.

Tierney, W. G. *Building Communities of Difference: Higher Education in the Twenty-first Century.* Westport, CT: Bergen & Garvey, 1993.

Ting-Toomey, S. Toward a theory of conflict and culture. In W. Gudykunst, L. Stewart & S. Ting-Tommey (Eds.), *Communication, Culture, and Organizational Processes.* Beverly Hills, CA: Sage, 1985.

Ting-Toomey, S. Conflict communication styles in Black and White subjective cultures. In Y. Y. Kim (Ed.), *Interethnic Communication: Current Research.*

Beverly Hills, CA: Sage, 1986.

Tinker, J. N. Intermarriage and assimilation in a plural society: Japanese Americans in the United States. In G. A. Crester & J. J. Leon (Eds.), *Intermarriage in the United States.* New York: Haworth, 1982.

Tjosvold, D. *Learning to Manage Conflict: Getting People to Work Together Productively.* New York: Lexington, 1993.

Tomaskovic-Devey, D. Labor process inequality and the gender and race composition of jobs. *Research in Social Stratification & Mobility*, 1993, 12, 215-247.

Triandis, H. C. (Ed.). *Handbook of Cross-Cultural Psychology* (6 Volumes). Boston: Allyn & Bacon, 1980.

Triandis, H. C. Acculturation indices as a means of confirming cultural differences. In R. Diaz-Guerrero (Ed.), *Cross-Cultural and National Studies in Social Psychology.* 23rd Proceedings of the International Congress of Psychology of the International Union of Psychological Science, Acapulco, Mexico, September 2-7, 1984. Volume 2. Amsterdam: North-Holland, 1985.

Triandis, H. C., Bontemp, R. & Villareal, M. J. Individualism and collectivism: Cross-cultural perspectives on self-ingroup relationships. *Journal of Personality & Social Psychology*, 1988, 54, 323-338.

Triandis, H. C., Marin, G., Lisansky, J. & Betancourt, H. Simpatia as a cultural script of Hispanics. *Journal of Personality & Social Psychology*, 1984, 47, 1363-1375.

Trickett, E. J., Watts, R. J. & Birman, D. Toward an overarching framework for diversity. In E. J. Trickett, R. J. Watts & D. Birman (Eds.), *Human Diversity: Perspectives on People in Context.* San Francisco: Jossey-Bass, 1994.

Trimble, J. E., Bolek, C. S. & Niemeryk, S. J. *Ethnic and Multicultural Drug Abuse: Perspective on Current Research.* New York: Haworth, 1993.

Tsai, M., Teng, L. N. & Sue, S. Mental status of Chinese in the United States. In A. Kleinman & T. Y. Lin (Eds.), *Normal and Deviant Behavior in Chinese Culture.* Hingham, MA: Reidel, 1980.

Tsang, C. L. Informal assessment of Asian Americans. In B. Gifford (Ed.), *Test Policy and Test Performance: Education, Language, and Culture.* Boston: Kluwer, 1989.

Tseng, W.-S. & Char, W. F. The Chinese of Hawaii. In W. S. Tseng, J. F. McDermott & T. W. Maretzki (Eds.), *Peoples and Cultures in Hawaii.* Honolulu: University Press of Hawaii, 1974.

Tseng, W.-S. & Hsu, J. *Culture and Family: Problems and Therapy.* New York: Haworth, 1991.

Tseng, W.-S. & Wu, D. Y. H. (Eds.). *Chinese Culture and Mental Health.* New York: Academic, 1985.

Tsui, P. & Schultz, G. L. Failure of rapport: Why psychotherapeutic engagement fails in the treatment of Asian clients. *American Journal of Orthopsychiatry*, 1985, 55, 561-569.

Tuchman, G. & Levine, H. G. New York Jews and Chinese food: The social construction of an ethnic pattern. *Journal of Contemporary Ethnography*, 1993, 22 (3), 382-407.

Tulloch, H. *Black Canadians: A Long Line of Fighters.* Toronto: NC Press, 1975.

Turner, J. H. & Bonacich, E. Toward a composite theory of middleman minorities. *Ethnicity*, 1980, 7, 144-158.

Turner, M., Fix, M. & Struyk, R. *Opportunities Denied, Opportunities Diminished: Racial Discrimination in Hiring.* Washington, D.C.: Urban Institute Press, 1991.

United States Department of Housing & Urban Development. *Hispanic Americans in the United States: A Selective Bibliography 1963-1974.* Washington, D.C.: United States Department of Housing & Urban Development, 1975.

United States Justice Department. *Uniform Crime Reports, 1990: Crime in the United States.* Washington, D.C.: United States Justice Department, 1991.

Valdez, A. Chicano used car dealers: A social world in microcosm. *Urban Life*, 1984, 13, 229-246.

Valdivieso, R. & Davis, C. *U.S. Hispanics: Challenging Issues for the 1990s.* Washington, D.C.: Population Reference Bureau, 1988.

Vallee, F. G. Kinship, the family and marriage in the Central Keewatin. In K. Ishwaran (Ed.), *The Canadian Family: A Book of Readings.* Toronto: Holt, Rinehart & Winston, 1971.

Vanier Institute of the Family. *Profiling Canada's Families.* Ottawa: Vanier Institute of the Family, 1994.

Vazquez-Nuttall, E., Romero-Garcia, I. & DeLeon, R. Sex roles and perceptions of femininity and masculinity of Hispanic women: A review of the literature. *Psychology of Women Quarterly*, 1987, 2, 409-425.

Vega, W. A. & Rumbaut, R. G. Ethnic minorities and mental health. *Annual Review of Sociology*, 1991, 17, 351-383.

Velez-Ibanez, C. G. & Greenberg, J. B. Formation and transformation of funds of knowledge among U.S.-Mexican households. *Anthropology & Education Quarterly*, 1992, 23 (4), 313-336.

Verma, R., Kwok, C. B. & Lam, L. The Chinese-Canadian family: A socio-economic profile. In K. Ishwaran (Ed.), *Canadian Families: Ethnic Variations.* Toronto: McGraw-Hill Ryerson, 1980.

Vigod, B. L. *The Jews in Canada.* Ottawa: Canadian Historical Association, 1984.

Vinovskis, M. *An "Epidemic" of Adolescent Pregnancy? Some Historical and Policy Considerations.* New York: Oxford University Press, 1988.

Vogel, E. The go-between in a developing society: The case of the Japanese marriage arranger. *Human Organization*, 1967, 20, 112-120.

Volti, R. *Society and Technological Change* (2nd ed.). New York: St. Martin's Press, 1992.

Wacquant, L. J. D. & Wilson, W. J. The costs of racial and class exclusion in the inner city. *Annals of the American Academy of Political & Social Sciences*, 1989, 501, 8-25.

Wagner, R. Changes in extended family relationships for Mexican American and Anglo single mothers. *Journal of Divorce*, 1987a, 11, 69-87.

Wagner, R. Changes in the friendship network during the first year of single parenthood for Mexican American and Anglo women. *Journal of Divorce*, 1987b, 11, 80-109.

Walker, J. W. St. G. *A History of Blacks in Canada: A Study Guide for Teachers and Students.* Ottawa: Minister of Supply & Services, 1980.

Walker, J. W. St. G. *The West Indians in Canada.* Ottawa: Canadian Historical Association, 1984.

Wall, J. A. Community mediation in China and Korea: Some similarities and differences. *Negotiation Journal*, 1993, 9, 141-142.

Walsh, F. Conceptualization of normal family processes. In F. Walsh (Ed.), *Normal Family Processes* (2nd ed.). New York: Guilford, 1993.

Ward, W. P. *The Japanese in Canada.* Ottawa: Canadian Historical Association, 1982.

Ward, W. P. *White Canada Forever: Popular Attitudes and Public Policy Towards Orientals in British Columbia* (2nd ed.). Kingston, ON: McGill-Queen's University Press, 1990.

Watson, M. F. & Protinsky, H. O. Black adolescent identity development: Effects of perceived family structure. *Family Relations*, 1988, 37 (3), 288-292.

Watson, W. H. *Black Folk Medicine: The Therapeutic Significance of Faith and Trust.* New Brunswick, NJ: Transaction Books, 1984.

Waxler-Morrison, N., Anderson, J. & Richardson, E. (Eds.). *Cross-Cultural Caring: A Handbook for Health Professionals in Western Canada.* Vancouver, BC: University of British Columbia Press, 1991.

Waxman, C. I. Are American Jews experiencing a religious revival? *Qualitative Sociology*, 1992, 15 (2), 203-211.

Webster, C. & D'Allesandro, F. *Teenage Mothers: A Life of Poverty and Welfare?* Olympia, WA: Washington State Institute for Public Policy, 1989.

Weick, K. E. *The Social Psychology of Organizing.* Reading, MA: Addison-Wesley, 1969.

Weinberg, S. S. *The World of Our Mothers: The Lives of Jewish Immigrant Women.* Chapel Hill, NC: University of North Carolina Press, 1988.

Weinfeld, M., Shaffir, W. & Cotler, I. (Eds.). *The Canadian Jewish Mosaic.* Toronto: Wiley, 1981.

Weinstein, L. A. *Moving a Battleship with Your Bare Hands: Governing a University System.* Madison, WI: Magna Publications, 1993.

Weiss, J. L. *Valley City: A Chinese Community in America.* Cambridge, MA: Schenkman, 1974.

Weissler, C. *Making Judaisim Meaningful: Ambivalence and Tradition in a Havurah Community.* New York: AMS Press, 1989.

Wenger, M. G. State responses to Afro-American rebellion: Internal neocolonialism and the rise of a new black petite bourgeoisie. *Insurgent Sociologist*, 1980, 10, 61-72.

Westbrook, F. D. & Sedlacek, W. E. Forty years of using labels to communicate about nontraditional students: Does it help or hurt? *Journal of Counseling & Development*, 1991, 70 (1), 20-28.

Westermeyer, J. (Ed.). *Anthropology and Mental Health: Setting a New Course.* The Hague, Netherlands: Mouton 1976.

Wetzel, P. Are 'powerless' communication strategies the Japanese norm? *Language in Society*, 1988, 17, 555-564.

White, J. & Parham, T. A. *The Psychology of Blacks: An Afro-American Perspective* (2nd ed.). Englewood Cliffs, NJ: Prentice Hall, 1990.

White, P. M. The Indo-Chinese in Canada. *Canadian Social Trends*, 1990, 18, 7-10.

Wickberg, E., Con, H., Johnson, G. & Willmot, M. E. *From China to Canada: A History of the Chinese Community in Canada.* Toronto: McClelland & Stewart, 1982.

Wilcox, J. R. & Ebbs, S. L. Promoting an ethical campus culture: The values audit. *National Association of Student Personnel Administrators Journal*, 1992, 29 (4), 253-260.

Wilkinson, C. B. & Spurlock, J. The mental health of Black Americans. In C. B. Wilkinson (Ed.), *Ethnic Psychiatry.* New York: Plenum Medical Books, 1986.

Williams, C. L. *An Annotated Bibliography on Refugee Mental Health.* Washington,

D.C.: United States Department of Health & Human Services, Pub. No. 87-1517, 1987.

Willie, C. V. The Black family and social class. *American Journal of Orthopsychiatry*, 1974, 44, 50-60.

Willie, C. V. & Greenblatt, S. L. Four classic studies of power relationships in Black families: A review and look to the future. *Journal of Marriage & the Family*, 1978, 40 (4), 691-696.

Wilson, E. (Ed.). *The Wisdom of Confucius*. New York: Avernel Books, 1982.

Wilson, K. L. & Portes, A. Immigrant enclaves: An analysis of the labor market experiences of Cubans in Miami. *American Journal of Sociology*, 1980, 86 (2), 295-319.

Wilson, M. N. The black extended family: An analytical consideration. *Developmental Psychology*, 1986, 22, 246-256.

Wilson, W. J. The urban underclass in advanced industrial societies. In P. E. Petersen (Ed.), *The New Urban Reality*. Washington, D.C.: Brookings Institute, 1985.

Wilson, W. J. *The Truly Disadvantaged: The Inner City, the Underclass, and Public Policy*. Chicago: University of Chicago Press, 1987.

Wilson, W. J. The underclass: Issues, perspectives, and public policy. Annals of the *American Academy of Political and Social Science*, 1989, 501, 182-192.

Wilson, W. J. Studying inner-city dislocations. *American Sociological Review*, 1991, 56, 1-14.

Winks, R. W. *The Blacks in Canada: A History*. Montreal: McGill-Queen's University Press, 1971.

Winn, C. The socio-economic attainment of visible minorities: Facts and policy implications. In J. Curtis (Ed.), *Social Inequality in Canada: Patterns, Problems, Policies*. Toronto: Prentice-Hall, 1988.

Wirth, L. *The Ghetto*. Chicago: University of Chicago Press, 1928.

Wolcott, H. F. *Transforming Qualitative Data: Description, Analysis, and Interpretation*. Thousand Oaks, CA: Sage, 1994.

Woldemikael, T. M. *Becoming Black American: Haitians and American Institutions in Evanston, Illinois*. New York: AMS Press, 1989.

Wong, B. Elites and ethnic boundary maintenance: A study of the roles of elites in Chinatown, New York City. *Urban Anthropology*, 1977, 6 (1), 1-22.

Wong, B. A comparative study of the assimilation of the Chinese in New York City and Lima, Peru. *Comparative Studies of Social History*, 1978, 20, 335-358.

Wong, B. *Economic Adaptation and Ethnic Identity of the Chinese*. New York: Holt, Rinehart & Winston, 1982.

Wong, B. Family, kinship, and ethnic identity of the Chinese in New York City, with comparative remarks on the Chinese in Lima, Peru and Manila, Philippines. *Journal of Comparative Family Studies*, 1985, 16, 231-254.

Wong, B. The Chinese: New immigrants in New York's Chinatown. In N. Foner (Ed.), *New Immigrants in New York*. New York: Columbia University Press, 1987.

Wong, B. *Patronage, Brokerage, Entrepreneurship and the Chinese Community of New York*. New York: AMS Press, 1988.

Wong, F. E. Diversity and community: Right objectives and wrong arguments. *Change*, 1991, 23 (4), 50-54.

Wong, R. R. Divorce mediation among Asian Americans: Bargaining in the shadow of diversity. *Family & Conciliation Courts Review*, 1995, 33 (1), 110-128.

Woolbright, C. (Ed.). *Valuing Diversity on Campus: A Multicultural Approach*.

Bloomington, IN: Association of College Unions-International, 1989.

Wright, D. J. (Ed.). *Responding to the Needs of Today's Minority Students.* New Directions for Student Services, #38. San Francisco: Jossey-Bass, 1987.

Wright, E. N. *The Retention and Credit Accumulation of Students in Secondary School: A Follow-Up from the 1980 Grade Nine Student Survey.* Toronto: Toronto Board of Education, Information Sevices Division, No. 176, 1985.

Wurzer, J. S. (Ed.). *Toward Multiculturalism: A Reader in Multicultural Education.* Yarmouth, ME: Intercultural Press, 1988.

Wylan, L. & Mintz, M. Ethnic differences in family attitudes towards psychotic manifestations, with implications for treatment programmes. *International Journal of Social Psychiatry,* 1976, 22, 86-95.

Yamamoto, J. Japanese-American suicides in Los Angeles. In J. Westermeyer (Ed.), *Anthropology and Mental Health: Setting a New Course.* The Hague, Netherlands: Mouton 1976.

Yamamoto, J. Japanese Americans. In A. Gaw (Ed.), *Cross-Cultural Psychiatry.* Boston, MA: John Wright-PSG, 1982.

Yamamoto, J. Therapy for Asian Americans and Pacific Islanders. In C. B. Wilkinson (Ed.), *Ethnic Psychiatry.* New York: Plenum Medical Books, 1986.

Yee, A. H. Asians as stereotypes and students: Misperceptions that persist. *Educational Psychology Review,* 1992, 4 (1), 95-132.

Yee, P. *Saltwater City.* Vancouver, BC: Douglas & McIntyre, 1988.

Ying, Y. W. Depressive symptomatology among Chinese-Americans as measured by the CES-D. *Journal of Clinical Psychology,* 1988, 44, 739-746.

Yinger, M. Ethnicity. *Annual Review of Sociology,* 1985, 11, 151-180.

Yip, G. *Cross Cultural Childrearing: An Annotated Bibliography.* Vancouver, BC: Centre for the Study of Curriculum & Instruction, University of British Columbia, 1985.

Young, N. F. Changes in values and strategies among Chinese in Hawaii. *Sociology & Social Research,* 1972, 56, 228-241.

Yu, L. C. Acculturation and stress within Chinese-American families. *Journal of Comparative Family Studies,* 1984, 15, 77-94.

Yu, L. C. & Wu, S.-C. Effects of length of stay in the United States on how the Chinese fulfill their filial obligations. In L. L. Adler (Ed.), *Cross-Cultural Research in Human Development.* New York: Praeger, 1989.

Yuan, D. Y. Chinatown and beyond: The Chinese population in metropolitan New York. *Phylon,* 1966, 27, 321-332.

Yum, J. O. The impact of Confucianism on interpersonal relationships and communication patterns in East Asia. *Communication Monographs,* 1988, 55 (4), 374-388.

Yung, J. *Chinese Women of America: A Pictorial History.* Seattle, WA: University of Washington Press, 1986.

Zander, A. The value of belonging to a group in Japan. *Small Group Behavior,* 1983, 14, 3-14.

Zayas, L. H. & Bryant, C. Culturally sensitive treatment of adolscent Puerto Rican girls and their families. *Child & Adolescent Social Work,* 1984, 1 (4), 235-253.

Zborowski, M. Cultural components in response to pain. *Journal of Social Issues,* 1952, 8, 16-30.

Zborowski, M. & Herzog, E. *Life Is With People.* New York: Schocken, 1952.

Zinn, M. B. Familism among Chicanos: A theoretical review. *Humboldt Journal of Social Relations,* 1982/1983, 10, 224-238.

Zuk, G. H. A therapist's perspective on Jewish family values. *Journal of Marriage & Family Counseling*, 1978, 4, 101-111.

Index

About the Author

MICHAEL BENJAMIN is a sociologist and, until recently, was Research Coordinator of the Student-Environment Study Group at the University of Guelph. He has published widely. On an occasional basis, he teaches at the university level, and is a family therapist and mediator. He currently works as a research and policy consultant in higher education, specializing in cultural diversity and student satisfaction.

ISBN 0-275-95544-3

9 780275 955441

90000>

EAN

HARDCOVER BAR CODE